A SAFETY NET THAT WORKS

IMPROVING FEDERAL PROGRAMS FOR LOW-INCOME AMERICANS

Douglas J. Besharov • Richard V. Burkhauser

Douglas M. Call • James C. Capretta • Kevin C. Corinth

Maura Corrigan • Mary C. Daly • Robert Doar

Ron Haskins • Bruce D. Meyer • Edgar O. Olsen

Angela Rachidi • Katharine B. Stevens • Russell Sykes

Edited by **Robert Doar**

AMERICAN ENTERPRISE INSTITUTE

ISBN-13: 978-0-8447-5004-0 (hardback)
ISBN-0-8447-5004-2 (hardback)
ISBN-13: 978-0-8447-5005-7 (paperback)
ISBN-10: 0-8447-5005-0 (paperback)
ISBN-13: 978-0-8447-5006-4 (ebook)
ISBN-10: 0-8447-5006-9 (ebook)

American Enterprise Institute
1789 Massachusetts Avenue, NW
Washington, DC 20036
www.aei.org

Contents

Preface

Americans are frustrated that too little progress is being made in reducing poverty and expanding opportunity. In a recent AEI/ *Los Angeles Times* survey, 70 percent of Americans said they believe the conditions for the poor had either stayed the same or gotten worse over the past 10 or 15 years, and 60 percent believe that most poor people will probably remain in poverty. Clearly the promise of upward mobility has not felt like a reality for many families stuck at the bottom of the economic ladder. In fact, one study from Pew Charitable Trusts found that 43 percent of Americans born in the bottom fifth of the income distribution remain there as adults, and more than 20 percent of children lived in poverty in 2014.

To be sure, the official poverty rate is a flawed metric because it does not consider a significant amount of government-provided assistance that raises many families' incomes above the poverty line. Better measures of poverty show that we have made progress in reducing material hardship, and experts from the left and right agree that the poor today are better off materially than in the past.

But they are better off largely because of government assistance, not because they are working or earning more on their own—and therein lies the current dissatisfaction. Poverty fighters across the political spectrum have consistently said that helping low-income Americans achieve sufficient earnings should be the goal of our anti-poverty efforts. The AEI/*Los Angeles Times* survey found that more than half of Americans living in poverty said that the main purpose of welfare programs should be helping poor people get back on their feet again, not simply providing for their material needs.

Thankfully, most mainstream leaders understand the key principles of a better approach. Able-bodied adults need to work because steady employment almost always leads a family out of poverty, provides opportunities for upward mobility, and is a source of dignity and purpose. Children are best off when they are raised by two committed parents, which is most likely to happen in marriage. And society must maintain a safety net that reduces material hardship, ensures that children can be raised in healthy environments, and rewards individuals who work.

However, translating these principles into effective public policy and detailed legislation is a difficult task. My hope is that this volume will be a useful resource for those trying to do just that. In the pages that follow, we have brought together academics and practitioners with decades of experience studying and implementing the crucial federal programs that assist low-income Americans. Each essay will discuss a program's history, what research and personal experience show about its effects, and one expert's view of how to help it work better.

Of course, not all of the problems facing low-income Americans will be solved by federal antipoverty programs. But political reality dictates that these major programs are not going to disappear anytime soon, meaning leaders who are serious about helping poor Americans should learn how they work and develop an agenda for improving them. Moreover, many of these assistance programs do reduce poverty and, with thoughtful reform, could be even more effective in helping struggling Americans move up. This volume intends to help policymakers understand how each program functions—its strengths, as well as its weaknesses.

Policymakers have an important responsibility, along with the rest of civil society, to develop a safety net that works and better helps poor Americans increase their earnings. When President Johnson declared our nation's "war on poverty," he defined our task as striving to "replace despair with opportunity." While none of the authors presented here have all the answers, I hope these analyses and proposals can help us move toward finally living up to that mission.

Robert Doar
Morgridge Fellow in Poverty Studies
American Enterprise Institute

The Earned Income Tax Credit

BRUCE D. MEYER

*University of Chicago; American Enterprise Institute;
National Bureau of Economic Research*

Since its inception in 1975, the federal earned income tax credit (EITC) has grown dramatically and is now the largest antipoverty program for the non-aged in the United States. In 2014, 28.5 million tax units received EITC payments totaling $68.3 billion, according to IRS data. As a result, the EITC lifted an estimated 7.3 million individuals above the poverty line. In addition to directly raising incomes, the EITC has sharply changed work incentives, currently increasing the after-tax wage by up to 45 percent for those with low earnings.

The EITC is part of the tax system and does not require people to have a tax liability that the credit offsets. A person without a net tax liability receives it as a payment that, in 2016, could be as large as $6,269.

The fundamental problem in designing tax and transfer programs for those with few resources is that such programs typically undermine work. The EITC's goal has been to transfer income while encouraging work. This feature led to the political support for its initial adoption and subsequent expansions.[1] The program has become increasingly prominent during a time when policymakers have sought to reduce the dependence encouraged by welfare programs.

In this paper, I first summarize how the EITC operates and describe the characteristics of recipients. I then discuss empirical work on the EITC's effects on income distribution, labor supply, and other outcomes. Next, I discuss a few policy concerns about the EITC: possible negative effects on hours of work and marriage and problems of compliance with the tax system. Finally, I briefly discuss the likely effects of further expanding the credit in ways suggested by several proposals.

How the EITC Works

The EITC provides an earnings subsidy to families that satisfy three criteria. First, a family must have a wage earner, since only those who work are eligible. Second, a family must have low income. In 2016, a single-parent family with one child was eligible if its income was below $39,296, while a family with two children could earn up to $44,648, and a family with three children could earn up to $47,955. A two-parent family could earn $5,550 more than these amounts and still receive the credit. Third, while a small EITC (up to $506 in 2016) is available to the childless, to receive a significant EITC, a family has to have resident children. In 2016, the maximum credit was $3,373 for a family with one child, $5,572 for a family with two children, and $6,269 for a family with three or more children (see Table 1).

Because the EITC is refundable, a family can receive the credit even if it does not have an income tax liability. In the vast majority of cases, the credit is received as a lump sum as part of a tax refund early the following year. The tax filer must fill out a one-page form with information on the qualifying child or children that is submitted with the rest of the tax return. In summary, the credit subsidizes poor parents' work as it transfers income to them.

To help visualize the EITC, Figure 1 shows the schedule for two types of households in 2016. The top schedule, for single-parent families with two children, provides a much larger credit at all income levels than that for childless individuals, shown underneath. Both schedules provide an earnings subsidy initially as the credit is phased in: 40 cents for each dollar earned for the first $13,930 for those with two children, and 7.65 cents for each dollar earned for the first $6,610 for the childless. For example, a single mother with two children who earned $10,000 would receive a $4,000 credit.

Table 1. Earned Income Tax Credit Schedule Parameters, 2016

	Phase-In Rate (%)	Phase-In Ends ($)	Maximum Credit Amount ($)	Phase-Out Begins ($)	Phase-Out Rate (%)	Phase-Out Ends ($)
Filing Status: Single						
Childless	7.65	6,610	506	8,270	7.65	14,880
1 Child	34	9,920	3,373	18,190	15.98	39,296
2 Children	40	13,930	5,572	18,190	21.06	44,648
>2 Children	45	13,930	6,269	18,190	21.06	47,955
Filing Status: Married Filing Jointly						
Childless	7.65	6,610	506	13,820	7.65	20,430
1 Child	34	9,920	3,373	23,740	15.98	44,846
2 Children	40	13,930	5,572	23,740	21.06	50,198
>2 Children	45	13,930	6,269	23,740	21.06	53,505

Source: Tax Policy Center, "Earned Income Tax Credit Parameters, 1975–2016," January 5, 2016, http://www.taxpolicycenter.org/sites/default/files/legacy/taxfacts/content/PDF/historical_eitc_parameters.pdf.

In the flat, or plateau, part of the schedule, the total credit received does not change with earnings. However, with additional earnings beyond the plateau, the credit is decreased in the phaseout region, resulting in an implicit tax on earnings at a rate just over 21 percent for those with two children. For those with one child, earnings subsidies, credits, and implicit taxes are somewhat lower, while for those with three or more children, everything is higher.

Who Receives the EITC

The eligibility requirements mean the EITC targets certain types of families: those headed by a single mother and large families. As Table 2 indicates, in recent years, more than 61 percent of the dollars spent on the EITC went to single parents (those with a head of household filing status). Larger families received most of the dollars as well. In 2014, 60 percent of all dollars were received by families with two

Figure 1. Earned Income Tax Credit Schedule for Childless and Those with Two Children

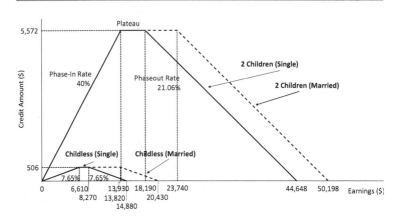

Source: Tax Policy Center, "Earned Income Tax Credit Parameters, 1975–2016," January 5, 2016, http://www.taxpolicycenter.org/sites/default/files/legacy/taxfacts/content/PDF/historical_eitc_parameters.pdf.

or more eligible children. While qualifying households without a child were more than a quarter of recipient households, they received just 3 percent of the dollars paid through the credit.

How the EITC Affects the Distribution of Income

The EITC's effect on the income distribution is among its most important effects. A convenient way to gauge the EITC's distributional effects is to ask how many people it raises above the poverty line.[2] The EITC raises more people above the poverty line than any other government program or tax policy except Social Security. In 2014, 7.3 million individuals were raised above poverty, more than four million of whom were children.[3] If we believe investments in children are especially productive,[4] then the EITC is particularly well targeted.

While no other antipoverty program reduces the poverty rate as much as the EITC, its effects are concentrated just under the poverty

Table 2. Earned Income Tax Credit Benefit Amounts and Number of Recipients, by Number of Qualifying Children, 2014

Recipient Characteristics	Number (Millions)	Amount ($ Millions)
By Filing Status of Recipient (Estimates)*		
Head of Household	13.98	41,686.90
Joint	6.56	20,501.75
Single	7.99	6,150.53
Total	28.54	68,339.18
By Number of Qualifying Children		
Without a Qualifying Child	7.38	2,120.94
With One Qualifying Child	10.49	24,976.43
With Two Qualifying Children	7.21	27,075.03
With Three or More Qualifying Children	3.45	14,166.78
Total	28.54	68,339.18

Note: Numbers and amount by filing status are estimated using percentages reported in *The Earned Income Tax Credit (EITC): An Overview* by Gene Falk and Margot L. Crandall-Hollick.
Source: IRS, " SOI Tax Stats — Individual Income Tax Returns Publication 1304," Table 2.5, https://www.irs.gov/uac/soi-tax-stats-individual-income-tax-returns-publication-1304-complete-report; IRS, Earned Income Tax Credit, "Statistical Sample," https://www.eitc.irs.gov/EITC-Central/press/statistics/statsmpl; and Gene Falk and Margot L. Crandall-Hollick, *The Earned Income Tax Credit (EITC): An Overview,* Congressional Research Service Report, January 19, 2016, https://www.fas.org/sgp/crs/misc/R43805.pdf.

line.[5] The largest percentage changes in incomes from the EITC tend to be for families with incomes near 75 percent of the poverty line, in contrast to other programs such as Temporary Assistance for Needy Families (TANF) and the Supplemental Nutrition Assistance Program (SNAP), which are targeted to those with the very lowest income.

The minimum wage is a policy alternative to the EITC that has often been promoted as helping low-wage workers. But the minimum wage is more poorly targeted than these transfer programs, with a large share going to children and secondary workers in well-off families.[6]

In interpreting changes in poverty due to the EITC and transfer programs, one must keep in mind that changes in taxes and transfers may alter pretax and pretransfer incomes. A full analysis of the behavioral effects of these programs is beyond the scope of this paper. However, one would expect that the mechanical effects of the EITC on poverty indicated here understate the effects on incomes, given the evidence in the literature (summarized below) of mostly positive labor supply effects. On the other hand, transfer programs such as TANF and SNAP likely reduce pretransfer earnings, suggesting that any direct poverty-reducing effects of these programs overstate the effects once incorporating behavioral responses. Thus, this consideration would indicate that the calculations summarized here understate the EITC's true effects but overstate the effects of the other programs.

Researchers have examined whether the increase in income for recipients and the form of the payment affect several outcomes. In contrast to social programs that pay benefits evenly over the year, most EITC recipients receive their benefits in a single check, averaging more than $1,500. Lisa Barrow and Leslie McGranahan explored whether the lumpy nature of EITC payments induces changes in expenditure patterns among recipients, finding that consumption rises, particularly for durable goods, in the months in which EITC refunds are received.[7] Thus, the evidence suggests that the EITC facilitates the purchase of big-ticket items by low-income families.

Additionally, Timothy Smeeding, Katherin Ross Phillips, and Michael O'Connor examined a large sample of individuals filing 1997 income tax returns in Chicago.[8] These recipients tended to report plans to use their credit for purposes beyond current consumption, including savings, car purchases, tuition payments, residential moves, and other uses that lead to economic and social mobility.

The EITC and Employment

I will now summarize the EITC's effects on work, particularly for single mothers.[9] The EITC encourages work by making it unequivocally more attractive to single parents who are considering participating in the labor market at all over a year. Regardless of the hours level, the gain from working has increased. Given that for many single mothers the net return to working is so low (weighing what is gained by work compared to what is lost in welfare and other benefits), a few thousand dollars can dramatically change the calculation in favor of working.

I calculated with Dan Rosenbaum that the average net return to working—defined as after-tax earnings plus the cash value of benefits received if a woman worked minus the cash value of benefits received if she did not work and averaged over the earnings distribution of single women—was $7,270 in 1984.[10] Tax changes, primarily the EITC, raised that net return to work by an average of $1,442 by 1996 (in 1996 dollars). The increase in incentives was especially high for the lowest-skilled single mothers, those likely to receive welfare benefits and who, if they worked, were likely to be on the phase-in or plateau portions of the EITC schedule.

I also examined with Rosenbaum the EITC's effect on the employment of single mothers using a simple structural model and found that the employment of single mothers in 1996 was 7 percentage points higher because of the EITC.[11] We determined the labor supply effects in this study by contrasting employment changes for single mothers with those of single women without children and employment differences across women with different numbers of children, state taxes, and the real value of the credit relative to state living costs. Other studies have found results that imply similar or even larger estimates, exploiting mostly the same types of contrasts.[12]

Hours of Work. The EITC's expected effects on hours of work for single parents are complicated. Most recipients are on the plateau or phaseout section of the credit schedule, shown in Figure 1.[13] Workers whose level of earnings put them on the plateau section or on the phaseout portion are in principle encouraged to reduce their hours under the EITC. However, this theoretical prediction has not been borne out in the data analyzed to date. This lack of an "hours effect" is one of the more puzzling yet robust findings in the literature.[14]

Various explanations have been offered for this surprising finding. The most common are: (1) workers' inability to freely vary their hours because of employers' preferences for certain hours, (2) measurement error in hours reported, and (3) imperfect perception of marginal tax rates.[15] I think the most plausible explanation is imperfect perception of marginal rates. It would not be surprising if recipients do not fully understand the tax schedule given the complexity of eligibility rules and instructions.[16] In recent years, the instructions for the EITC have been a dense 13 or 14 pages. The marginal rates are not reported on the tax forms anywhere, unlike the base income tax rates, for which marginal rates are reported quite clearly on the tax rate schedules. Most recipients do not fill out the tax forms themselves,[17] and those who prepare tax returns for them do not routinely explain marginal rates to clients. Thus, a lack of a response to the incentive to reduce hours may not be too surprising.

The EITC's expected effects on work and hours among couples are even more complicated. Since at least one parent likely is working, the effects have some similarities to the hours effects for single current recipients, which in principle means the working parent is encouraged to work fewer hours. With couples, overall hours can be reduced by one of the partners leaving the workforce or by one or more partners reducing hours. The main evidence on this occurrence comes from research from Nada Eissa and Hilary Hoynes and from Bradley Heim.[18] While Eissa and Hoynes found that the main effect is a reduction in participation by wives, Heim found mainly a change in hours by those who do work. Both papers found a small reduction in overall hours.

A caveat on the labor supply effects of the EITC is in order. The increase in the number of low-wage workers caused by the EITC has likely pushed down wages in low-skilled labor markets in general. This wage reduction decreases the earnings and employment of others. While estimating this effect is harder than estimating the labor supply of recipients,[19] the overall EITC labor supply effects are likely overstated by the estimated effect on recipients alone.

Welfare Caseloads. The EITC reduces welfare receipt by making work more attractive than welfare for a substantial number of single mothers. In response to the welfare reforms of the mid-1990s and the almost contemporaneous EITC expansions, welfare caseloads fell from more than five million families in 1994 to just over two million by 2001. Caseloads have drifted downward since, reaching 1.6 million in 2014.[20]

In his study of welfare receipt among female-headed families, Jeffrey Grogger estimated the EITC's effect by comparing those with different EITC maximum benefit amounts due to schedule changes over time and differences in the number of children.[21] He concluded that the EITC was responsible for about 15 percent of the decline in welfare receipt in the 1990s. He argued that most of the reduction in welfare cases is through a reduction in welfare entry.

Other Effects of the EITC. There is substantial evidence that the EITC has beneficial effects on health and education, through either increased household income or increased maternal work. Hilary Hoynes, Douglas Miller, and David Simon found that the EITC expansions in the 1990s reduced the chance of a low birth weight delivery, an important indication of infant health.[22] Gordon Dahl and Lance Lochner found that EITC payments appear to increase child test scores, but only in the short run.[23] William Evans and Craig Garthwaite found improvements in women's mental health.[24] In all these cases, it is unclear whether the improvements come from the adult recipients' higher income or their increased likelihood of working.

Problems with the EITC: Hours, Marriage, and Compliance

Three important problems with the EITC are its predicted negative effects on hours, its potential to discourage marriage among low-income workers, and the receipt of credits by ineligible filers. The first issue, hours of work, has already been discussed. A concern is that even if we cannot see in the data a reduction in hours among single-mother recipients, the theoretical prediction is sufficiently clear that it is likely to happen. If the reason we do not see an hours response is that recipients do not understand the marginal incentives, then if recipients' understanding improves, the situation might change, and an hours reduction may emerge.

Raj Chetty and Emmanuel Saez field-tested a novel program using tax preparers to educate recipients on the marginal incentives to work under the EITC.[25] Somewhat surprisingly, they found that providing additional information on EITC incentives does not affect average earnings. This result may be due to the difficulty in getting tax preparers to successfully convey information about the phase-out range marginal tax rates. In more recent work, Raj Chetty, John Friedman, and Emmanuel Saez found that there seems to be learning over time about some features of the EITC, but this improved knowledge does not clearly carry over to marginal tax rates for wage and salary workers.[26]

A second concern is marriage incentives. The EITC as currently designed has complicated incentives for marriage. The schedule is the same for singles and couples except for the longer plateau for couples, with the maximum benefit available to someone who earns slightly more than full-time work at the minimum wage (see Figure 1).

Because of this structure, the EITC encourages marriage for some: those who have children but have little or no earnings. It discourages marriage for others: those with children who are working full time but remain poor. On net, more couples and potential couples increase their EITC payments by divorcing or staying unmarried than increase them by marrying or staying married. Thus, the EITC discourages marriage somewhat overall.

Of the two most detailed studies that estimate the effects on marriage, one found no effect, the other little or no effect on marriage. David Ellwood conducted two analyses: (1) he examined changes in marriage rates of women at different wage quartiles, with the lowest quartile expected to be affected by the EITC, and (2) he examined whether cohabiting couples marry, comparing those whose EITC amount would rise with marriage to those whose credit would fall.[27] Nada Eissa and Hilary Hoynes determined marriage effects by comparing marriage rates for a sample of married or cohabiting couples that differ in how tax and welfare provisions affect their marriage incentives because their earnings differ (and provisions change over time).[28]

The final major concern about the EITC, and the one most in the popular press, is noncompliance. Noncompliance means not paying taxes that are due, either intentionally or unintentionally. The IRS estimates that in recent years about 30 percent of credit dollars were claimed in error.[29] The most common source of error is a claim for which a child is not eligible, most often because the child does not reside with the claimant.

There are two different ways of thinking about EITC noncompliance. If one's reference point is state welfare systems, the credit seems low on administrative expenses but high on take-up and noncompliance. Because tax refunds are paid quickly and only a small share have eligibility later verified through an audit, many ineligibles receive the credit, and many eligibles receive overpayments. While it is difficult to determine the share of such payments that are fraud, certainly some are.

If one's reference point is tax administration, it is not clear that EITC noncompliance is higher than for other tax provisions. Furthermore, a high share of tax-enforcement efforts has been devoted to making sure those who receive the EITC are in fact eligible. EITC recipients have been subject to a large share of audits relative to the potential lost revenue. In fiscal year 2004, the EITC accounted for 48 percent of individual income tax return audits, despite it being only 3–4 percent of the tax gap (taxes due that were not collected). Even this share is probably overstated given the IRS methodology that counts as an overpayment payments that should go to another household member or relative.

In addition, a large share of cases in which payments are denied are overturned when assistance is provided to filers to help them understand the required documentation. Much of noncompliance is probably driven by needless complexity—14 pages of instructions in the overall tax guide and 56 pages in the EITC instruction booklet.

EITC Reforms

In an earlier paper, I discussed four types of EITC reforms: (1) providing a more generous EITC for three-child families; (2) modifying the tax schedule to reduce marriage penalties; (3) simplifying eligibility criteria for the credit; and (4) providing a more generous credit for single, childless individuals or noncustodial fathers.[30] The first was adopted as part of the American Recovery and Reinvestment Act of 2009, and the second was addressed in a limited way under Presidents George W. Bush and Barack Obama. Because marriage penalties (and subsidies) remain, I will discuss this issue and the third briefly here. The fourth, which I will also discuss, has been proposed by Speaker Paul Ryan and President Obama.

Marriage Penalties. One can reduce marriage penalties in several ways. One could change the married credit to be always twice the credit for single parents, but that would be expensive. Other alternatives that balance increased costs and penalty reductions have been considered by Janet Holtzblatt and Robert Rebelein.[31] For example, one could extend the plateau of the schedule or lower phaseout tax rates and thus extend the phaseout range for couples. Alternatively, one could add a second-earner deduction, which would reduce the amount of income subject to income tax for families with two earners in the phaseout range of the credit, thus flattening and extending the phaseout. This last option is inexpensive relative to the alternatives as nearly all the lost revenue goes toward reducing marriage penalties, but it would require another worksheet to be added to the tax forms.[32] The approach adopted by Presidents Bush and Obama was to extend the plateau of the EITC schedule for joint filers.

EITC Simplification. The EITC could be simplified in many ways. The rules and instructions are extraordinarily complicated, which is also true of other income tax provisions. As already mentioned, the main instruction booklet includes 14 dense pages on the EITC, and the dedicated booklet on the EITC is 56 pages.

Much of the complication with the EITC is determining who is a child for EITC purposes. Current tax law has several definitions of a child that apply to different tax credits. A clear simplification proposed by the President's Advisory Panel on Federal Tax Reform would use the same definition of a child in terms of relationship to the taxpayer, residency, and age for the EITC, the Child Tax Credit, and the determination of dependents (per child deduction from income).[33] One could also consider combining these three tax reductions for those with children. This is a much greater change in the overall shape of the tax schedule and could be more expensive but has been proposed by others, including David Ellwood and Jeffrey Liebman.[34]

An Expanded EITC for Those Without Coresident Children. Finally, recent proposals have circulated to expand the EITC for the childless.[35] Such an approach necessarily increases marriage penalties somewhat since it increases credits for the unmarried.

Variants on this idea were implemented in New York State and the District of Columbia. These jurisdictions supplement the federal EITC for noncustodial parents who have paid all child support that accrued during the tax year. An excellent description of noncustodial parent EITCs can be found in research by Laura Wheaton and Elaine Sorensen.[36] The New York and DC noncustodial parent EITCs have different age restrictions, with all those 18 and over eligible in New York, but only those age 18–30 eligible in DC. The New York credit is currently two-thirds of the state EITC for a single taxpayer with one child, while the DC credit is 40 percent of the federal credit for families with resident children (which depends on the number of children).

These noncustodial parent EITCs and broader EITCs for all childless adults are not likely to affect labor supply per dollar transferred as much as the current single-mother-focused EITC does, given that most men already work, despite the low participation rate for some groups, noted by Nicholas Eberstadt and others.[37] It seems unlikely that a childless EITC would have appreciable positive labor supply effects. Considering that marginal tax rates are likely to increase for most recipients who will be on the phaseout portion of the schedule, and that the additional income from the credit may make recipients feel less of a need to work as hard, the labor supply effects may even be negative. An expanded EITC for the childless would, however, provide a way to transfer income to another segment of the poor without significantly discouraging work.

Conclusions

In summary, the evidence indicates that the income-distribution features of the EITC are quite good. The credit targets resources at those below the poverty line, particularly families with children. It raises more than 7.3 million people above the poverty line. While it is especially aimed at people right under the poverty line, it also raises 2.8 million people above half the poverty line.

The empirical evidence on labor supply and marriage indicates that the incentives of the EITC are remarkably favorable given the resources transferred. Studies of the EITC's effects on employment imply that the credit has sharply increased the portion of single mothers that work.

Paul Ryan and others have proposed to expand the credit for the childless. Two jurisdictions, New York and the District of Columbia, have such credits, but for noncustodial parents. While they will transfer income to those with few resources, EITCs for those without resident children are unlikely to stimulate employment as successfully as the current EITC because the vast majority of this population already works.

Notes

1. Jeffrey B. Liebman, "The Impact of the Earned Income Tax Credit on Incentives and Income Distribution," *Tax Policy and the Economy* 12 (1998); and Denis J. Ventry Jr., "The Collision of Tax and Welfare Politics: The Political History of the Earned Income Tax Credit," in *Making Work Pay: The Earned Income Tax Credit and Its Impact on America's Families*, ed. Bruce D. Meyer and Douglas Holtz-Eakin (New York: Russell Sage Foundation Press, 2001), 15–66.

2. This approach accounts for differences across family size using the same method as the Census Bureau when calculating the poverty rate.

3. Because of pronounced underimputation of EITC receipt in the CPS documented in Meyer, Mok, and Sullivan, these numbers were calculated from the 2014 Current Population Survey data and then scaled up by the 2011 ratio of families with children who received the EITC as reported

in Statistics of Income Data divided by the number of EITC families with children recorded in the CPS. See Bruce Meyer, Wallace Mok, and James Sullivan, "The Under-Reporting of Transfers in Household Surveys: Its Nature and Consequences" (working paper, National Bureau of Economic Research, July 2009), Table 10. For tables with these calculations and tables describing the EITC recipient population, see Bruce D. Meyer, "Background Tables for 'The Earned Income Tax Credit,'" December 2016, https://harris.uchicago.edu/sites/default/files/BackgroundTablesAEI-December-2016.pdf.

4. James J. Heckman and Dimitriy V. Masterov, "The Productivity Argument for Investing in Young Children" (working paper, National Bureau of Economic Research, April 2007).

5. See Liebman, "The Impact of the Earned Income Tax Credit on Incentives and Income Distribution."

6. Richard V. Burkhauser, Kenneth A. Couch, and Andrew J. Glenn, "Public Policies for the Working Poor: The Earned Income Tax Credit Versus Minimum Wage Legislation," *Research in Labor Economics* 15 (1996): 65–109; David Neumark and William Wascher, "Using the EITC to Help Poor Families: New Evidence and a Comparison with the Minimum Wage," *National Tax Journal* 54 (2001): 281–317; Saul D. Hoffman and Laurence S. Seidman, *Helping Working Families: The Earned Income Tax Credit* (Kalamazoo, MI: Upjohn Institute for Employment Research, 2003); and Thomas MaCurdy, "How Effective Is the Minimum Wage at Supporting the Poor?," *Journal of Political Economy* 123, no. 2 (2015): 497–545.

7. Lisa Barrow and Leslie McGranahan, "The Effects of the Earned Income Tax Credit on the Seasonality of Household Expenditures" in *Making Work Pay: The Earned Income Tax Credit and Its Impact on America's Families*, ed. Bruce D. Meyer and Douglas Holtz-Eakin (New York: Russell Sage Foundation Press, 2001), 329–65.

8. Timothy M. Smeeding, Katherin Ross Phillips, and Michael A. O'Connor, "The Earned Income Tax Credit: Expectation, Knowledge, Use and Economic and Social Mobility," in *Making Work Pay: The Earned Income Tax Credit and Its Impact on America's Families*, ed. Bruce D. Meyer and Douglas Holtz-Eakin (New York: Russell Sage Foundation Press, 2001), 301–28.

9. For excellent summaries of the labor supply effects of the EITC, see V. Joseph Hotz and John Karl Scholz, "The Earned Income Tax Credit," in *Means-Tested Transfer Programs in the United States*, ed. Robert A. Moffitt

(Chicago, IL: University of Chicago Press, 2003); Nada Eissa and Hilary Hoynes, "Behavioral Responses to Taxes: Lessons from the EITC and Labor Supply," *Tax Policy and the Economy* 20 (2006): 163–92; and Austin Nichols and Jesse Rothstein, "The Earned Income Tax Credit," in *Economics of Means-Tested Transfer Programs in the United States, Volume I*, ed. Robert A. Moffitt (Chicago, IL: University of Chicago Press, 2016).

10. Bruce D. Meyer and Dan T. Rosenbaum, "Making Single Mothers Work: Recent Tax and Welfare Policy and Its Effects," *National Tax Journal* 53 (2000): 1027–62; and David Neumark and William Wascher, "Using the EITC to Help Poor Families: New Evidence and a Comparison with the Minimum Wage," *National Tax Journal* 54 (2001): 281–317.

11. Bruce D. Meyer and Dan T. Rosenbaum, "Welfare, the Earned Income Tax Credit, and the Labor Supply of Single Mothers," *Quarterly Journal of Economics* CXVI (2001): 1063–114.

12. For example, see Nada Eissa and Jeffrey B. Liebman, "Labor Supply Response to the Earned Income Tax Credit," *Quarterly Journal of Economics* 112, no. 2 (May 1996): 605–37; Jeffrey Grogger, "The Effects of Time Limits, the EITC, and Other Policy Changes on Welfare Use, Work, and Income Among Female-Headed Families," *Review of Economics and Statistics* 85, no. 2 (2003): 394–408; and V. Joseph Hotz, Charles H. Mullin, and John Karl Scholz, "The Earned Income Tax Credit and the Labor Market Participation of Families on Welfare," Mimeo, University of Wisconsin, 2005.

13. IRS data from 1994 indicate that 26.6 percent of recipients with children are on the phase-in portion of the schedule, 13.9 percent are on the plateau, and 59.5 percent are on the phaseout portion. US General Accounting Office, *Earned Income Credit: Profile of Tax Year 1994 Credit Recipients*, July 16, 1996, http://www.gao.gov/products/GGD-96-122BR.

14. Eissa and Liebman, "Labor Supply Response to the Earned Income Tax Credit"; Bruce Meyer and Dan Rosenbaum, "Welfare, the Earned Income Tax Credit, and the Labor Supply of Single Mothers" (working paper, National Bureau of Economic Research, September 1999); Bruce D. Meyer, "Labor Supply at the Extensive and Intensive Margins: The EITC, Welfare and Hours Worked," *American Economic Review* 92 (May 2002): 373–79; and Eissa and Hoynes, "Behavioral Responses to Taxes."

15. Meyer, "Labor Supply at the Extensive and Intensive Margins"; and Eissa and Hoynes, "Behavioral Responses to Taxes."

16. For a discussion of worker perceptions of EITC provisions, see Jennifer L. Romich and Thomas Weisner, "How Families View and Use the EITC: Advance Payment Versus Lump Sum Delivery," *National Tax Journal* 53 (2000): 1245–64.

17. See US General Accounting Office, *Earned Income Credit.*

18. Nada Eissa and Hilary Hoynes, "Taxes and the Labor Market Participation of Married Couples: The Earned Income Tax Credit," *Journal of Public Economics* 8 (2004): 1931–58; and Bradley T. Heim, "The Impact of the Earned Income Tax Credit on the Labor Supply of Married Couples: Structural Estimation and Business Cycle Interactions" (working paper, US Department of the Treasury, 2006).

19. Andrew Leigh, "Who Benefits from the Earned Income Tax Credit? Incidence Among Recipients, Coworkers and Firms," *B. E. Journal of Economic Analysis & Policy* 10, no. 1 (2010); and Jesse Rothstein, "Is the EITC as Good as an NIT? Conditional Cash Transfers and Tax Incidence," *American Economic Journal: Economic Policy* 10, no. 1 (2010).

20. Center on Budget and Policy Priorities, "Chart Book: TANF at 20," August 5, 2016.

21. Grogger, "The Effects of Time Limits, the EITC, and Other Policy Changes"; and Jeffrey Grogger, "Welfare Transitions in the 1990s: The Economy, Welfare Policy, and the EITC," *Journal of Policy Analysis and Management* 23, no. 4 (2004): 671–95.

22. Hilary W. Hoynes, Douglas L. Miller, and David Simon, "Income, the Earned Income Tax Credit, and Infant Health," *American Economic Journal: Economic Policy* (2013).

23. Gordon Dahl and Lance Lochner, "The Impact of Family Income on Child Achievement: Evidence from the Earned Income Tax Credit," *American Economic Review* 102, no. 5 (2012): 1927–56.

24. William N. Evans and Craig L. Garthwaite, "Giving Mom a Break: The Impact of Higher EITC Payments on Maternal Health," *American Economic Journal: Economic Policy* 6, no. 2 (2014): 258–90.

25. Raj Chetty and Emmanuel Saez, "Teaching the Tax Code: Earnings Responses to an Experiment with EITC Recipients," *American Economic Journal: Applied Economics* 5, no. 1 (2009): 1–31.

26. Raj Chetty, John N. Friedman, and Emmanuel Saez, "Using Differences in Knowledge Across Neighborhoods to Uncover the Impacts of the

EITC on Earnings," *American Economic Review* 103, no. 7 (2013): 2683–721.

27. David Ellwood, "The Impact of the Earned Income Tax Credit and Other Social Policy Changes on Work and Marriage in the United States," *National Tax Journal* 53 (2000): 1063–106.

28. Nada Eissa and Hilary Hoynes, "Tax and Transfer Policy, and Family Formation: Marriage and Cohabitation" (working paper, University of California at Davis, 2000), http://www.econ.ucdavis.edu/faculty/hoynes/working_papers.html.

29. Internal Revenue Service, "Compliance Estimates for the Earned Income Tax Credit Claimed on 2006-2008 Returns," August 2014.

30. Bruce D. Meyer, "The U.S. Earned Income Tax Credit: Its Effects and Possible Reforms," *Swedish Economic Policy Review* 14, no. 2 (Fall 2007): 55–80.

31. Janet Holtzblatt and Robert Rebelein, "Measuring the Effect of the Earned Income Tax Credit on Marriage Penalties and Bonuses" in *Making Work Pay: The Earned Income Tax Credit and Its Impact on America's Families*, ed. Bruce D. Meyer and Douglas Holtz-Eakin (New York: Russell Sage Foundation Press, 2001), 166–95.

32. Ibid.

33. President's Advisory Panel on Federal Tax Reform, *Simple, Fair, and Pro-Growth: Proposals to Fix America's Tax System*, US Government Printing Office, November 2005, https://www.treasury.gov/resource-center/tax-policy/Documents/Report-Fix-Tax-System-2005.pdf.

34. David T. Ellwood and Jeffrey B. Liebman, "The Middle Class Parent Penalty: Child Benefits in the U.S. Tax Code," *Tax Policy and the Economy* 15 (2001).

35. Paul Ryan, "Expanding Opportunity in America: A Discussion Draft from the House Budget Committee," House Budget Committee Majority Staff, July 24, 2014, http://budget.house.gov/uploadedfiles/expanding_opportunity_in_america.pdf.

36. Laura Wheaton and Elaine Sorensen, "Extending the EITC to Non-custodial Parents: Potential Impacts and Design Considerations," Urban Institute, 2009.

37. Nicholas Eberstadt, *Men Without Work: America's Invisible Crisis* (West Conshohocken, PN: Templeton Press, 2016).

Viewing the Food Stamp Program Through a 44-Year Lens

RUSSELL SYKES

American Public Human Services Association

As a novice to the social services world, I began employment in 1972 as an outreach worker in the Emergency Food and Medical Services Program of a rural Community Action Agency (CAA) in Gettysburg, Pennsylvania.[1] The Food Stamp Program (FSP), now the Supplemental Nutrition Assistance Program (SNAP), was optional for localities at the time and was not yet nationwide.

My job was to travel the rural back roads to locate low-income families and help them enroll in the program. We also worked to fulfill another CAA goal, which is now largely defunct: "maximum feasible participation" by the poor in social programs. Practically, this meant recruiting a council of poor individuals to be involved in discussing and helping design programs that would improve their economic future.

Since then, I have continued to work in social services, including the FSP/SNAP, at every level of government and in many capacities outside of government. I have been a direct service provider; a researcher; a deputy commissioner in New York State, where I administered SNAP; a congressionally appointed member of the National Commission on Hunger; and a consultant on a variety of human service issues to major research and policy organizations. I currently direct the American Public Human Services Association's Center for Employment & Economic Wellbeing (APHSA-CEEWB). It is hardly a stretch to say that I have been in or around the program since its inception.

Over that time, I have seen the FSP/SNAP grow from a small, inexpensive, and fairly straightforward elective program to a large and increasingly complex program that is the principal means by which the federal government reduces food insecurity (as distinguished from abject hunger and malnutrition, which are rare in the US). It has improved the material well-being of many people and is a crucial support. But it is also ripe for change in some areas. This chapter's purpose is to outline the program, describe how it developed into its current form, and address several questions policymakers would do well to consider moving forward.

The Supplemental Nutrition Assistance Program

SNAP is our nation's principal nutrition assistance program for low-income Americans and is one of the largest means-tested programs in both reach and cost. For most, it is an entitlement—if you meet the eligibility criteria and apply, you receive the benefit—and the federal government pays for the benefits in their entirety. In 2015, SNAP provided 45 million people with benefits in the average month, and benefits averaged about $125 per person per month for a total annual federal cost of about $70 billion.[2]

Benefits are provided to enrolled households via an Electronic Benefit Transfer (EBT) card, which is similar to a debit card and is refilled with funds each month. Benefits can be used to purchase nearly any food item available in participating stores, and there are more than 250,000 authorized retailers across the country.[3] Items such as alcohol, tobacco, and paper products are not eligible for purchase with SNAP benefits.

SNAP is designed to supplement a household's spending on food but not pay for a household's food costs in their entirety. Households receiving the benefit are expected to contribute 30 percent of their own net income after certain deductions toward food costs. The US Department of Agriculture (USDA) determines the maximum monthly amount of benefits for a given household size based on the cost of its Thrifty Food Plan, which is a basket of foods that provide adequate nutrition at minimal cost.

If a household has no net income after certain deductions, the USDA issues that household the maximum monthly benefit (in 2016, $511 per month for a family of three). For households with some net income, the maximum benefit is determined by subtracting 30 percent of the household's income from the maximum benefit amount for that household size.[4] This means that as households earn more, they are expected to contribute more of their own income toward food. It also means that they lose about $0.25 of SNAP benefits with each additional dollar earned, after deductions.

Eligibility is determined at the household level. Households are defined as groups of people who prepare food together rather than groups of people who live together; multiple SNAP households can live in one residence. To be eligible, households must have monthly gross incomes below 130 percent of the federal poverty level (in 2016, $2,117 per month for a household of three) and net incomes below 100 percent of the federal poverty level. Net incomes are calculated by deducting from gross income portions of the cost of various living expenses such as rent, utilities, and child care. A portion of any earned income is also deducted. Eligibility is also subject to an asset test: the typical household cannot have more than $2,250 in liquid assets to be eligible. This requirement can be waived. (I will discuss why this is problematic later.) Typically, a principal residence is not counted, and neither is the household's primary vehicle, although there is some variation among states.[5]

SNAP benefits flow disproportionately to those struggling the most—a surprisingly diverse population. In 2014, 58 percent of SNAP benefits flowed to the 43 percent of SNAP households with gross incomes of 50 percent or less of the federal poverty guidelines.[6] In that same year, 22 percent of households receiving SNAP reported no gross income; 41 percent reported no net income; and only 31 percent had earnings. (Public benefits, such as Temporary Assistance for Needy Families and Supplemental Security Income, count as income but not earnings.) Furthermore, 10 percent of recipients were elderly; 44 percent were children; and the rest were nonelderly adults. Among adults, SNAP recipients are disproportionately female, at 62 percent of nonelderly adults and 63 percent of elderly adults.[7]

How We Got Here

A program that now serves about one in five American children and 45 million people did not appear overnight. SNAP has evolved and grown into its current form over roughly the past 50 years.

Food assistance was initially as much a farm subsidy program as an antihunger effort. In the late 1930s, farmers were producing surpluses they could not sell. Many cities were plagued by high unemployment, and some people could not afford food.

In response, the Department of Agriculture developed a program to solve both issues. It allowed households to purchase orange coupons, which could then be used to purchase food. One dollar would purchase a coupon worth one dollar, which could be redeemed for one dollar's worth of any food at participating retailers. Orange coupons were intended to replace existing purchases. For each dollar of orange coupons purchased, households would receive $0.50 in blue coupons at no cost. Blue coupons were redeemable only for food items determined to be surplus goods. But the program ended when unemployment fell and surpluses evaporated.

Under President Lyndon B. Johnson, the FSP became permanent, following a host of pilot projects initiated under the Kennedy administration. The Food Stamp Act of 1964 maintained the general structure of purchasing food coupons worth more than the dollars paid for them. Over the next decade, program rules were standardized nationally, including the 30 percent household contribution, and states were required to expand the program to all jurisdictions. Participation grew from 500,000 to 15 million individuals between 1965 and 1974.[8]

The program changed significantly in the late 1970s, when the rallying cry for change became elimination of the purchase requirement (EPR). The push grew from the concern that households had difficulty finding the upfront cash to buy their food-stamp allotment. After EPR was implemented in 1979, the 30 percent household food contribution became a paper expectation rather than an upfront cash outlay. Participation increased by 1.5 million in the month following the bill's passage.[9]

Calls to destigmatize the program gained momentum in the mid-1980s. The concern was that requiring recipients to use paper stamps to purchase food caused some to decline participation for fear that they would be frowned on by cashiers and other shoppers. This led to the EBT card, which made food stamps far less distinguishable from other forms of payment. In the late 1980s, Congress officially allowed all states to use EBT and passed other changes that expanded program access.

But as program participation and costs continued to grow, the Clinton administration and Congress enacted sweeping welfare reform, which included major changes to the FSP in the Personal Responsibility and Work Opportunities Reconciliation Act of 1996 (PRWORA). Changes included eliminating eligibility for most legal immigrants, imposing stronger work requirements on able-bodied adults without dependents (ABAWDs) by limiting benefits to three months in any 36-month period for those who were not working or participating in a work program for at least 20 hours per week, and establishing stricter sanctions for noncompliance. PRWORA also made EBT mandatory for all states.

The focus on tighter eligibility and work requirements soon waned. The 2002 Farm Bill restored eligibility to qualified aliens who had been in the US for five years and to qualified alien children regardless of how long they had been in the US. It also adjusted the standard deduction by family size and indexed it to inflation; simplified reporting, which greatly relaxed how often households needed to report changes in income; and lengthened certification periods. Participation increased substantially to 26 million people in July 2006.[10]

The 2008 Farm Bill maintained emphasis on outreach and access. The legislation further simplified income reporting, allowed states to submit waiver requests to replace face-to-face interviews with telephone interviews and signatures, and extended transitional benefits to those leaving state cash assistance programs. To further destigmatize assistance receipt, the federal program changed its name from the Food Stamp Program to the Supplemental Nutrition Assistance Program (SNAP).

The Great Recession and modifications to the program in response to it further expanded participation. Under the American Recovery and Reinvestment Act, projected future benefit increases were fronted, increasing SNAP benefit amounts by 13.6 percent. Participation and costs hit all-time highs: by 2013, 47.6 million people received SNAP benefits worth more than $76 billion.[11] Ultimately this increase turned out to be higher than actual food price inflation and was rolled back starting in November 2013, in part to pay for spending on other social programs.

With the economy improving, the 2014 Farm Bill shifted focus back to reducing costs and increasing work. The final bill reduced spending by an estimated $8 billion over 10 years by narrowing the "Heat-and-Eat" loophole. This loophole allowed nominal state contributions (as little as $0.10 per month) toward the utility costs of SNAP households through the Low-Income Heating and Energy Assistance Program (LIHEAP) to permit participants to claim a substantial "standard utility deduction." But many recipients lived in housing where utility costs were included in the cost of rent. Because utility costs and a portion of rent are both separately deducted from gross income in calculating SNAP benefits, this amounted to a legal double-counting of utility costs that increased household SNAP benefits by as much as $90 per month.

States aggressively pushed the LIHEAP as a mechanism to draw down federal dollars. The final legislation responded by requiring a $20 annual minimum utility assistance contribution from states to qualify households for these deductions.[12] Anecdotal evidence suggests that it probably did not close the door entirely—the gains in additional SNAP benefits are still several times higher than the new utility contribution floor.

The debate over the bill also raised concerns about nonworking able-bodied SNAP beneficiaries. The final bill included $200 million to fund pilot projects in 10 states to test the effectiveness of various education and training programs for SNAP recipients. Target populations included ABAWDs, those with low skills, and those working low-wage or part-time jobs.[13]

SNAP's Strengths

SNAP benefits provide crucial supports for eligible low-income families and individuals to assist them in purchasing food, support work for those with low earnings, and respond quickly to economic downturns.

SNAP appears to be effective in achieving its primary goal: reducing food insecurity. The best measure is very low food security (VLFS), which the USDA defines as a household in which "eating patterns of one or more household members were disrupted and their food intake reduced, at least some time during the year, because they couldn't afford enough food." This is distinct from low food security (LFS), which is defined as "reduced quality, variety, or desirability of diet [but] little or no indication of reduced food intake."[14] In 2014, 5.6 percent of households in the United States contained at least one family member who experienced VLFS.[15]

Measuring SNAP's impact on VLFS is difficult for a variety of reasons—for example, SNAP recipient households differ in important ways from non-SNAP households—and research on the question is mixed. My view is that the best evidence points to SNAP substantially reducing VLFS, although there are anomalies. A recent evaluation from the USDA estimated that participation in SNAP reduced the share of households experiencing VLFS by between 12 and 19 percent. Less severe LFS was reduced by between 6 and 17 percent.[16] SNAP receipt is generally associated with increased food availability and caloric intake.

SNAP also reduces poverty. Analysis from the Center on Budget and Policy Priorities, using the government's Supplemental Poverty Measure, which counts SNAP as a financial resource, found that SNAP kept 4.8 million people out of poverty in 2013, including 2.1 million children. SNAP appears to be particularly effective for the most vulnerable, lifting 1.3 million children out of deep poverty (50 percent or less of the poverty threshold) in 2013.[17] This is no surprise because SNAP is most generous to those with the lowest incomes. Some have even suggested that SNAP is best understood as an income-transfer program rather than an antihunger program and, relatedly, questioned which congressional committees are best suited to legislate it. (This is mostly beyond my scope here, but I discuss it briefly in the concluding section.)

Receipt of food assistance may also have beneficial long-term impacts, especially for children. I find most interesting a recent pair of studies that use the FSP's staggered rollout across states in the 1960s and early 1970s.[18] They find that maternal access to food stamps reduced the incidence of low birth weight. New work from Hilary Hoynes, Diane Schanzenbach, and David Almond referenced in a 2016 White House report on SNAP suggests that access to food stamps in utero and during early life decreased rates of obesity by 16 percentage points and increased high school graduation rates by 18 percentage points.[19] The authors also find positive impacts on measures of earnings and self-sufficiency for women.

SNAP is also highly responsive to economic conditions. In times of economic distress, more people become eligible for the program and more people receive benefits—as evidenced by the substantial increase in enrollment and spending during the Great Recession. Poor communities typically benefit the most from SNAP's economic responsiveness. VLFS actually decreased among low-income households during the recession, even as millions more enrolled in the program, although VLFS for the general population rose during this period.[20] This stands in contrast to other safety-net programs, such as housing assistance, which do not respond to fluctuations in need.

Second, its reach among eligible people is very high by safety-net program standards. In 2012, the program provided benefits to 83 percent of those eligible.[21] Perhaps more significantly, the program provided 96 percent of the total benefits that would be disbursed if 100 percent of eligible individuals participated in the program. This is because those most in need participate at the highest rates and receive the largest SNAP benefit amounts.[22] This is an astounding percentage.

Finally, as measured by a mandatory quality control (QC) system, the vast majority of its payments are issued appropriately. The program correctly issues 96.34 percent of its payments (neither substantially overpaying nor underpaying households).[23] This stands in contrast to other public assistance programs, such as Medicaid, which in 2015 improperly issued 9.8 percent of payments, valued at $29.1 billion.[24] SNAP's improper-payment rate has improved substantially over time, falling by half since 2000. Of course, some of this progress is due to loosened eligibility criteria. Recently, however, the Office of the Inspector General and the USDA have expressed concerns with how states are operating their QC systems and have taken steps to further improve it. (This process is ongoing and beyond my scope here.)

Key Questions for SNAP Reform

While the program certainly has many positive aspects, it is far from perfect. Its deficits demand attention. What follows is a discussion of key questions surrounding SNAP that should be addressed.

Are current levels of nonwork among SNAP recipients concerning? The short answer is "yes." But first it is important to clarify who we are talking about regarding work. The majority of SNAP recipients are not expected to work; 64 percent of the caseload is comprised of children, the elderly, and individuals with disabilities. The relevant question about work and SNAP concerns the 36 percent of the caseload comprised of nonelderly, able-bodied adults, particularly those without dependent children.[25]

These are people we would expect to be working or engaged in allowable work-preparation activities, but most of them are not. In 2013, only 33 percent of nonelderly and nondisabled adults reported any earnings in the year they received SNAP, falling from 37 percent in 2000.[26] In raw numbers, the growth has been dramatic. From 2000 to 2013, the number of nondisabled, nonelderly adults receiving SNAP but reporting no earnings more than tripled, from 3.1 million to 11.3 million.[27] Among able-bodied adults age 18–49 without dependent children—those most expected to work—work rates are even lower. In 2014, 4.7 million ABAWDs received SNAP, up from about 2 million in 2000. Only 24 percent reported any income from earnings.[28]

SNAP is structured to soften the blow when people lose their jobs. It is no surprise that enrollment rose substantially during the economic downturn. And there are many nuances—many of these individuals receive SNAP for only a brief period before returning to work. But SNAP is often sold as a work support that helps low earnings go further. When about two-thirds of able-bodied adults and about three-quarters of ABAWDs receiving SNAP are not working, this characterization becomes somewhat misleading. SNAP, working with other programs, must do a better job addressing the issue that often makes work-able adults eligible for the program in the first instance: nonwork.

A strong case could be made for stricter enforcement of the existing work requirement for ABAWDs. This requirement has never been as effective as it should be—the 1996 legislation allowed states to exempt 15 percent of the ABAWD caseload from the requirement and request waivers related to the requirement. States have varied widely in how aggressively the requirement is enforced.

Work requirements were waived in most states during the recession, but states are being required to reinstitute them now that the economy has improved.[29] Initial evidence from early movers, such as Kansas, shows positive impacts on work levels and earnings. That said, concerns remain that earnings levels are still quite low.

The availability of work programs is also a concern. Many states are scrambling to provide adequate slots either in job search, work experience, or other allowable activities for those currently not employed, and historically, the USDA Food and Nutrition Service (FNS) and many states have paid too little attention to making these programs available and accessible to unemployed ABAWDs. States too often do not track the success of ABAWDs who exit the program to get a sense of how they are affected.

Moving forward, the requirement should be enforced more aggressively and uniformly, but with an eye toward these issues. In my view, if states cannot provide sufficient opportunities for engagement activities or actual job placement, ABAWD participants should not be denied benefits.

For the broader able-bodied adult population, SNAP has long had work-registration rules. But several times more people are registered for work than actually participate in allowable work activities.[30]

This is because states have significant discretion in determining the level at which they attempt to place recipients in employment or otherwise engage them in assigned activities at all. Until recently, the USDA-FNS and most states, with a few notable exceptions, have not aggressively pursued job placement or sought to make sure that able-bodied adults are actually assigned to activities under SNAP Employment and Training (E&T). At a minimum, states should be required to assign able-bodied adults in SNAP to work activities, giving then an extra nudge toward employment or the training and assistance that may help them find a job. I am hopeful that results from the 10 state pilot projects will provide more concrete guidance on strategies in this regard.

For too long, SNAP has been a transactional program. It has become adept at accurately issuing benefits to those meeting its eligibility criteria. It is less successful at asking this second question: what has put you in a position to need SNAP, and how can we help you get a job? The program must do a better job of making employment central to its interactions with beneficiaries and providing the support they need to secure employment.

To its credit, the USDA, since the enactment of the Workforce Innovation and Opportunity Act in 2014, which tied together multiple employment-related programs, has expanded its emphasis and commitment to SNAP E&T. It has moved from a token one-person overseer nationally to a solid team of five or more full-time staff and a staff person in each regional office assigned to work with states to truly emphasize employment in SNAP. But while there are increasingly some small bright spots, years of complacency and inattention will take time to overcome.

Are expansion efforts such as broad-based categorical eligibility a good use of funding? Do the program's asset tests make sense? There are two tiers of categorical eligibility under SNAP. One is basic categorical eligibility (Cat-El), and it is quite simple. Recipients of cash benefits through Supplemental Security Income, Temporary Assistance for Needy Families (TANF), or state General Assistance are made automatically ("categorically") eligible for SNAP and do not need to be deemed eligible through the program's customary income and asset tests. The rationale is that making recipients go through separate determination processes for two low-income programs, when the eligibility requirements of both programs are quite similar, adds unnecessary administrative cost.

Broad-based categorical eligibility (BBCE) is different. It allows states to confer SNAP eligibility to households by providing *noncash* services through TANF. For example, many states provide households with a TANF-funded brochure or a referral to a 1-800 telephone hotline and count households receiving these services as categorically eligible for SNAP. Under BBCE, states may make eligible all households with gross incomes below a level that they set—as high as 200 percent of the federal poverty level (versus 130 percent under SNAP eligibility rules). However, these households must still meet the *net* income threshold for SNAP to be eligible.

States may waive asset tests entirely under BBCE and still confer eligibility. Forty states, the District of Columbia, Puerto Rico, and Guam use BBCE to waive SNAP resource limits entirely or increase the amount of allowable resources significantly and still remain eligible. In all but five of these jurisdictions, no asset test is required for SNAP eligibility conferred via BBCE.[31]

The workaround on income rules confers eligibility to many households that otherwise would not be eligible for SNAP because their gross incomes exceed 130 percent of poverty. In 2010, 473,000 households in the states that apply BBCE were eligible for SNAP despite having gross incomes in excess of 130 percent of poverty.[32] Because states that have waived the asset/resource test for SNAP do not keep data on household resources, it is impossible to know the number of households that have become eligible via BBCE despite having resources in excess of traditional SNAP asset thresholds.

Cat-El is useful because recipients must pass strict eligibility and asset tests as part of receiving significant benefits through programs in which states have a financial stake. It reduces administrative duplication. BBCE is different. Recipients of the services that trigger BBCE do not have to pass such tests, and states need not spend a lot of money to provide services. Although BBCE's real impact on SNAP enrollment and spending is relatively small, waiving traditional program eligibility rules for this population weakens the targeting of SNAP to those most in need and raises questions about program integrity and congressional intent. It should be ended.

There may be some merit to arguments that net incomes matter more than gross incomes, especially in areas with a high cost of living. But BBCE is not the right way to address this. Any eligibility changes should be made intentionally in the federal program by federal policymakers—for example, by increasing gross income limits or expanding deductions for child care and shelter costs—not by giving states license to expand eligibility to previously ineligible families, whether or not they have substantial expenses.

The same principle applies to SNAP asset tests. Federal policymakers should definitively decide on the appropriate asset limit in SNAP and expect and require states to adhere to that limit. They should not provide an outlet for states to define asset limits as they see fit or waive them entirely, particularly because SNAP benefits are entirely federally funded. Few states balk at the chance to draw down more federal dollars.

That said, a strong argument should be raised for increasing federal asset limits for all SNAP participants. The current $2,250 in countable assets ($3,000 for households with an elderly member) is very low and likely discourages savings and participation in formal financial institutions.[33] I would propose raising this limit to at least $7,000, while repealing BBCE to prevent states from waiving asset tests, making asset rules more realistic and uniform across states. This would allow more households to accrue modest savings while assuring the public that means-tested benefits are not flowing to households not intended to receive them.

Should we be concerned about SNAP's high caseload and its slow decline after the recession? Yes, but with important caveats. By early 2016, the SNAP caseload declined by 2.6 million people after peaking at an all-time high of 47.6 million in 2012. Annual costs have also declined from more than $76 billion to just under $70 billion.[34]

But SNAP participation has remained far above its levels before the recession (27 million in 2007), and the caseload's decline has been quite slow. Given that the unemployment rate has halved since 2011, one would expect faster declines in the caseload and spending as more people find work. This raises questions as to whether the program is as economically responsive as some claim.

Changes to SNAP are an important part of the story. Expanded use of BBCE has contributed to higher caseloads. Benefit increases through the American Recovery and Reinvestment Act of 2009 increased participation. The ABAWD work-requirement waiver has not pushed the people most expected to work to take jobs as the economy has begun to strengthen. Unreported income that would be surfaced by a stronger emphasis on work requirements has also likely played a role. These factors have likely contributed to higher caseloads and slowed caseload declines in recent years. But elevated benefit levels have now returned to normal, and the ABAWD waivers are expiring in most places. Policy is returning to normal, except for BBCE. It is likely that moving forward, the caseload will therefore decline more.[35]

But perhaps the largest contributors are nonwork and continued weakness in the labor market. The unemployment rate does not tell the complete story: it describes only how likely someone looking for work is to secure employment and does not count those who have given up the search. Many have. The labor force participation rate among those who could and want to work and whose unemployment insurance benefits have expired is near an all-time low of 62.7 percent, having declined steadily since 2008.[36] The overall employment rate (the share of people age 16 and older who have a job) remains 3.4 percentage points below prerecession levels.[37]

Slow wage growth for those at the bottom is also a likely contributor. A much larger share of the population continues to have incomes below 130 percent of the poverty line than before the recession, and as a result, more people continue to be eligible for SNAP.[38]

This underscores that SNAP needs to do more to connect nonworking recipients with a job. With unemployment hovering around 5 percent, finding work is no longer unrealistic in many communities around the country. The program should not be content to provide benefits to those who are out of work—it should engage them in programs and activities that help them reenter employment. As it stands, SNAP could be faulted more with a sin of omission than of commission.

The employment issue became more important with the passage of the Workforce Innovation and Opportunity Act (WIOA) in 2014 and subsequent final regulations in 2016. The main aspect of WIOA is the integration of fragmented employment-related programs, such as those run out of the Department of Labor through local American Job Centers, TANF in the Administration for Children and Families within the US Department of Health and Human Services (HHS), and SNAP E&T programs.

Are current household benefit levels under SNAP adequate? Yes, in general. The purpose of SNAP is to supplement a household's income to allow them to afford a sufficient level of basic nutrition. The USDA bases the maximum value of benefits on the cost of the Thrifty Food Plan (TFP), which is a basket of basic foods that will meet a given family's nutritional needs at minimal cost. The USDA calculates the cost of this basket of foods on a monthly basis to account for food costs changing over time.

There are 15 different "market baskets" under the TFP that are designed to meet the different nutritional needs of households with people of different ages and genders. They contain ratios of dairy, proteins, vegetables, and other foods in accordance with the USDA's Recommended Dietary Allowances and Dietary Guidelines for Americans.

A leading critique of the TFP—and the maximum benefit levels based on it—is that it does not account for the time cost of preparing food.[39] This argument suggests that households may not have the time to prepare foods afforded under the TFP and, as a result, they purchase foods that require less time to prepare. These foods tend to be more expensive, leaving households short on funds and at higher risk for food insecurity. In response, some have proposed adopting the USDA's more generous Low-Cost Food Plan, which provides 130 percent of the benefits of the TFP.

This critique has some truth, but I see several problems with it. One is that SNAP benefits based on the TFP do not account for the 30 percent contribution of net income after deductions that households themselves are meant to spend on food. Second, SNAP benefits based on the TFP do not account for outside nutritional resources that many children in SNAP households take advantage of. Many receive free lunch through their schools, and some receive free breakfast as well. A substantial number of SNAP households receive benefits through the Special Supplemental Nutrition Assistance Program for Women, Infants and Children (WIC). Many also participate in summer programs that provide free lunch or breakfast or in a pilot EBT program that increases SNAP benefits over the summer to households with children (and is likely to be expanded). Arguments concerning inadequate preparation time often refer to households with children. But on a per-meal, per-person basis, these families often already have resources exceeding TFP levels because of their own purchase contribution and a substantial share of meals that are not being paid for through SNAP.

Second, it would be expensive. If SNAP benefit levels today were suddenly changed to adopt the more generous food plan costs, the aggregate cost of SNAP would rise from $69.6 billion to roughly $90 billion. This does not account for the likely uptick in participation due to an increase in maximum benefits.[40] Even a more modest increase, such as a 15 percent increase in the TFP cost as suggested by Diane Schanzenbach, would represent a significant expense in the current budget environment.[41]

Third, even if lack of time for food preparation leads to higher levels of VLFS, the proposals seeking to address that issue go far beyond the claimed problem. They would raise benefit levels for everyone to address an issue associated with employment: lack of time. But does this make sense when a large share of the adult caseload is not reporting any earnings or is not expected to work at all? Probably not. Few would argue that it is unreasonable to expect those with time to prepare basic foods. And for the purchase of a basic selection of nutritious foods to be prepared in the home, the TFP is, by and large, sufficient.

This said, more research could be done to explore the extent to which lack of time affects VLFS, among which populations, and whether benefit adequacy needs to be addressed. Should it be a significant issue, small and rigorously evaluated demonstration projects targeting the most affected populations could explore whether increased benefits are needed—for example, contrasting an increase in the TFP to the current level or the Low-Cost Food Plan with the TFP in a small area, concerning the impact on both food preparation time and VLFS in general. It seems this is the proper way to address this concern, rather than rushing into a major new expenditure.[42]

Should SNAP more aggressively address health issues, such as obesity? The United States has an obesity problem. Rates are higher among the poor and even higher among those participating in SNAP. Over the period 2007–10, 40 percent of SNAP beneficiaries were obese, compared to 30 percent of higher-income Americans and 32 percent of the non-SNAP poor.[43]

This raises legitimate questions about the extent to which SNAP addresses one of our nation's most pressing public health issues. I believe that the program should take tough, but needed, steps to ensure that public dollars are flowing toward nutritious foods, not junk foods. Other government nutrition programs—such as the WIC and, increasingly, school lunches—place strict limits on the types or nutritional content of foods to which public dollars are devoted. SNAP should consider doing the same.

A first step, endorsed by the National Commission on Hunger, is to eliminate sugar-sweetened beverages (SSBs) from the list of items that can be purchased through SNAP. SSBs are not nutritious, and their effects on obesity are significant. By one estimate, SNAP beneficiaries spend $1.7–2.1 billion per year of their assistance on SSBs.[44] A recently released survey by the USDA found that 47.7 percent of SNAP participants reported drinking a regular soda on the day covered by the dietary recall survey, and 24.6 percent reported consuming noncarbonated sweetened beverages.[45] An earlier USDA analysis of the National Health and Nutrition Examination Survey data estimated that 83 percent of SNAP participants consumed some type of SSB on the intake day.[46]

That change will be difficult, which I learned through my role in an unsuccessful effort to restrict SNAP use for purchasing SSBs in New York. In the city, the overlap between the consumption of SSBs and the obesity epidemic—with its attendant health problems (diabetes and heart disease) and Medicaid costs—was significant in many of the poorest boroughs. We asked: why should SNAP, unlike other programs operated by the USDA-FNS and applauded by anti-hunger advocates, have no nutritional standards, while all the others clearly outline either the allowable food packages or nutritional standards? Our proposal made this case and included an evaluation component to review whether the proposed ban reduced the purchase of SSBs or if SNAP recipients substituted their own money to make the same purchases.

The proposal for the demonstration project revealed a disturbing gulf between antihunger advocates aligned with the beverage industry, which vehemently opposed the project, and a broad array of public health organizations that fully supported it. While the denial letter from the USDA was based (in my view) on slim reeds—for example, that it is difficult for retailers to implement or that it is too large a catchment area—the real reason was that the USDA succumbed to the louder, better-funded voices of the antihunger and beverage industries, which argued that free choice to buy any items with SNAP dollars other than those already prohibited should trump broad public health concerns.[47] A strong case can be made to the contrary.

The USDA has thrown its support behind incentivizing the purchase of healthy foods through the Healthy Incentives Project, which is laudable. But instead of allowing or encouraging states to experiment broadly with restrictions as a research counterpoint, they have, for the most part, resisted such efforts. (Proposals from Maine, Minnesota, and New York City have all been rejected.) This is despite evidence that providing summer meal assistance to children using WIC's purchase restrictions resulted in better nutrition for children than meal assistance provided through SNAP, with no significant difference in VLFS between the two groups.[48] It would be useful to know which approach or combination of approaches produces better nutritional outcomes. States should be given greater leeway to experiment with these approaches, so long as they are rigorously evaluated.

The concept of banning the purchase of SSBs with SNAP benefits, with a strong evaluation component, is a sound and rational policy and should receive serious consideration in future legislation around SNAP. I fully support the National Commission on Hunger's final assessment that a carefully defined class of SSBs should be excluded from the list of allowable purchases in SNAP; that SNAP benefits should help families meet nutritional needs, not contribute to negative health outcomes through poor nutritional choices; and that the technology already exists to exclude certain items at the retail store level.[49]

Are SNAP's efforts to improve food buying and preparation habits working? The Nutrition Education and Training Program (SNAP-Ed), the program's principal effort to improve the food purchasing and preparation habits of SNAP households, is well-intentioned but expensive and broadly ineffective. It could be improved in many ways.

SNAP-Ed lacks a substantial base of evidence. Few of the interventions conducted through SNAP-Ed have been evaluated, and many of those evaluated have not been cause for celebration. An effort completed in 2012 aimed at increasing daily at-home consumption of fruits and vegetables among young children showed no outcomes impact in any of the three interventions evaluated.[50] A second wave of demonstrations completed in late 2013 was more positive, showing statistically significant positive impacts for two interventions aimed at increasing daily intake of fruits and vegetables among children.[51] Still, there is broad agreement that we do not really know how effective SNAP-Ed is. We have scant evidence for a program that spent $388 million on nutrition in 2012.

This should be corrected. One option is to devote a larger share of SNAP-Ed funds to rigorous impact evaluations with the goal of establishing a suite of proven interventions for bringing about specific, desired outcomes that align with the objectives of improving food purchase, preparation, and consumption decisions. Knowing which models are not effective is also useful. Over time, an increasing share of SNAP-Ed dollars could be tied to programs backed by at least two rigorously evaluated demonstration projects.

My preferred alternative, shared by others, is to greatly reduce or simply end the SNAP-Ed program and reinvest the funds in other purposes that more directly help participants increase their food purchasing power and improve their health. If SNAP-Ed were ended, it could free funding to explore other program improvements, such as evaluating the effectiveness of benefit increases through a modest pilot approach testing an alternative to the TFP, increasing the current paltry asset test, and expanding other nutrition-oriented programs. One such program, the Healthy Incentives Pilot approach (which is not a SNAP-Ed program), has been shown to significantly increase participants' purchase of healthier foods, predominantly more fruits and vegetables.[52]

Addressing the retailer side of the nutrition-decision equation is also important, although it is not a part of SNAP-Ed. Retailers are where individuals in SNAP ultimately make their purchase decisions. Two things could be done here. First, an expanded array of food items should be required offerings among SNAP participating retailers. An effort is already underway by the USDA-FNS to curtail small retailers from carrying only items of little or no nutritional value. The USDA announced in February 2016—following requirements contained in the 2014 Farm Bill—that participating retailers would need to provide SNAP participants with increased access to healthy foods by requiring stores to stock a wider array of choices.[53] This should be continued, expanded, and enforced.

Second, the FNS should implement minimal shelf display rules for retailers that will make healthier food items more visibly and conveniently available to help curtail impulse buying. For example, the USDA could require that stores accepting SNAP provide a minimum of 15 feet of shelf space for healthy foods or that no more space is devoted toward junk food than healthy food.[54]

Conclusion

SNAP is one of the nation's best defenses against VLFS and times of economic distress. It responds quickly to increased household need. It substantially reduces poverty. It likely generates long-term positive outcomes for many beneficiaries, including children, particularly in their early development stage. But, like all social programs, it could be improved.

With the growing debate as to whether SNAP is more of an income transfer and antipoverty program than a nutrition program, it is worth exploring whether USDA-FNS and the Agriculture Committees in Congress are the proper venues for oversight of SNAP, given its close programmatic relationship to TANF, Medicaid, and employment programs under WIOA. For better coordination, consideration should be given to having HHS administer SNAP and transfer congressional oversight authority to the House Ways and Means and Senate Finance Committees.[55]

Whether or not such a change in oversight is made, basic eligibility rules should be established federally and enforced uniformly and consistently, and loopholes that allow states to expand eligibility and benefits beyond federal program rules should be closed. If changes in the basis for program benefits or any expanded deductions for earnings, housing, or child care are to be explored, they should occur only within carefully evaluated, small pilot efforts that analyze their effectiveness in reducing VLFS. Any broader expansion should address the affordability of bringing policy changes to scale.

The program should focus more aggressively on connecting its able-bodied beneficiaries with work, not just providing them with services to ease the burden of nonwork. Increased state flexibility on this and many other fronts—such as improving nutritional outcomes, including purchase restrictions, and targeting benefits to those most in need—should be encouraged and facilitated, although rigorously evaluated. And dollars in nutritional education should be limited only to interventions that demonstrate results and ended for those that do not.

Notes

1. CAAs are local entities—remnants of President Johnson's War on Poverty—that operate a variety of assistance programs. Johnson envisioned local entities governed in part by the low-income people they served. Many still exist, but they are less prevalent than in the past. For more, see Rich Lucas, "History of Community Action," Illinois Association of Community Action Agencies, http://www.iacaanet.org/history.php.

2. US Department of Agriculture, Food and Nutrition Service, "Supplemental Nutrition Assistance Program: Number of Persons Participating," accessed April 28, 2016, http://www.fns.usda.gov/sites/default/files/pd/29SNAPcurrPP.pdf; and Henry J. Kaiser Family Foundation, "Average Monthly Food Stamp Benefits Per Person: FY 2014," September 4, 2015, http://kff.org/other/state-indicator/avg-monthly-food-stamp-benefits/.

3. US Department of Agriculture, Food and Nutrition Service, *Fiscal Year 2015 at a Glance*, March 9, 2016, http://www.fns.usda.gov/sites/default/files/snap/2015-SNAP-Retailer-Management-Year-End-Summary.pdf.

4. US Department of Agriculture, Food and Nutrition Service, "Supplemental Nutrition Assistance Program (SNAP): Eligibility," February 25, 2016, http://www.fns.usda.gov/snap/eligibility.

5. Ibid.

6. Kelsey Farson Gray and Shivani Kochhar, *Characteristics of Supplemental Nutrition Assistance Program Households: Fiscal Year 2014*, US Department of Agriculture, December 2015, http://www.fns.usda.gov/sites/default/files/ops/Characteristics2014.pdf.

7. Ibid.

8. US Department of Agriculture, Food and Nutrition Service, "A Short History of SNAP," November 20, 2014, http://www.fns.usda.gov/snap/short-history-snap.

9. Ibid.

10. Ibid.

11. US Department of Agriculture, "Supplemental Nutrition Assistance Program."

12. Randy Alison Aussenberg and Libby Perl, *The 2014 Farm Bill: Changing the Treatment of LIHEAP Receipt in the Calculation of SNAP Benefits*, Congressional Research Service, February 12, 2014, http://nationalaglawcenter.

org/wp-content/uploads/assets/crs/R42591.pdf.

13. US Department of Agriculture, Food and Nutrition Service, "USDA Awards $200 Million for Skills Training to Help SNAP Recipients Get Good Jobs," press release, March 20, 2015, http://www.fns.usda.gov/pressrelease/2015/007115.

14. US Department of Agriculture, Economic Research Service, "Definitions of Food Security," September 8, 2015, http://www.ers.usda.gov/topics/food-nutrition-assistance/food-security-in-the-us/definitions-of-food-security.aspx.

15. US Department of Agriculture, Economic Research Service, "Food Security Status of U.S. Households in 2014," September 8, 2015, http://www.ers.usda.gov/topics/food-nutrition-assistance/food-security-in-the-us/key-statistics-graphics.aspx.

16. James Mabli and Jim Ohls, "Supplemental Nutrition Assistance Program Participation Is Associated with an Increase in Household Food Security in a National Evaluation," *Journal of Nutrition* 145, no. 2 (2014): 344–51.

17. Brynne Keith-Jennings, "SNAP Kept Nearly 5 Million People out of Poverty Last Year, New Figures Show," Center on Budget and Policy Priorities, October 16, 2014, http://www.cbpp.org/blog/snap-kept-nearly-5-million-people-out-of-poverty-last-year-new-figures-show.

18. Douglas Almond, Hilary W. Hoynes, and Diane Whitmore Schanzenbach, "Inside the War on Poverty: The Impact of Food Stamps on Birth Outcomes," *Review of Economics and Statistics* 93, no. 2 (2011): 387–403.

19. Hilary W. Hoynes, Diane Whitmore Schanzenbach, and Douglas Almond, "Long Run Impacts of Childhood Access to the Safety Net," *American Economic Review* 106, no. 4 (2016): 903–34, https://www.aeaweb.org/articles?id=10.1257/aer.20130375; and Executive Office of the President, *Long-Term Benefits of the Supplemental Nutrition Assistance Program*, December 2015, https://www.whitehouse.gov/sites/whitehouse.gov/files/documents/SNAP_report_final_nonembargo.pdf.

20. VLFS for those below the poverty line fell from 19.3 percent in 2008 to 18.0 percent in 2014. See Mark Nord, Margaret Andrews, and Steven Carlson, *Household Food Security in the United States, 2008*, US Department of Agriculture, Economic Research Service, November 2009; and Alisha Coleman-Jensen et al., *Household Food Security in the United States in 2014*, US

Department of Agriculture, Economic Research Service, September 2015.

21. Karen E. Cunnyngham, *Reaching Those in Need: Estimates of State Supplemental Nutrition Assistance Program Participation Rates in 2012*, US Department of Agriculture, February 2015, http://www.fns.usda.gov/sites/default/files/ops/Reaching2012.pdf.

22. Rich Lucas, email to author, March 7, 2016.

23. US Department of Agriculture, Food and Nutrition Service, "Supplemental Nutrition Assistance Program (SNAP)," July 2, 2015, http://www.fns.usda.gov/snap/quality-control.

24. Centers for Medicare & Medicaid Services, "Payment Error Rate Measurement Program (PERM) Medicaid Error Rates," November 2015, https://www.cms.gov/Research-Statistics-Data-and-Systems/Monitoring-Programs/Medicaid-and-CHIP-Compliance/PERM/Downloads/PERMMEDICAIDERRORRATES201511192015.pdf.

25. Kelsey Farson Gray and Shivani Kochhar, *Characteristics of Supplemental Nutrition Assistance Program Households: Fiscal Year 2014*, US Department of Agriculture, Office of Policy Support, December 2015, http://www.fns.usda.gov/sites/default/files/ops/Characteristics2014.pdf.

26. Analysis from the Center on Budget and Policy Priorities provided to the American Enterprise Institute.

27. Ibid.

28. Steven Carlson, Dorothy Rosenbaum, and Brynne Keith-Jennings, *Who Are the Low-Income Childless Adults Facing the Loss of SNAP in 2016?*, Center on Budget and Policy Priorities, February 8, 2016, http://www.cbpp.org/research/food-assistance/who-are-the-low-income-childless-adults-facing-the-loss-of-snap-in-2016.

29. US Department of Agriculture, "Supplemental Nutrition Assistance Program—Expiration of Statewide ABAWD Time Limit Waivers," March 4, 2015, http://www.fns.usda.gov/sites/default/files/snap/SNAP-Expiration-of-Statewide-ABAWD-Time-Limit-Waivers.pdf.

30. The exact numbers here are murky. Some federal reports suggest that in 2014, 6.9 million SNAP participants were registered for work but only 2.8 million participated in any allowable activities. See Gray and Kochar, *Characteristics of Supplemental Nutrition Assistance Program Households*. Other reports indicate that states reported 13.3 million SNAP participants who were subject to the work requirement in SNAP

and registered for work, but placed only about 640,000 participants in E&T services. See Randy Alison Aussenberg, *SNAP and Related Nutrition Provisions of the 2014 Farm Bill (P.L. 113–79)*, Congressional Research Service, April 24, 2014, http://nationalaglawcenter.org/wp-content/uploads/assets/crs/R43332.pdf.

31. One- and two-person households still receive the minimum benefit. Gene Falk and Randy Alison Aussenberg, *The Supplemental Nutrition Assistance Program (SNAP): Categorical Eligibility*, Congressional Research Service, July 22, 2014, https://www.fas.org/sgp/crs/misc/R42054.pdf.

32. US Government Accountability Office, *Supplemental Nutrition Assistance Program: Improved Oversight of State Eligibility Expansions Needed*, August 2, 2012, http://www.gao.gov/products/GAO-12-670.

33. US Department of Agriculture, Food and Nutrition Service, "Supplemental Nutrition Assistance Program (SNAP): Eligibility."

34. US Department of Agriculture, Food and Nutrition Service, "Supplemental Nutrition Assistance Program (SNAP)," accessed April 28, 2016, http://www.fns.usda.gov/pd/supplemental-nutrition-assistance-program-snap.

35. Chad Stone, Arloc Sherman, and Brynne Keith-Jennings, *No Mystery Why SNAP Enrollment Remains High: It's Still the Economy*, Center on Budget and Policy Priorities, March 18, 2016, http://www.cbpp.org/research/no-mystery-why-snap-enrollment-remains-high-its-still-the-economy.

36. US Bureau of Labor Statistics, "Civilian Labor Force Participation Rate," retrieved from FRED, Federal Reserve Bank of St. Louis, June 3, 2016, https://research.stlouisfed.org/fred2/series/CIVPART.

37. US Bureau of Labor Statistics, "Civilian Employment-Population Ratio," retrieved from FRED, Federal Reserve Bank of St. Louis, June 3, 2016, https://research.stlouisfed.org/fred2/series/EMRATIO.

38. Center on Budget and Policy Priorities, "Chart Book: SNAP Helps Struggling Families Put Food on the Table," March 24, 2016, http://www.cbpp.org/research/food-assistance/chart-book-snap-helps-struggling-families-put-food-on-the-table.

39. Diane Whitmore Schanzenbach, "Strengthening SNAP for a More Food-Secure, Healthy America" (Hamilton Project Discussion Paper, Brookings Institution, December 2013).

40. Lucas, email to author, March 7, 2016.

41. Schanzenbach, "Strengthening SNAP for a More Food-Secure, Healthy America."

42. National Commission on Hunger, *Freedom from Hunger: An Achievable Goal for the United States of America*, 2015, http://cybercemetery.unt.edu/archive/hungercommission/20151216222324/https://hungercommission.rti.org/Portals/0/SiteHtml/Activities/FinalReport/Hunger_Commission_Final_Report.pdf.

43. US Department of Agriculture, Food and Nutrition Service, *Diet Quality of Americans by SNAP Participation Status: Data from the National Health and Nutrition Examination Survey, 2007–2010: Summary*, May 2015, http://www.fns.usda.gov/sites/default/files/ops/NHANES-SNAP07-10-Summary.pdf.

44. T. Andreyeva et al., "Grocery Store Beverage Choices by Participants in Federal Food Assistance and Nutrition Programs," *American Journal of Preventative Medicine* 43, no. 4 (October 2012): 411–18, http://www.ncbi.nlm.nih.gov/pubmed/22992359.

45. Elizabeth Condon et al., *Diet Quality of Americans by SNAP Participation Status: Data from the National Health and Nutrition Examination Survey, 2007–2010*, US Department of Agriculture, Food and Nutrition Service, May 2015, Table C-4, http://www.fns.usda.gov/sites/default/files/ops/NHANES-SNAP07-10.pdf.

46. Jessica E. Todd and Michele Ver Ploeg, *Restricting Sugar-Sweetened Beverages from SNAP Purchases Not Likely To Lower Consumption*, US Department of Agriculture, Economic Research Service, March 2, 2015, http://www.ers.usda.gov/amber-waves/2015-march/restricting-sugar-sweetened-beverages-from-snap-purchases-not-likely-to-lower-consumption.

47. Jessica Shahin, letter to Elizabeth Berlin, August 19, 2011, http://www.foodpolitics.com/wp-content/uploads/SNAP-Waiver-Request-Decision.pdf.

48. Phil Gleason, *Does Limiting Choice in Food Assistance Programs Affect Dietary Quality Among School-Aged Children?*, Mathematica Policy Research, http://www.appam.org/assets/1/7/Philip_Gleason__Panel_2___slides.pdf.

49. National Commission on Hunger, *Freedom from Hunger*.

50. Vivian Gabor et al., *SNAP Education and Evaluation Study (Wave I): Final Report*, US Department of Agriculture, January 2012, http://www.fns.usda.gov/sites/default/files/SNAPEdWaveI_0.pdf.

51. US Department of Agriculture, Food and Nutrition Service, Office of Policy Support, *Supplemental Nutrition Assistance Program Education and Evaluation Study (Wave II) (Summary)*, December 2013, http://www.fns.usda.gov/sites/default/files/SNAPEdWaveII_Summary.pdf.

52. US Department of Agriculture, Food and Nutrition Service, Office of Policy Support, *Evaluation of the Healthy Incentives Pilot (Hip) Final Report—Summary*, September 2014, http://www.fns.usda.gov/sites/default/files/HIP-Final-Summary.pdf.

53. US Department of Agriculture, Food and Nutrition Service, "USDA Proposes Policies to Improve Food Access, Healthy Choices for Low-Income Americans," press release, February 16, 2016, http://www.fns.usda.gov/pressrelease/2016/004516.

54. Thomas A. Farley and Russell Sykes, "See No Junk Food, Buy No Junk Food," *New York Times*, March 20, 2015, http://www.nytimes.com/2015/03/21/opinion/see-no-junk-buy-no-junk.html.

55. Primary advocates of SNAP in the antihunger world and major research organizations that study SNAP increasingly discuss the program as being an income and work-support program that lifts many individuals and children out of poverty. And new poverty measures, such as the Supplemental Poverty Measure, treat SNAP as income. SNAP benefits, along with recipients' own food expenditures, do help more than 45 million households obtain a nutritionally adequate diet, and SNAP has been shown to reduce food insecurity. Additionally, SNAP's close connection to other agricultural programs in the Farm Bill has dissipated since the time when the program, then known as Food Stamps, was a major avenue for eligible households to purchase agricultural surplus and commodities. The erosion of this link raises additional questions as to whether the House Ways and Means and Senate Finance Committees should more appropriately reauthorize SNAP with other programs operated out of the US Department of Health and Human Services because of its income-support function. Adding to that argument is the increasing alignment of SNAP with programs such as TANF and Medicaid, as there is a major crossover of clients served by all three programs. Additionally, a case can be made that the administration of SNAP could just as well fall under HHS rather than the USDA to foster greater integration and alignment of these programs, particularly from a systems and eligibility determination

standpoint. Lawmakers should reevaluate the long tradition of SNAP being related to other agriculture programs and being reauthorized as part of the Farm Bill.

Medicaid

JAMES C. CAPRETTA
American Enterprise Institute

In 1965, the authors of Medicaid thought they were creating a program that would provide federal structure, uniformity, and some funding for the many state programs that were already providing relatively inexpensive "indigent care" services to low-income households. They did not foresee the transformation they were setting in motion. Medicaid has grown into the largest health care program in the country by enrollment, with 66 million participants and with annual federal and state costs of more than $550 billion. It is by far our nation's largest program serving low-income households.[1]

Medicaid's purpose is to provide access to medically necessary health care to persons who, because of limited resources and lack of health insurance coverage, have less capacity to secure care for themselves. The definition of the services paid for by Medicaid has expanded over the years through legislative changes, administrative decisions, and court cases. Today, the program pays for hospital and physician care, prescription drugs, screening and preventive services, and long-term care services and supports for elderly and disabled persons.

Medicaid spending has increased rapidly nearly every year since the program was enacted, creating significant pressure in federal and state budgets. Medicaid, along with other major entitlement programs, is a primary reason for today's large federal budget deficit and for the massive deficits projected for the coming decades. Its growth has forced federal and state policymakers to limit spending on other priorities, including many programs that also serve low-income households.

There are several reasons for Medicaid's growth, including eligibility liberalizations enacted by Congress and cost trends that have rapidly increased health spending for all insurance plans. But Medicaid's original federal-state design is also an important factor, especially the "matching" system through which the federal government pays for more than half of state Medicaid spending.

The Medicaid FMAP and Split Political Accountability

Medicaid is a shared federal-state responsibility. The program was created in federal law, but it is largely administered by the states. States pay for the medical and social services that enrollees use and then receive funds from the federal government to partially pay for the program's costs.

Most federal funding provided to the states under Medicaid is determined by a standard state-specific formula called the federal medical assistance percentage (FMAP). The FMAP is based on the ratio of per capita income in the states relative to the national average. States with lower per capita incomes get higher FMAPs. For instance, in 2016, the FMAP for Arkansas is 70 percent, meaning that for every $1.00 the state spends on standard Medicaid benefits, the federal government pays for $0.70 of the bill. Medicaid law puts a floor on the standard FMAP at 50 percent, so states with higher per capita incomes, such as California, Massachusetts, and New York, which might otherwise have FMAPs below 50 percent, get half their Medicaid bill paid for by the federal government.[2]

Special matching rates apply to different subparts of Medicaid. For instance, the federal government generally applies a uniform FMAP of 50 percent for all state administrative expenses. In addition, the Affordable Care Act (ACA) allows states to expand Medicaid eligibility to all households with incomes below 138 percent of the federal poverty line. For three years (2014 through 2016), the federal government is paying 100 percent of the costs for newly eligible Medicaid enrollees. After 2016, the FMAP for this "expansion population" will be 90 percent.[3] On average, the federal government pays for between 62 and 64 percent of total Medicaid spending, depending on the year.[4]

The Medicaid FMAP is the fundamental flaw in the program's current design and the main reason it is so costly. States can initiate new spending in Medicaid—spending that often will boost economic activity in the state—and federal taxpayers pay for at least half the cost. At the same time, savings from state-initiated Medicaid-spending cuts are also shared with federal taxpayers.

For instance, in a state where the FMAP is 60 percent, the governor and state legislators face the unattractive prospect of keeping only $1.00 of every $2.50 in Medicaid savings they can identify and implement. The other $1.50 goes to the federal treasury. Put another way, governors and state legislators are reluctant to impose $2.50 in budgetary pain for a $1.00 gain to their bottom line. Powerful health-sector interests, including hospital systems, nursing-home operators, physician groups, and insurers, also make it difficult for states to restrict total funding on the program, although payment rates for individual services can be quite low.

Medicaid's current federal-state design also undermines political accountability. Neither the federal government nor the states are fully in charge. As a result, each side has tended to blame the other for the program's shortcomings, and neither believes it has sufficient power to unilaterally impose effective reforms.

Incentives for Higher Spending

Federal Medicaid spending has no upper limit. The federal government continues to make matching payments to the states as long as the spending is within the boundaries of allowable Medicaid expenditures.

The only check on runaway expenditures is the state contribution to the program. The FMAP establishes both the federal government's matching payments for Medicaid costs and the state share (1 − FMAP). The requirement of a state contribution for every extra dollar of spending should serve as a disincentive for wasteful and excessive expenditures.

Figure 1. Medicaid Enrollment as a Percentage of the US Population

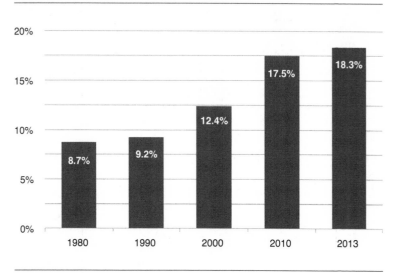

Sources: US Census Bureau and CMS Actuary.

Unfortunately, the discipline that comes from requiring a state contribution to program costs has been partially undermined by schemes that have effectively lowered states' shares of Medicaid expenditures. These schemes generally involve grossly inflating state payment rates to certain narrowly defined sets of providers of services. These high payments draw additional federal matching funds. The state then imposes a special, narrowly drawn tax on those same providers of services, which has the effect of reimbursing the state for its presumed share of the higher Medicaid payment rates. The net effect is more federal spending on Medicaid and no additional burden on taxpayers in the state.[5]

States can also reduce their budgetary costs if they are able to move programs traditionally financed with state-only funds under the Medicaid programmatic umbrella, thus drawing partial federal support. Not surprisingly, this has been a common practice in states for many years as well.[6]

Medicaid Enrollment Growth

Congress enacted a series of program liberalizations in the 1980s and 1990s that fueled program enrollment growth. These changes extended public insurance coverage to tens of millions of people nationwide, mainly women and children.

But it was not just federal action that expanded the program. The pressures that pushed Congress to broaden Medicaid's reach also pushed states to adopt some of the optional coverage expansions allowed in federal law. The FMAP paved the way for these state decisions by lowering the cost barrier to higher program enrollment.

The combined effect of these factors has been a remarkable and uninterrupted increase in the percentage of the US population participating in Medicaid. As shown in Figure 1, in 1980, national Medicaid enrollment was 8.7 percent of the US population. By 2013, it had risen to 18.3 percent.

Federal Cost Growth

Medicaid-spending growth over the past 50 years is an important reason the federal government is under fiscal stress today. Moreover, continued growth in program spending is expected to contribute substantially to large deficits and growing federal debt over the coming decades.

As shown in Figure 2, federal spending on Medicaid in 1972 was only 0.4 percent of gross domestic product (GDP). Today, it is 2 percent of GDP.

The Congressional Budget Office expects spending on the program to continue to rise rapidly. Current long-term projections show combined spending for Medicaid, the Children's Health Insurance Program, and the subsidies for health insurance provided under the ACA increasing from about 2.2 percent of GDP today to 3.2 percent in 2050.[7]

Figure 2. Historical Medicaid Spending

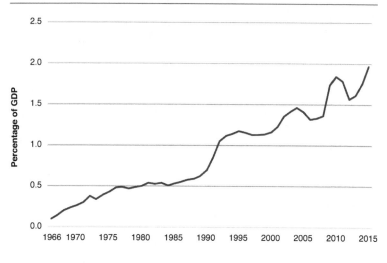

Source: Congressional Budget Office, Historical Tables, January 2016.

Medicaid's Diverse Beneficiary Population

There are different program beneficiaries within Medicaid, with different service needs. Specifically, Medicaid provides insurance to lower-income households needing access to traditional medical services, and it provides assistance to the severely disabled and the frail elderly in need of nursing-home care or other support services to help them with their activities of daily living.

As shown in Figure 3, Medicaid eligibility is dominated by children and nondisabled adults, including pregnant women. In 2015, these beneficiaries made up 79 percent of all persons enrolled in the program. The elderly and the disabled comprised just 21 percent of enrollment.

The distribution of Medicaid spending is a different matter. In 2015, more than half of all federal Medicaid spending went toward services used by the elderly or the disabled, and less than half went to services used by children and nondisabled adults. The higher

Figure 3. 2015 Medicaid Eligibility Categories and Spending

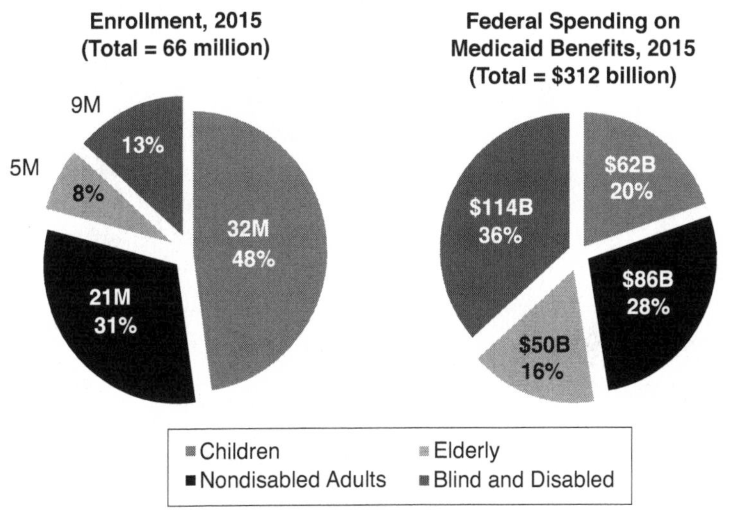

Enrollment, 2015
(Total = 66 million)

9M
13%
5M
8%
32M
48%
21M
31%

Federal Spending on
Medicaid Benefits, 2015
(Total = $312 billion)

$62B
20%
$114B
36%
$86B
28%
$50B
16%

- Children
- Nondisabled Adults
- Elderly
- Blind and Disabled

Source: Congressional Budget Office, "Detail of Spending and Enrollment for Medicaid—CBO's March 2015 Baseline," March 2015.

concentration of spending on the elderly and disabled is due to the much more expensive and intensive services needed for these populations. In 2012, the federal and state governments spent, on average, $17,848 for every disabled Medicaid enrollee, but only $2,679 for every child enrolled in the program.[8]

Medicaid Waivers and Budget Neutrality

Medicaid's cumbersome rules and federal mandates have led many states to seek more flexibility in running the program through program waivers. These waivers, authorized by Section 1115 of the Social Security Act, allow the Department of Health and Human Services (HHS) to set aside certain Medicaid requirements as part of "demonstrations," or tests, of new approaches to providing health benefits to lower-income households. States also seek waivers to help them manage their programs outside of the normal and lengthy federal constraints that otherwise apply to the program.

The federal government has approved many state waiver requests, but not all that have been submitted. Some have been approved only after a lengthy and contentious negotiation between federal and state officials over the content of the waiver program. According to the HHS online database, 407 current waiver programs of all types have been approved by HHS and are in operation, of which 40 are existing Section 1115 waivers.[9] Twenty-six waiver requests are now pending at HHS.

The most important consideration in any significant waiver request is federal funding. More specifically, the waiver requests from states are assessed by federal officials to determine whether they are budget neutral, meaning whether the federal government would pay more to the state under the waiver than it would without it. Not surprisingly, this is the source of frequent disagreements between states and the federal government.

The concept of budget neutrality in Medicaid waiver assessments dates back to the early 1980s. Before that time, HHS could approve state Medicaid requests without regard to the waivers' impact on federal spending. The statute never mentions budget neutrality as a requirement for federal approval of the demonstration programs. As HHS approved more and more requests by the states to waive certain Medicaid statutory provisions, the White House Office of Management and Budget (OMB) became concerned that the state programs being approved by HHS were actually costing the federal government substantially more than the regular Medicaid program.

In 1983, the OMB and HHS came to an agreement that all future Section 1115 waivers must be budget neutral to the federal government over the life of the demonstration.[10] This agreement also gave the OMB the authority to reject demonstration requests that did not meet the test of neutrality. Since then, the OMB has played a central role in virtually all federal-state negotiations over significant waiver requests.

Figure 4. Medicaid Payments Versus Medicare and Private Insurance

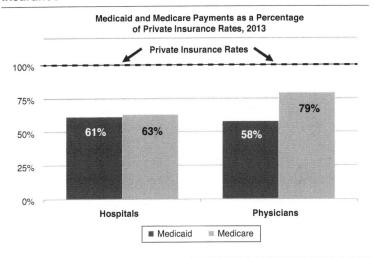

Medicaid and Medicare Payments as a Percentage of Private Insurance Rates, 2013

Source: John D. Shatto and M. Kent Clemens, "Projected Medicare Expenditures Under an Illustrative Scenario with Alternative Payment Updates to Medicare Providers," Office of the Actuary, Centers for Medicare and Medicaid Services, July 22, 2015, https://www.cms.gov/Research-Statistics-Data-and-Systems/Statistics-Trends-and-Reports/ReportsTrustFunds/Downloads/2015TRAlternativeScenario.pdf.

Medicaid's Access and Quality Problems

The Medicaid program struggles to provide its enrollees with sufficient access to care. The easiest way for states to slow cost growth has been to limit payment-rate increases for hospitals and physicians, so much so that payments are now well below what private insurers and the Medicare program pay for the same services. As shown in Figure 4, in 2013, Medicaid's payment rates were only 61 percent of what private insurers paid for the same inpatient hospital services. Similarly, Medicaid's payment rates for physicians were only 58 percent of what private insurers paid on behalf of their enrollees.[11]

Physicians and other service providers respond to these low payment rates by explicitly limiting the number of Medicaid patients they will see or by employing other business practices, such as the location of their offices and facilities, to cater to patients with higher-paying commercial insurance. Medicaid's inadequate network of willing providers makes it difficult for some patients to access care when they need it, or from the most qualified practitioners.

Several academic studies have documented the problems that occur when access to care is inadequate. A 2010 study published in the *Annals of Surgery* found that, after controlling for important demographic and risk factors, Medicaid patients fared much worse than their private-insurance counterparts in terms of outcomes from major surgical interventions. The study examined nearly 900,000 cases from a large patient-care database compiled from hospitals nationwide. The authors found that patients with Medicaid coverage were much more likely to die from surgical interventions than the privately insured and that Medicaid patients even had higher mortality rates than those who were uninsured.[12]

Medicaid's low payment rates for services would seem to contradict the program's high and rapidly rising costs. But Medicaid's costs have been driven mainly by large increases in program enrollment and a growth in the volume and intensity of the services provided to each patient. States have responded by limiting what they pay for each service, but that has only served to erode the quality of care provided to each enrollee without keeping spending growth to acceptable levels.

Medicaid Reform: Per Person Allotments to the States

Medicaid reform needs to start with a restructured relationship between the federal government and the states and a reformed approach to financing the program that does not rely on open-ended federal matching funds.

Medicaid funding should be divided into two funding streams, one for the disabled and elderly and the other for everyone else. The services provided to these two populations vary greatly, as do the state approaches to administering Medicaid for them. Breaking Medicaid funding up into two streams would begin the process of implementing different kinds of reforms for the different populations of Medicaid participants.

The other important structural change would be the switch to some form of fixed federal funding to states. The federal government would continue to heavily support the Medicaid program, but the commitment would have a limit, which would give states a strong incentive to manage the program for efficiency and cost control.

One approach would be a block grant. Under a block grant, the federal government would make fixed, aggregate payments to the states based on historical spending patterns. Cost overruns at the state level would require the state to find additional resources within the state budget. Conversely, states that were able to control costs would enjoy the full benefits of their efforts. The block grant would not be reduced when states found ways to root out waste and inefficiency from the program.

The key issue in converting to a block grant is establishing the basis by which the federal government will make payments to states. One option would be to examine the federal government's historical Medicaid-spending levels in various states over a particular number of preceding years. The block grant's first year could then be calculated as the average of federal Medicaid spending in the state per year during that time, inflated to the year in question by the national Medicaid-spending growth rate.

Once the first year is settled, the question becomes how to inflate the federal Medicaid block-grant amounts in future years. The indexing options include using the consumer price index, which historically is well below medical inflation; the growth rate of the national economy as measured by GDP; or perhaps a measure of national or regional health spending growth. The decision on indexing is highly consequential because alternative approaches can result in large differences in federal spending over time. If the block grant is pursued in part to help ease the nation's severe, long-term budgetary challenges, then indexing the block-grant amounts to something below the historical rate of growth for Medicaid can produce significant savings estimates, especially over the long term.

Opponents of the block-grant concept argue that it will necessarily reduce services for vulnerable populations. But that is far from certain. The current program, with open-ended federal matching payments, provides strong incentives to states to move as much spending as possible under the Medicaid umbrella. With a block grant, states would have strong incentives to eliminate waste without undermining coverage for those who truly need it.

In 1996, similar arguments were made about the block granting of welfare funding, with predictions that it would lead to significant hardship for the program's enrollees. Instead, states reviewed who was on the cash assistance program and quickly found that many of them were capable of entering the workforce and improving their household incomes from wages instead of government assistance. By 2000, the cash welfare rolls had fallen by about half, even as the population in the bottom fifth of the income distribution experienced substantial gains in their real incomes.[13]

Health coverage is more complicated than cash welfare, but there is every reason to expect that substantial inefficiency exists in Medicaid and that a block grant would provide the incentive to find and eliminate it. Among other things, states would seek to remove from the program persons who are erroneously enrolled today. The Centers for Medicare and Medicaid Services reports that the program has an improper payment rate of 9.4 percent and that much of the wasteful spending is associated with persons who are ineligible for Medicaid enrollment.[14] Further, states would seek to design their programs so that households that could enroll in more privately financed coverage, including employer plans, do so. Taking steps to minimize erroneous or unnecessary Medicaid spending would allow states to concentrate on ensuring high-quality care for those who remain on the program.

Still, concerns about the effect that a block grant might have on health services for the vulnerable has led to proposals that mitigate against some of the financial risks a block grant would entail. The most prominent example of such a proposal is per capita caps.

Under per capita caps, the federal government would establish for each state a per-person payment for each of the main eligibility categories in the Medicaid program: the elderly, the blind and disabled, nondisabled adults, and children. The federal government would then make payments to the states based on the number of Medicaid enrollees in each of these categories. The per capita payment would be based on historical spending rates for the various categories of beneficiaries in each state and, again, would be indexed to a predetermined growth rate.[15]

Per capita caps in Medicaid would have the same advantages as a block grant in that the states would have strong incentives to use federal funding wisely. The amount of the federal payment per person would be the same regardless of how much the state spends on each enrollee. The only difference with the block grant is that the states would not be at risk for increased Medicaid enrollment because the federal government's payments to the states would be made on a per-enrollee basis, including for enrollees who might not have been expected to sign up and would have been excluded from the block-grant formula. This could be important in times of slow economic growth or during a recession, when Medicaid enrollment typically surges.

Perhaps most important, per capita caps have enjoyed bipartisan support in the past. In 1995 and 1996, the Clinton administration proposed Medicaid per capita caps as part of a larger balanced-budget plan. That proposal was explicitly endorsed by 46 Senate Democrats in a letter to the president in December 1995.[16]

The per capita allotment approach to federal funding allows for more enrollment flexibility and perhaps more bipartisan support. For these reasons, policymakers should make implementation of per capita federal payments to states the centerpiece of a Medicaid reform plan.

Conclusion

The Medicaid program is an important component of the nation's safety net. The program serves tens of millions of people who would otherwise struggle to secure access to needed medical care and long-term care services. But it is no longer possible to ignore the immense budgetary pressures the program has created for the federal government and the states. Indeed, state governors and legislators, on a bipartisan basis, have been calling for fundamental Medicaid reform for many years because they see the program crowding out their ability to address other important state priorities.

What is needed is a reworking of the federal-state relationship concerning the program's financing and governance. The federal government should step back from micromanaging every aspect of program administration and instead provide the overall framework and a predictable funding stream to the states. States should pay for a portion of the program's cost. They should also be given the freedom and responsibility to make the major decisions over program design and be held accountable for the results.

Notes

1. Congressional Budget Office, "Detail of Spending and Enrollment for Medicaid—CBO's March 2015 Baseline," March 2015, https://www.cbo.gov/sites/default/files/51301-2015-03-Medicaid.pdf.

2. For an explanation of the FMAP, see Laura Snyder and Robin Rudowitz, "Medicaid Financing: How Does It Work and What Are the Implications," Kaiser Family Foundation, May 2015, http://files.kff.org/attachment/issue-brief-medicaid-financing-how-does-it-work-and-what-are-the-implications.

3. As enacted, the ACA required states to expand their Medicaid program to this population. That requirement was ruled unconstitutional by the Supreme Court in a June 2012 decision. Consequently, states have the option to expand their programs to this population, but are not required to do so. As of March 2016, 31 states plus the District of Columbia have opted into the ACA's Medicaid expansion, while 19 states have declined to do so. See Kaiser Family Foundation, "Status of State Action on Medicaid Expansion Decision," March 14, 2016, http://kff.org/health-reform/state-indicator/state-activity-around-expanding-medicaid-under-the-affordable-care-act/.

4. CBO, "Detail of Spending and Enrollment for Medicaid."

5. Marjorie Kanof, "Medicaid Financing: Long-Standing Concerns About Inappropriate State Arrangements Support Need for Improved Federal

Oversight," testimony before the Committee on Oversight and Government Reform, US House of Representatives, November 1, 2007, http://www.gao.gov/assets/120/118488.pdf.

6. For instance, in 2010 the state of Connecticut moved a state-funded and capped health insurance assistance program for low-income adults without children under Medicaid to secure federal matching funds. Ironically, M. Jodi Rell, the governor at the time, argued against the shift on the basis that it would be more difficult to control enrollment once the program became part of a broader Medicaid entitlement. See Keith M. Phaneuf, "Bill Cuts Most of This Year's Deficit," *Connecticut Mirror*, April 15, 2010, http://www.westportnow.com/index.php?/v3/comments/bill_cuts_most_of_this_years_deficit/. Between 2010 and 2013, enrollment in the program grew from 45,000 to 86,000 people. See Keith M. Phaneuf, "Malloy Takes to Air to Rebut Budget Critics," *Connecticut Mirror*, May 6, 2013, http://www.ctmirror.org/story/2013/05/06/malloy-takes-air-rebut-budget-critics.

7. Congressional Budget Office, *The 2015 Long-Term Budget Outlook*, June 2015, https://www.cbo.gov/sites/default/files/114th-congress-2015-2016/reports/50250-LongTermBudgetOutlook-4.pdf.

8. Medicaid and CHIP Payment and Access Commission, *MACStats: Medicaid and CHIP Data Book*, Exhibit 22, December 2015, https://www.macpac.gov/wp-content/uploads/2015/01/EXHIBIT-22.-Medicaid-Benefit-Spending-Per-Full-Year-Equivalent-FYE-Enrollee-by-State-and-Eligibility-Group-FY-2012.pdf.

9. For the HHS waiver database, see Centers for Medicare and Medicaid Services, "Waivers," http://www.medicaid.gov/Medicaid-CHIP-Program-Information/By-Topics/Waivers/Waivers.html.

10. Cynthia Shirk, "Shaping Medicaid and SCHIP Through Waivers: The Fundamentals," National Health Policy Forum, July 2008, http://www.nhpf.org/library/background-papers/BP64_MedicaidSCHIP.Waivers_07-22-08.pdf.

11. John D. Shatto and M. Kent Clemens, "Projected Medicare Expenditures Under an Illustrative Scenario with Alternative Payment Updates to Medicare Providers," Office of the Actuary, Centers for Medicare and Medicaid Services, July 22, 2015, https://www.cms.gov/Research-Statistics-Data-and-Systems/Statistics-Trends-and-Reports/ReportsTrustFunds/Downloads/2015TRAlternativeScenario.pdf.

12. Damien J. LaPar et al., "Primary Payer Status Affects Mortality for Major Surgical Operations," *Annals of Surgery* 253, no. 3 (September 2010), http://journals.lww.com/annalsofsurgery/Abstract/2010/09000/Primary_Payer_Status_Affects_Mortality_for_Major.16.aspx.

13. Pamela J. Loprest, "How Has the TANF Caseload Changed over Time?," Urban Institute, March 2012, www.acf.hhs.gov/sites/default/files/opre/change_time_1.pdf; and Congressional Budget Office, *Changes in the Economic Resources of Households with Low-Income Children*, May 2007, www.cbo.gov/sites/default/files/cbofiles/ftpdocs/81xx/doc8113/05-16-low-income.pdf.

14. Centers for Medicare and Medicaid Services, *Medicaid Improper Payment Report: FY 2010*, https://www.cms.gov/Research-Statistics-Data-and-Systems/Monitoring-Programs/Medicaid-and-CHIP-Compliance/PERM/Downloads/2010_long_version.pdf.

15. Fred Upton and Orrin Hatch, "Making Medicaid Work: Protect the Vulnerable, Offer Individualized Care, and Reduce Costs," US Congress, May 2013, http://energycommerce.house.gov/sites/republicans.energycommerce.house.gov/files/analysis/20130501Medicaid.pdf.

16. "Congressional Record—Senate," Cong. Rec. 141, no. 207 (December 22, 1995): S19185, www.gpo.gov/fdsys/pkg/CREC-1995-12-22/pdf/CREC-1995-12-22-pt1-PgS19185.pdf.

Empowering Child Support Enforcement to Reduce Poverty

ROBERT DOAR
American Enterprise Institute

Of all the programs that help low-income Americans, Child Support Enforcement (CSE) stands apart from the others. While most social services programs involve providing government-funded assistance to families, CSE requires absent parents to take responsibility for their children and provide financial support from their own resources. This difference between CSE and traditional government programs leaves CSE alone in the world of antipoverty policy. "The orphan child of social services" is how a county administrator described the program to me soon after I became the state child support enforcement director in New York in 1995.

To be sure, the program, which provides assistance to families by emphasizing parental responsibility, has enjoyed periods of broad support by coalitions of unconventional partners. President Bill Clinton and his appointees were especially supportive and fostered the program's renaissance in the 1990s. David Ellwood, one of the chief architects of Clinton's social policy agenda, emphasized child support's importance in his landmark 1988 book *Poor Support*, stating that "expecting more from absent parents makes both moral and economic sense."[1] When Donna Shalala, Clinton's secretary for the Department of Health and Human Services, testified before the Ways and Means Committee in 1995, she attacked the Republican welfare reform bill for not being *strong enough* on child support.[2] And President Clinton recounts in his autobiography that he personally urged the Republican Congress to toughen child support provisions in the bipartisan welfare reform law.[3]

The CSE program also benefited from a particularly effective alliance of political interests. Supporters of middle-class women's independence, including feminists, joined forces with poverty fighters who felt that greater financial support from the absent partners of welfare moms would go a long way to reduce poverty. Their mutual goal was to make the legal process of determining and collecting child support payments fast, efficient, and reliable.

When President Clinton signed the historic legislation in 1996, a quarter of the pages of the welfare reform law were dedicated to child support enforcement.[4] These tougher provisions paid off: total collections for custodial parents increased by 74 percent, from $15.7 billion in 1994 to $27.4 billion in 2004 in inflation-adjusted dollars.[5] Further, Census survey data show that the percentage of all poor single parents who had an agreement to receive child support (a proxy for CSE's reach) increased from 50.6 percent in 1993[6] to 58.7 percent in 2003.[7]

Unfortunately, this record of success has reversed, and a program that was collecting more for custodial parents (the single parent with the child in the household, which is the mother 83 percent of the time)[8] has become far less effective. In 2015, the program still lifted 1.4 million people out of poverty, but its reach has clearly declined.[9] Inflation-adjusted total collections peaked in 2008 and have been decreasing since.[10] In 2013, Census data showed that only 45 percent of poor custodial parents had an agreement for payment of child support, down from 58.7 percent in 2003.[11]

What accounts for this loss of momentum is a legitimate, although exaggerated, concern about being too tough on poor noncustodial parents, the parent who is not living with the child. A false wisdom has emerged in the policy community—from academics to the media—that the child support system forces noncustodial dads to, as the headline of a 2015 *New York Times* story put it, "Skip Child Support. Go to Jail. Lose Job. Repeat."[12] Some influential commentators even see the system as fundamentally unjust by imposing on poor men burdens that are viewed as the government's responsibility.

Obama administration officials appear to be undisturbed by the CSE program's diminished role. Under the leadership of Vicki Turetsky, the federal Office of Child Support Enforcement commissioner, the administration has promoted a shift away from strong enforcement policies that increase collections.[13] Supporters of strong child support policies have noticed the administration's attitude. In published comments on regulations proposed by the Obama administration, the National Child Support Enforcement Association expressed concern about the proposed regulations' "over-lenience toward noncustodial parents" and said that parts of the proposed rule would "undermine the program's fundamental purpose to collect support for children."[14]

Certainly, some poor noncustodial parents are struggling and need help to live up to their obligations. But most noncustodial parents, poor and nonpoor alike, are capable of working and could contribute something—even a regular payment of $25 per month has value. Analysts who are critical of the program seem to forget that the parent raising the child full time is often poor too. In 2013, for poor custodial parents who received child support payments, the noncustodial parent's payments represented 49 percent of their income.[15] Allowing parents to completely walk away from their financial responsibility to their children should not be an option.

Meanwhile, conservatives have hardly been running to the rescue and have long been uncomfortable with the program. The idea of empowering a government bureaucracy to coerce private action, even in furtherance of a legally established order of support (not to mention a value as important as parental responsibility), can be anathema to small-government Republicans. As Ron Haskins recounts in his history of the passage of welfare reform, one Republican member of Congress said he felt "sick to his stomach" after hearing about this government program's powers to force the absent parent to pay.[16]

This lack of support from both sides is troubling because CSE is uniquely positioned to help address our most pressing social problems: more than 40 percent of children born to unmarried mothers,[17] an official poverty rate for people in single-mother families of more than 30 percent,[18] and more than seven million prime-age men totally disconnected from the labor force.[19]

Why Is the Child Support Enforcement Program Important?

The formal child support system provides additional income to families with children. Often these families are poor: 29 percent of custodial parents were below the poverty line in 2013, and only 45 percent of those parents have a child support agreement.[20] If the share of poor custodial parents with agreements had held steady at 58.7 percent (the share in 2003) instead of declining over the past decade, an additional 500,000 poor custodial parents would have had orders to receive support in 2013. Surely a substantial fraction of these parents would have received enough in payments for them and their children to be lifted above the poverty line—74 percent of cases with orders had at least some payments during the year.[21] Reinvigorating the child support system would help ensure that more single mothers benefited from this often-forgotten piece of our safety net.

But CSE is extremely valuable beyond the resources it delivers to households with children. The program sends a clear message to all potential parents: if you play a role in bringing a child into the world, you have a responsibility to help support him or her. Strong child support enforcement not only communicates that essential American value, it changes the incentives around fathering children outside of marriage by making it impossible to abandon the responsibilities of parenthood. These cultural and economic signals appear to have resulted in changed behavior. Research from Irwin Garfinkel and coauthors in 2003 and Anna Aizer and Sara McLanahan in 2006, as well as others, have found stricter child support enforcement to be linked to reduced nonmarital childbearing.[22]

Additionally, when child support obligations force an absent parent to be reminded of his financial responsibilities, he is also more likely to take up his other fatherly duties and be more involved in the child's life. A host of studies have made it clear that child support payments from the noncustodial parent are associated with increased contact and time spent with the absent parent.[23]

Unsurprisingly then, receiving child support is also linked to better outcomes for the children involved. "The research says that a dollar of child support," explains Turetsky, "improves children's educational outcomes more than any other income source."[24]

Studies have found that formal child support payments are associated with fewer behavioral problems, better academic performance, and increased self-esteem.[25] Both social science and common sense confirm that having two active and involved parents contributing financially and emotionally to child-rearing is extremely valuable for children's development, and a strong CSE program makes it more likely to happen.

Finally, while it may seem counterintuitive, the CSE program offers one of policy's best opportunities to address the crisis of prime-age male nonwork in America. Nicholas Eberstadt shows in *Men Without Work* that roughly seven million men age 25 to 54 are not working or even looking for work. His analysis shows that these men are disproportionately less educated and never married; many are almost certainly noncustodial parents. These declining employment rates are not only bad for men—women see unemployed men as less "marriageable," and children suffer from having fathers who are absent and less reliable in contributing to the household.

But unlike poor single mothers, poor noncustodial parents receive little in means-tested assistance and are largely left out of the system of work requirements and work subsidies created by welfare reform, which led never-married mothers to increase their work rates. Policy largely ignores single men, except for expecting them to pay child support—but therein lies the potential for CSE to help. CSE could have an ongoing relationship with these men, and if the program were reinvigorated with an eye toward helping men who have been unable to make their payments find work, it could provide the combination of help and hassle that enabled single mothers to leave the welfare rolls for work after welfare reform.

Despite these potential benefits and its impressive cost effectiveness (in 2015 the CSE program collected $5.26 in support for every dollar of administrative expense),[26] the reach and effectiveness of the child support enforcement system has been diminishing. How that has happened and what we should do about it is the subject of this paper.

How the Child Support Enforcement Program Works

CSE is undoubtedly one of government's most complicated programs. Administered by states but with strong oversight and generous funding from the federal government, the program offers the following core services to the custodial parent:

1. Locating the noncustodial parent using employment, tax, public assistance, and other government data;

2. Determining whether the noncustodial parent identified is indeed the biological parent;

3. Establishing a "child support order," which determines the noncustodial parent's obligation;

4. Collecting and enforcing those orders and distributing collections to the custodial parent; and

5. Modifying orders when appropriate (e.g., changes in ability to pay).

A key step in the process is determining the correct amount mandated to be paid each month when establishing the order. Setting order amounts that correspond to ability to pay has been shown by research to lead to more regular payments and prevent large debts from accruing.[27]

While procedures vary from state to state, all states follow their own carefully calculated guidelines that take into account the noncustodial parent's income and the number of children covered, and many cap the award amounts demanded from poor noncustodial parents. Most states have minimum mandatory amounts that should be manageable even for low-income noncustodial parents. Some states use a guideline model that explicitly factors in both parents' basic needs before ordering a support amount.

A recent survey of state child support directors shows the progress that has been made in setting more reasonable orders. If the noncustodial parent is incarcerated at the time of order establishment, 41 states say they would not impute income—usually leading to a $0 order or no order established at all. When a noncustodial parent returns from prison but is having a hard time finding more than 20 hours of work a week, more states than not indicate they will not impute income above what he is actually earning.[28] Efforts to ensure that order amounts are affordable for poor noncustodial parents have led to significant changes in practice. In New York City more than 15 percent of all orders of support are set at $50 or less per month, and in the past year in Los Angeles, a stunning 49 percent of all new orders required less than $50 per month in support.[29]

Many of these protections of the noncustodial parent, however, depend on his participating in the process and providing information about his income. Failure to attend hearings can result in "default orders" that sometimes are set beyond the noncustodial parent's ability to pay and can contribute to a work disincentive by garnishing such a large share of his low wages.

But even in these cases, states and the Office of Child Support Enforcement (OCSE) have developed a range of strategies to right-size orders. Federal statute requires state agencies to periodically review orders to see if they should be adjusted and to reexamine the order at either parent's request. Approximately 20 states have developed specific "review and adjustment" programs to make sure order amounts are promptly brought into line with ability to pay.[30] These initiatives can use technology to simplify the process for requesting a change, contact newly unemployed noncustodial parents to help them adjust the order, or conduct public information campaigns to inform parents of their ability to request a modification when their economic situation changes.

In New York City, for example, several programs have been implemented and expanded in recent years to reflect this change of approach and help poor noncustodial parents overcome a variety of challenges. The Arrears Cap program helped noncustodial parents lower their arrears by a combined $10 million as of December 2012, and the Modify Department of Social Services Order program helped them rightsize their orders. The city's jobs program for poor noncustodial parents increased the number of participants making child support payments by 29 percent from 2008 to 2012.[31]

Reforms nationwide have clearly improved the situation: inflation-adjusted total arrears have declined by 11 percent since 2005, in spite of an economic downturn one might expect to reduce compliance and increase arrears.[32] Critics of the child support system need to recognize that the system has already made significant progress in limiting the establishment and enforcement of unfair orders.

Once orders are established, the child support system has a host of tools that can automatically collect owed support. For example, CSE agencies can garnish wages, intercept income tax refunds and lottery winnings, suspend driver's licenses, and use a handful of other technologies to make sure that noncustodial parents meet their obligations. Importantly, these techniques can be used only once the custodial parent has helped identify the noncustodial parent and established an order that can be enforced.

If the enforcement methods listed above are not successful, all states have civil or criminal contempt-of-court procedures and criminal nonsupport laws. Finally, all states' child support agencies have the authority to seek a judicial order that remands nonpaying noncustodial parents to a work program—essentially requiring the absent parent to attend work activities, pay owed child support, or go to jail.[33] As of 2014, 30 states and Washington, DC, were operating child support work programs, but only three states had statewide programs.[34]

The History of the Child Support Enforcement Program

In 1974, Congress passed the Social Service Amendments, which enacted Title IV-D of the Social Security Act, known as the CSE program. Title IV-D created the OCSE and required states to participate in the OCSE's programs for parent location, paternity establishment, and child support order enforcement.[35] In a memo to President Gerald Ford on the day the law was signed, Secretary of Health, Education, and Welfare Caspar Weinberger clearly explained the intent of the program:

Over 75 percent of the AFDC [welfare] caseload involves an absent parent. Less than 15 percent of the cases are receiving any child support payment. This indicates the magnitude of the problem and the extent to which certain parents have shifted their support obligation to the public. Studies demonstrate that existing state and local child support programs can produce child support collections far in excess of corresponding administrative expenses. Therefore, the new child support program could reduce AFDC costs by substantially increasing child support collections.[36]

The secretary closed the memo by stating that child support could help many families remain independent and thus reduce the need for public assistance. From the beginning, CSE was focused on requiring absent parents to take responsibility for their children and helping families acquire the resources needed to be independent, but it also had a third original charge: reimbursing the government for the cost of welfare benefits.

This makes conceptual sense—as Weinberger explains, absent parents whose children end up on welfare are shifting the costs from themselves to the public. But emphasizing cost recovery made child support's other two, arguably more important, missions more difficult. The fact that the CSE program was enforcing orders with absent fathers and taking the money for the government rather than distributing it to the family damaged the program's image, leading some to believe they were better off avoiding the program altogether.

Over the years, CSE has made remarkable progress in shifting away from cost recovery as a primary goal. In 2014, 95 percent of collections were distributed to families, with only 5 percent going to recover public assistance costs—a major improvement from 80 percent going to the custodial parent in 1996.[37]

A host of legislative changes strengthened CSE's ability to collect payments from the noncustodial parent. In 1984, the Child Support Enforcement Amendments, among other improvements, implemented mandatory wage withholding and the interception of income tax refunds for noncustodial parents who are behind on their payments. Then, the Family Support Act of 1988 took up a different set of problems in the program, namely judges setting inconsistent order amounts that were often insufficient for the family's needs.

Leading up to welfare reform in the 1990s, a broad bipartisan coalition continued to build momentum behind toughening enforcement. The US Commission on Interstate Child Support, which included Senator Bill Bradley (D-NJ), recommended in 1992 a series of provisions, such as establishing a system for withholding income across state lines, designed to increase collections from absent parents. The Congressional Caucus for Women's Issues saw strengthening child support as an opportunity to help struggling single mothers and turned those recommendations into proposed legislation.[38]

This bipartisan movement had backing from top academics. In *Poor Support,* Harvard Professor David Ellwood, the eventual co-chair of the Clinton administration's working group on welfare reform, argued that "what mothers desperately need is some nonwelfare supports they can count on . . . child support seems an obvious place to look for help." Further, Ellwood believed strengthening the child support enforcement system was "not a matter of economic efficiency; it is a matter of right and wrong. Parents have obligations."[39]

As Ron Haskins details in *Work over Welfare*, high-ranking Clinton administration officials and lawyers from the left-leaning Children's Defense Fund and National Women's Law Center worked on refining those ideas and included them in the Clinton proposed welfare reform legislation of 1994.[40] When Republicans in the House drafted their legislation that would become the welfare reform law, they were using child support plans created largely by liberals as their base text.

This strong support for strengthening child support enforcement led to a series of new powers for the program in the 1996 Personal Responsibility and Work Opportunity Act. Child support agencies gained access to more information on noncustodial parents and were given new authorities for penalizing noncustodial parents who do not pay, such as suspending drivers' licenses.

By the early 2000s, leaders of both parties had gradually transformed CSE into an effective program for requiring absent parents to contribute to their children's well-being and delivering needed resources to low-income families. At the time, it seemed no one would argue with ensuring that the payment of child support should be, in the words of Clinton administration official Paul Legler, "automatic and inescapable—like death or taxes."[41]

The Breakdown of Consensus

In recent years, the CSE program has lost its near-universal backing. Especially in the media and in the work of some important scholars, attention has shifted from the poor mother trying to raise a child without financial help to the poor father who struggles in the labor market.

Several studies have shown that nonresident fathers have limited ability to pay support. One paper found that the fathers in current assistance cases have poverty rates between 34 and 43 percent.[42] Some have hypothesized that increased child support enforcement functions like a tax that discourages noncustodial parents from working. And while the results were not definitive, research by Harry Holzer, Elaine Sorensen, and Paul Offner suggested a link between tougher CSE policies and decreased employment for 25- to 34-year-old black males.[43]

After writing *Doing the Best I Can* about low-income fathers in Philadelphia, Johns Hopkins Sociologist Kathryn Edin concluded that instead of disparaging absent fathers for not taking responsibility, we should recognize that "these men desperately want to be good fathers."[44] Because these men are struggling but, in her view, trying as hard as they can to support their children, Edin is skeptical of tough enforcement measures:

> Child support is a remnant of the days when we used to think that dads didn't matter. With our right hand we've pushed these men away; we've said, "you're worthless." With our left hand we're picking his pocket. . . . That's how it feels to him.[45]

This new conventional wisdom has influenced policymakers and, more importantly, administrators. As we have seen, Obama administration officials have adopted this new perspective on the program—a remarkable change for Democratic policymakers, who were formerly united on the need for collecting support for single mothers and their children. As a result, the Obama administration proposed new regulations that would require state agencies to take into account the noncustodial parent's subsistence needs when setting orders, prohibit states from allowing courts to consider what the noncustodial parent could be making so they will have to look at only available data on actual earnings instead, and allow states to spend federal child support dollars on employment and training programs for fathers, among other changes.

We should be concerned about disconnected men who are struggling to work regularly and make their child support payments, and some of the ideas in the regulation are helpful. In particular, prohibiting the treatment of incarceration as "voluntary unemployment," as all but a handful of states already do, is an appropriate way to keep orders in line with ability to pay and prevent the accrual of exorbitant debts that can discourage work.

But other aspects of the proposed regulation show an ambivalence about the goal of requiring noncustodial parents to support their children. For example, limiting state agencies so they can consider only available data on the noncustodial parent's current income would effectively disallow support orders for fathers who had only off-the-books income and thus had no available earnings record. It could also incentivize noncustodial parents to refuse to work to avoid a child support order. This provision ignores the complexity often present in real-life cases and would allow too many absent parents to avoid responsibility for providing for their children.

Despite the Obama administration's misgivings about the effect of tough child support enforcement on poor fathers, more than 40 percent of births today happen outside of marriage, making the program's mission of requiring both parents to provide for their children as important as ever. Accepting a decline in the program's reach, or further rolling back the infrastructure built by bipartisan effort over the past four decades, would likely hurt these poor single parents and their children and miss an opportunity to help absent fathers meet their obligations rather than avoid them.

The Two Problems in the Child Support Enforcement Program

CSE has the potential to provide valuable assistance to children in single-parent families and to empower noncustodial parents to live up to their parental responsibilities. However, a look at the evidence shows the system is neither reaching custodial parents nor promoting work among noncustodial parents in the way we should hope.

Declining Reach. CSE's reach has declined substantially among eligible families. Because of the increasing focus on noncustodial fathers, this decline has received little attention in public discussions surrounding the program, and that is a mistake. Given the strong poverty-reducing effects of the program for families with children and its positive effects on child outcomes, the program should reach more people who could use its help, not fewer.

My outline of the issue draws heavily on recent work published through AEI from Daniel Schroeder of the University of Texas at Austin's Ray Marshall Center. Schroeder has evaluated many of the employment programs for noncustodial parents who are unemployed or underemployed and are struggling to make their payments.[46]

The national CSE caseload peaked 15 years ago and has been declining since, despite overall population growth and a growing share of children being born to never-married mothers. The formal child support caseload peaked at roughly 19.4 million cases in 1998 and has since declined by about 20 percent to 15.1 million cases in 2014.

Further, Census data measuring the broader child support eligible population show that the share of custodial parents with an agreement for financial support is also in decline, especially in the past decade. From 2003 to 2013, the share of custodial parents with agreements declined by 11 percentage points, from 60 percent to 49 percent.

Census data also show a sharp decline in the number of custodial parents asking CSE for help from any number of its core services. Between 1993 and 2013, the share of custodial parents requesting help from a CSE service nearly halved, falling from 42 percent to

22 percent. In 2013, 2.8 million fewer custodial parents asked for help from CSE than did so in 1993.

Many factors certainly underlie this decline, and it is difficult to know with certainty the extent to which each factor has contributed. Schroeder identifies several potential factors in his analysis: for example, a rising share of male custodial parents (who are less likely to seek CSE services than female custodial parents) or an increased share of births to never-married mothers (order rates are higher among divorcees).

But by far the most compelling reason for the decline is a dramatically diminished pipeline of cases into the program through the Temporary Assistance for Needy Families (TANF) cash welfare program. Establishing a CSE case is *required* for individuals seeking a TANF cash benefit. This means that every applicant for TANF must cooperate with the CSE program by providing information about the noncustodial parent to receive assistance. Given that encouraging personal responsibility is a core objective of both CSE and TANF, this makes sense. It sends a strong message that custodial parents should not receive financial support from the government if they have not first asked the other parent to contribute.

However, TANF caseloads have more than halved since 1996, and far fewer people are applying for benefits. This is not necessarily a bad thing: work rates among never-married mothers, incomes, and child poverty rates remain better today than they were before welfare reform, in part due to TANF's changes.

But while poor single parents may no longer be seeking cash welfare through the state's TANF program, they are seeking and receiving help through the Supplemental Nutrition Assistance Program (SNAP), Medicaid, child care, and housing assistance programs— and these programs do not effectively require opening a child support case as a condition of receiving aid.[47] This is a lost opportunity to connect parents with additional support and make sure all parents take responsibility for their children.

Nonwork Among Noncustodial Parents. Policy should not have to choose between helping single mothers or low-income men. CSE is a rare government program (outside the criminal justice system) that interacts often with disconnected, low-skilled men, but it does not do enough to help them. Order amounts should be responsive to the noncustodial parent's ability to pay and his changing economic circumstances, and significant improvements have been made on this front. But a singular focus on reducing order amounts and forgiving arrears distracts from the main challenge these men face: not enough of them are working. Instead of reducing what we expect of these men, we should help them better meet their obligations to their families and society.

The reforms to the program in 1996 focused on tracking down and holding accountable "deadbeat" dads, but it did little to acknowledge or address those who really are dead broke. This is a difficult balance to strike—I know from my experience working in New York that many fathers who appear to have few assets and no earnings are working off-the-books or involved in illicit activities, but they are reluctant to make that known because they either do not want to pay or do not want the government to know of their off-the-books activities.

However, from what we know about noncustodial parents, it is clear that many are failing to work regularly. Reliable data on noncustodial parents are hard to come by because the Census Bureau's major surveys do not ask whether a man living alone is also a nonresident father.[48] But a survey from 1997 conducted by the Urban Institute found that only 43 percent of noninstitutionalized, nonresident fathers who were poor worked at all—and this was during the late 1990s economic boom.[49] Another study from the Urban Institute used administrative data from nine states in 2003 and 2004 and found that 25 percent of all obligors had no reported income.[50]

I suspect, given the evidence on young, low-skilled men generally, that these rates must look even worse today. In 2000, among African American men age 16–24 without a high school diploma and not in school, the employment rate was 40.8 percent, and for similarly positioned whites, it was 72.3 percent. By 2007 (like 2000, a year at the peak of the business cycle), the rates had fallen dramatically to 28.7 and 55.0 percent, respectively.[51]

Given that so many noncustodial parents fail to work at all, it is not surprising that 70 percent of arrears are owed by noncustodial parents who have no documented income or very little earnings (less than $10,000 a year).[52] Debt forgiveness or smaller orders alone do not solve these individuals' challenges. They need steady employment.

Reforms to Address These Challenges

Given the crucial role that CSE plays in reducing poverty among vulnerable children and families, child support leaders and legislators must work to reverse the program's decline in reach and its continued struggles in securing payment from poor noncustodial fathers.

Expanding CSE's Reach. A simple strategy to address the program's declining reach is to attach the CSE case-establishment requirement that currently accompanies TANF to other public benefit programs. The most obvious candidate would be SNAP, which reaches many more families than TANF and has a regular application and recertification process during which mothers could be automatically enrolled. In 2013, SNAP provided benefits to 47.6 million people in 23 million households, including 4.5 million custodial parents, or more than a third of custodial parents. In contrast, TANF served less than 5 percent of custodial parents.[53] This simple change would almost certainly increase the share of low-income custodial parents receiving child support and, as a result, would likely reduce child poverty.

Sensible exemptions to this requirement must be made for those with extenuating circumstances, such as abusive relationships. Such exemptions already exist in the context of the TANF-CSE interaction, and they should be applied to a CSE case-establishment requirement in the context of SNAP. To be clear, mothers who provide information about the father while applying for SNAP should receive 100 percent of the support generated—payments made by these noncustodial parents should not be reimbursing state or federal government costs.

Other reforms could likely help boost participation, too. For mothers receiving cash welfare from the TANF program, states are permitted to keep any money paid by the noncustodial parent to reimburse itself for the assistance it is providing. However, research has found that more generous "pass-through" policies that send a portion, or all, of a child support payment directly to the custodial parent are associated with increased collections at minimal cost to the government.[54]

Many states pass on a portion of the payments to families on assistance and keep the rest, and Colorado already passes through the full payment made by the noncustodial parent.[55] This gives custodial parents and noncustodial parents a stronger incentive to cooperate—mothers get more money if they do, and fathers know that at least a portion of their money is flowing directly to the family. To maximize participation and change the perception of citizens distrustful of the program, states should continue moving their distribution policies in the direction of supporting families first, before reimbursing government welfare spending.

Increasing Work Among Struggling Noncustodial Parents. Child support professionals and legislators must develop new strategies and expand effective ones to better help struggling noncustodial parents meet their obligations by working regularly. These efforts should be targeted toward noncustodial parents who are not paying their orders—slightly more than 25 percent of custodial parents with an order received no support in 2013.[56] There are already promising models of effective work programs for those who owe child support but do not have jobs or are having a hard time making payments.

For example, the NCP-Choices program in Texas has shown positive impacts on employment rates and child support paid among noncustodial parents. Relative to their peers in a rigorously evaluated pilot, noncustodial parents ordered into the program paid child support 47 percent more often, paid $57 more per month, were employed at 21 percent higher rates, and participated in workforce development programming at 82 percent higher rates than the comparison group. Positive effects persisted over several years.[57]

Workforce programs generally, and for noncustodial parents specifically, struggle to enroll and retain clients when participation is voluntary. NCP-Choices has been effective largely because an order by a CSE judge gives those who have been noncompliant with their orders a clear choice: you can either pay a significant amount toward your arrears, participate in the work program, or go to jail. Participants almost always showed up.

Programs that mandate participation may sound tough, but they show results in helping noncustodial parents get into employment and meet their child support obligations. In the words of Lawrence Mead, a professor at New York University who wrote an important book on work programs for poor men, these programs succeed for the same reason welfare reform succeeded: they provide both help and hassle.[58] They should be expanded.

However, these programs are expensive. And for judges to be able to remand large numbers of noncompliant noncustodial parents to work programs—to create a broad work requirement for absent parents—they will need to be expanded dramatically. State agencies need more flexibility and more funding to enroll more low-income noncustodial parents in effective work programs.

Long-standing federal policy has held that state child support agency spending on employment programs is not eligible for the 66 percent federal match that reimburses state spending on other child support administrative expenses. The Obama administration included in its regulation a provision that would reverse this position. Although this important change should be made through the legislative process, not through a regulation, the policy stands as a good one.

If we are going to require work among noncustodial parents, we should also take steps to make sure work pays—like we did with custodial parents in welfare reform. While momentum has been building in Washington for an expansion of the earned income tax credit (EITC) for all childless adults, this policy is not well-targeted. A better solution is to expand the EITC for noncustodial parents who work and pay current child support. As commissioner in New York State, I created and implemented such a program, and an Urban Institute analysis found that it increased the share of parents who paid their support in full.[59] This idea has bipartisan support; when President Obama was in the Senate, he proposed a bill that would double the EITC for noncustodial parents who paid current child support.[60]

Conclusion

CSE is a needed and effective program. It currently lifts more than one million families above the government's official poverty line, reduces single parenthood, and improves child outcomes, all by enforcing and facilitating personal responsibility at very low cost to taxpayers.

But the program has been on the decline. Its caseload has dropped, and its reach among eligible families has been declining substantially over the past decade. It should help more people, and it can. Efforts should be undertaken to reach more CSE-eligible families and help more struggling noncustodial parents fulfill their obligations through employment. The former ought to be pursued by requiring CSE participation as a condition of SNAP receipt and working to improve the program's image. The latter could be achieved by providing CSE with greater funding flexibility through the legislative process to expand effective workforce programs.

Notes

1. David Ellwood, *Poor Support: Poverty in the American Family* (New York: Basic Books, 1989).

2. Ron Haskins, *Work over Welfare: The Inside Story of the 1996 Welfare Reform Law* (Washington, DC: Brookings Institution Press, 2006).

3. Bill Clinton, *My Life* (New York: Knopf, 2004), 602.

4. Ann Marie Rotondo, "Helping Families Help Themselves: Using Child Support Enforcement to Reform Our Welfare System," *California Western Law Review* 33 (1997), http://scholarlycommons.law.cwsl.edu/cgi/viewcontent.cgi?article=1301&context=cwlr.

5. Daniel Schroeder, *The Limited Reach of the Child Support Enforcement System*, American Enterprise Institute, December 5, 2016, Appendix Panel A.

6. US Census Bureau, "Child Support: 1993," 1994, Table 4, http://www.census.gov/people/childsupport/data/files/chldsu93.pdf.

7. Timothy S. Grall, "Custodial Mothers and Fathers and Their Child

Support: 2003," US Census Bureau, July 2006, https://www.census.gov/prod/2006pubs/p60-230.pdf.

8. Timothy Grall, "Custodial Mothers and Fathers and Their Child Support: 2013," US Census Bureau, January 2016, https://www.census.gov/content/dam/Census/library/publications/2016/demo/P60-255.pdf.

9. David Waddington, "Income, Poverty, and Health Insurance Coverage: 2015," US Census Bureau, September 13, 2016, http://www.census.gov/content/dam/Census/newsroom/press-kits/2016/20160913_iphi_slides.pdf.

10. Schroeder, *The Limited Reach of the Child Support Enforcement System*, Appendix Panel A.

11. Grall, "Custodial Mothers and Fathers and Their Child Support: 2013."

12. Frances Robles and Shaila Dewan, "Skip Child Support. Go to Jail. Lose Job. Repeat.," *New York Times,* April 19, 2015, http://www.nytimes.com/2015/04/20/us/skip-child-support-go-to-jail-lose-job-repeat.html.

13. Jonathan Walters, "Is Jailing Deadbeat Dads Effective?," *Governing,* July 16, 2013, http://www.governing.com/topics/health-human-services/col-jailing-deadbeat-dads-effective-child-support-payments.html.

14. National Child Support Enforcement Association, "NCSEA Comments on NPRM," January 16, 2015, http://www.ncsea.org/documents/2015-1-14-NCSEA-comments-on-NPRM-FINAL.pdf.

15. Carmen Solomon-Fears, "Child Support: An Overview of Census Bureau Data on Recipients," Congressional Research Service, March 1, 2016, https://www.fas.org/sgp/crs/misc/RS22499.pdf.

16. Haskins, *Work Over Welfare.*

17. Brady E. Hamilton et al., "Births: Final Data for 2014," *National Vital Statistics Reports* 64, no. 12 (December 23, 2015), http://www.cdc.gov/nchs/data/nvsr/nvsr64/nvsr64_12.pdf.

18. Bernadette D. Proctor, Jessica L. Semega, and Melissa A. Kollar, "Income and Poverty in the United States: 2015," US Census Bureau, September 2016, Table B-1, https://www.census.gov/content/dam/Census/library/publications/2016/demo/p60-256.pdf.

19. Nicholas Eberstadt, *Men Without Work* (West Conshohocken, PA: Templeton Press, 2016).

20. Grall, "Custodial Mothers and Fathers and Their Child Support: 2013."

21. Ibid.

22. Irwin Garfinkel et al., "The Roles of Child Support Enforcement and Welfare in Non-Marital Childbearing," *Journal of Population Economics* 16 (2003): 55–70; and Anna Aizer and Sara McLanahan, "The Impact of Child Support Enforcement on Fertility, Parental Investments, and Child Well-Being," *Journal of Human Resources* 41 (2006): 28–45.

23. H. Elizabeth Peters et al., "Legislating Love: The Effect of Child Support and Welfare Policies on Father-Child Contact," *Review of Economics of the Household* 2 (2004): 255–74, http://link.springer.com/article/10.1007/s11150-004-5647-5; Lenna Nepomnyaschy, "Child Support and Father-Child Contact: Testing Reciprocal Pathways," *Demography* 44 (2007): 93–112, http://www.jstor.org/stable/4137223; Chien-Chung Huang, "Mothers' Reports of Nonresident Fathers' Involvement with Their Children: Revisiting the Relationship Between Child Support Payment and Visitation," *Family Relations* 58 (2009): 54–64, http://www.jstor.org/stable/20456836; and Judith A. Seltzer, Nora Cate Schaeffer, and Hong-Wen Chang, "Family Ties After Divorce: The Relationship Between Visiting and Paying Child Support," *Journal of Marriage and Family* 51 (1989): 1013–31, http://www.jstor.org/stable/pdf/353213.pdf.

24. Vicki Turetsky, "Working with Child Support—Effective Strategies from Model State and Local Partnerships" (webinar transcript, National Responsible Fatherhood Clearinghouse, March 28, 2013), https://www.fatherhood.gov/sites/default/files/webinar/transcript/2013.03_nrfc_webinar_transcript.pdf.

25. Virginia W. Knox, "The Effects of Child Support Payments on Developmental Outcomes for Elementary School-Age Children," *Journal of Human Resources* 31, No. 4 (1996): 816–40; and Paul R. Amato and Joan G. Gilbreth, "Nonresident Fathers and Children's Well-Being: A Meta-Analysis," *Journal of Marriage and Family* 61, no. 3 (1999): 557–73.

26. Vicki Turetsky, "FY 2015 Preliminary Data Report," Office of Child Support Enforcement, April 18, 2016, http://www.acf.hhs.gov/css/resource/fy-2015-preliminary-data-report.

27. Steven Eldred, "How Do Child Support Order Amounts Affect Payments and Compliance?," Orange County Department of Child Support Services, October 2011, http://www.ywcss.com/sites/default/files/pdf-resource/how_do_child_support_orders_affect_payments_and_compliance.pdf; and Maria Cancian, Carolyn Heinrich, and Yiyoon Chung, "Does Debt

Discourage Employment and Payment of Child Support? Evidence from a Natural Experiment," Institute for Research on Poverty, July 2009, http://www.irp.wisc.edu/publications/dps/pdfs/dp136609.pdf.

28. James C. Fleming, "National Council of Child Support Directors" (presentation at Annual Meeting and Conference of National Council of Child Support Directors, June 19–22, 2016).

29. New York City and Los Angeles administrators, email messages to author, October 2016.

30. National Conference of State Legislatures, "Child Support 101.2: Establishing and Modifying Support Orders," http://www.ncsl.org/research/human-services/enforcement-establishing-and-modifying-orders.aspx.

31. Paul Lopatto, "A Change in Approach: A Shift in Priorities and Caseload at the City's Office of Child Support Enforcement," New York City Independent Budget Office, July 2014, http://www.ibo.nyc.ny.us/iboreports/2014childsupport.pdf.

32. Schroeder, *The Limited Reach of the Child Support Enforcement System*, Appendix Panel A.

33. Carmen Solomon-Fears, Gene Falk, and Adrienne L. Fernandes-Alcantara, "Child Well-Being and Noncustodial Fathers," Congressional Research Service, February 12, 2013, 27, http://greenbook.waysandmeans.house.gov/sites/greenbook.waysandmeans.house.gov/files/R41431_gb.pdf.

34. Vicki Turetsky, "Work-Oriented Programs for Noncustodial Parents," Office of Child Support Enforcement, May 27, 2014, http://www.acf.hhs.gov/css/resource/work-oriented-programs-for-noncustodial-parents.

35. Naomi R. Cahn and Jane C. Murphy, "Collecting Child Support: A History of Federal and State Initiatives," *Clearinghouse Review* 34, no. 165 (2000), http://scholarship.law.gwu.edu/cgi/viewcontent.cgi?article=1406&context=faculty_publications.

36. Jerry H. Jones, "HEW Implementation of Child Support Law," Gerald R. Ford Presidential Library, April 28, 1975, https://www.fordlibrarymuseum.gov/library/document/0047/phw19750512-03.pdf.

37. Carmen Solomon-Fears, "Analysis of Federal-State Financing of the Child Support Enforcement Program," Congressional Research Service, July 19, 2012, http://greenbook.waysandmeans.house.gov/sites/greenbook.waysandmeans.house.gov/files/2012/documents/RL33422_gb.pdf.

38. Haskins, *Work over Welfare*.

39. Ellwood, *Poor Support*.

40. Haskins, *Work over Welfare*.

41. Ronald Mincy, Monique Jethwani, and Serena Klempin, *Failing Our Fathers: Confronting the Crisis of Economically Vulnerable Nonresident Fathers* (New York: Oxford University Press, 2014).

42. Maria Cancian and Daniel R. Meyer, "Fathers of Children Receiving Welfare: Can They Provide More Child Support?," *Social Service Review* 78 No. 2 (2004): 179–206, http://www.ssc.wisc.edu/~gwallace/Papers/ Cancian%20and%20Meyer%20(2004).pdf.

43. Harry Holzer, Paul Offner, and Elaine Sorensen, "Declining Employment Among Young Black Less-Educated Men: The Role of Incarceration and Child Support," Urban Institute, 2004, http://www.urban.org/research/ publication/declining-employment-among-young-black-less-educated-men.

44. Kathryn Edin, *Doing the Best I Can: Fatherhood in the Inner City* (Berkeley, California: University of California Press, 2013); and Kathryn Edin, "What About Fathers?," *Shriver Report,* 2014, http://shriverreport.org/what-about-the-fathers-kathryn-edin/.

45. Ruth Graham, "How 'Deadbeats' Can Still Be Good Dads," *Boston Globe,* December 5, 2014, https://www.bostonglobe.com/ideas/2014/12/05/ how-deadbeats-can-still-good-dads/EdiXe3spvu7hSOIhDJXWfJ/story.html.

46. Schroeder, *The Limited Reach of the Child Support Enforcement System*.

47. The federal statute has a state option to require custodial parents who receive SNAP to cooperate with the state child support agency, but only three states have implemented this option. See Rodney W. Hopkins and Robbi N. Poulson, *Food Stamp Child Support Cooperation Study*, University of Utah, Social Research Institute, August 29, 2014, http://le.utah.gov/interim/ 2014/pdf/00005534.pdf.

48. Solomon-Fears, Falk, and Fernandes-Alcantara, "Child Well-Being and Noncustodial Fathers," 4.

49. Elaine Sorensen and Chava Zibman, "Poor Dads Who Don't Pay Child Support: Deadbeats or Disadvantaged?," Urban Institute, April 2001, http://www.urban.org/sites/default/files/alfresco/publication-pdfs/310334-Poor-Dads-Who-Don-t-Pay-Child-Support.PDF.

50. Elaine Sorensen, Liliana Sousa, and Simon Schaner, "Assessing Child Support Arrears in Nine States and the Nation," Urban Institute, July 11, 2007,

http://tpcprod.urban.org/UploadedPDF/1001242_child_support_arrears.pdf.

51. Solomon-Fears, Falk, and Fernandes-Alcantara, "Child Well-Being and Noncustodial Fathers," 16.

52. Sorensen, Sousa, and Shaner, "Assessing Child Support Arrears in Nine States and the Nation."

53. Schroeder, *The Limited Reach of the Child Support Enforcement System*; and US Department of Agriculture, Food and Nutrition Service, "Supplemental Nutrition Assistance Program (SNAP)," October 7, 2016, http://www.fns.usda.gov/pd/supplemental-nutrition-assistance-program-snap.

54. Kye Lippold, Austin Nichols, and Elaine Sorensen, "Evaluation of the $150 Child Support Pass-Through and Disregard Policy in the District of Columbia," Urban Institute, November 2010, http://www.urban.org/sites/default/files/alfresco/publication-pdfs/412779-Evaluation-of-the-Child-Support-Pass-Through-and-Disregard-Policy-in-the-District-of-Columbia.PDF.

55. National Conference of State Legislatures, "Child Support Pass-Through and Disregard Policies for Public Assistance Recipients," September 21, 2016, http://www.ncsl.org/research/human-services/state-policy-pass-through-disregard-child-support.aspx.

56. Grall, "Custodial Mothers and Fathers and Their Child Support: 2013," 1.

57. Daniel Schroeder and Nicholas Doughty, "Texas Non-Custodial Parent Choices: Program Impact Analysis," Lyndon B. Johnson School of Public Affairs, September 3, 2009, http://raymarshallcenter.org/files/2005/07/NCP_Choices_Final_Sep_03_2009.pdf.

58. Lawrence M. Mead, *Expanding Work Programs for Poor Men* (Washington, DC: AEI Press, 2011).

59. Austin Nichols, Elaine Sorensen, and Kye Lippold, "The New York Noncustodial Parent EITC: Its Impact on Child Support Payments and Employment," Urban Institute, June 27, 2012, http://www.urban.org/sites/default/files/alfresco/publication-pdfs/412610-The-New-York-Noncustodial-Parent-EITC-Its-Impact-on-Child-Support-Payments-and-Employment.PDF.

60. Solomon-Fears, Falk, and Fernandes-Alcantara, "Child Well-Being and Noncustodial Fathers," 56.

Reducing Poverty by Reforming Housing Policy

EDGAR O. OLSEN
University of Virginia

L ow-income housing assistance is fertile ground for reforms that would provide better outcomes with less public spending. The majority of current recipients are served by programs whose cost is enormously excessive for the housing provided. Phasing out these programs in favor of the system's most cost-effective program would ultimately free up the resources to provide housing assistance to millions of additional people and reduce taxes.[1]

Furthermore, the current system of low-income housing assistance provides enormous subsidies to some households while offering none to others that are equally poor, and it provides subsidies to many people who are not poor while offering none to many of the poorest. Avoiding these excessive subsidies and focusing assistance on the poorest families will contribute further to poverty alleviation. Well-designed reforms of the current system of low-income housing assistance would substantially alleviate poverty with less public spending.

Overview of Current System

To appreciate the potential for alleviating poverty through housing policy reforms, it is essential to know the nature of current programs and the evidence about their performance.[2] The bulk of low-income housing assistance in the United States is funded by the federal government through a large number of programs with a combined cost of more than $50 billion a year. Unlike other major means-tested transfer programs in the US, low-income housing programs do not offer assistance to many of the poorest families that are eligible for them. Eligible families that want assistance must get on a waiting list.

Most low-income housing assistance in the US is for renting a unit, and the most important distinction among rental housing programs is whether the subsidy is attached to the dwelling unit (project-based assistance) or the assisted household (tenant-based assistance). If the subsidy is attached to a rental dwelling unit, families must accept the particular unit offered to receive assistance and lose the subsidy if they move, unless they obtain alternative housing assistance before moving.

Each family that is offered tenant-based assistance is free to occupy any unit that meets the program's minimum housing standards, that rents for less than the program's ceiling, that is affordable with the subsidy's help, and whose owner is willing to participate in the program. Families retain the subsidy if they move to another unit meeting these conditions. Figure 1 indicates the percentage of households that receive rental assistance of various types.

The Department of Housing and Urban Development (HUD) housing voucher program is the only significant program that provides tenant-based assistance. It is the second-largest low-income housing program, serving about two million households and accounting for about 32 percent of all households that receive low-income rental assistance.

There are two broad types of project-based rental assistance: public housing and privately owned subsidized projects. Both types have usually involved constructing new projects. In almost all other cases, they have required substantial rehabilitation of existing buildings. Many of these programs no longer subsidize the construction of projects, but most projects built under them still house low-income households with the help of subsidies for their operation and renovation. Overall, project-based assistance accounts for about 68 percent of all households that receive low-income rental assistance.

Public housing projects are developed and operated by local public housing authorities established by local governments, albeit

Figure 1. Percentage of Households That Receive Each Type of Rental Assistance

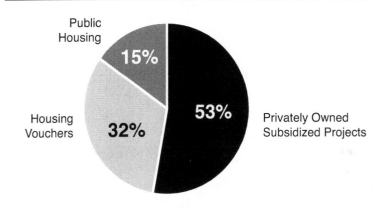

Public Housing — 15%

Housing Vouchers — 32%

53% — Privately Owned Subsidized Projects

Note: Includes assistance from US Department of Housing and Urban Development and other sources.
Source: Author's calculations based on 2013 American Housing Survey.

with substantial federal subsidies and regulations that restrict their choices. For example, regulations limit the circumstances under which housing projects can be sold and what can be done with the proceeds. In the public housing program, government employees make most of the decisions that unsubsidized for-profit firms would make in the private market—what to build, how to maintain it, and when to tear it down. Decisions about where to build projects have been heavily influenced by local political bodies. The public housing stock has declined by about 400,000 units since its peak in 1991. About one million households live in public housing projects.

Government agencies also contract with private parties to provide housing in subsidized projects. Most are for-profit firms, but not-for-profits have a significant presence. The largest programs of this type are the IRS's Low-Income Housing Tax Credit, HUD's Section 8 New Construction and Substantial Rehabilitation and Section 236 Rental and Cooperative Housing for Lower-Income Families programs, and the US Department of Agriculture's Section 515 and 521 programs.

Under these programs, in exchange for certain subsidies, private parties agree to provide rental housing meeting certain standards at restricted rents to eligible households for a specified number of years.

None of these programs provide subsidies to all suppliers who would like to participate. This is highly relevant for their performance. In general, subsidies to selected sellers of a good have very different effects than subsidies to all sellers. Subsidies to selected sellers lead to excessive profits and much greater wasteful rent seeking. About four million households live in projects of this type.

Performance of US Low-Income Housing Programs

Many aspects of the performance of low-income housing programs have been studied, such as their effects on recipients' labor earnings and the types of neighborhoods occupied by them.[3] We certainly do not have evidence on all aspects of performance for all programs, and the evidence leaves much to be desired in many cases. However, we cannot avoid making a decision about reforms until we have excellent evidence on all aspects of performance for all programs. Enough evidence exists to give policymakers confidence that certain changes would move the program in the right direction. Making no change in current policies is a decision.

Of all the differences in the performance of various methods for delivering housing assistance to low-income families, differences in cost-effectiveness are by far the most consequential for poverty alleviation. Evidence on housing programs' performance indicates that project-based assistance is much more costly than tenant-based assistance when it provides equally good housing. These studies define equally good housing to be housing that would rent for the same amount in the same locality in the unsubsidized market. This measure accounts for the desirability of the neighborhood and the housing itself. In the best studies, the estimated magnitude of the excess cost is enormous.[4]

The best study of Section 8 New Construction and Substantial Rehabilitation, HUD's largest program that subsidized the construction of privately owned projects, found an excess total cost of at least

44 percent.[5] That is, the total cost of providing housing under this program was at least 44 percent greater than the total cost of providing equally good housing under the housing voucher program. This translates into excessive taxpayer cost of at least 72 percent for the same outcome. It implies that housing vouchers could have served all the people served by this program equally well and served at least 72 percent more people with the same characteristics without any increase in public spending.

The best study indicates even larger excess costs for public housing.[6] More recent evidence has confirmed the large excess cost of the Section 8 New Construction and Substantial Rehabilitation Program, and US General Accounting Office (GAO) studies have produced similar results for the major active construction programs: LIHTC, HOPE VI, Section 202, Section 515, and Section 811.[7] In contrast, a succession of studies over the years have found that the total cost of various types of tenant-based housing assistance have exceeded the market rent of the units involved by no more than the modest cost of administering the program.[8]

The preceding evidence on the cost-effectiveness of project-based assistance applies to units built or substantially rehabilitated under a subsidized construction program and still under their initial use agreement. Evidence from the Mark-to-Market program indicates the excessive cost of renewing use agreements for privately owned subsidized projects. In most cases, owners are paid substantially more than market rents for their units.[9]

The results concerning the cost-effectiveness of different housing programs illustrate the virtue of substantially relying on market mechanisms to achieve social goals, especially the virtue of forcing sellers to compete for business. Under a program of tenant-based assistance, only suppliers who provide housing at the lowest cost given its features can remain in the program. If the property owner attempts to charge a voucher recipient a rent in excess of the market rent, the tenant will not remain in the unit indefinitely because he or she can move to a better unit without paying more for it. Under programs of project-based assistance, suppliers who receive payments in excess of market rents for their housing can remain in the program indefinitely because their tenants would lose their subsidies if they moved. These suppliers have a captive audience.

Recent events in Washington, DC, vividly illustrate the pitfalls of providing subsidies to selected suppliers.[10] The mayor has proposed spending about $4,500 per month per apartment to lease units in buildings owned mainly by contributors to her campaign. This cost does not include services to these families, and most units are dormitory style. It has been estimated that these agreements would increase the market value of the properties tenfold. At the same time, families with HUD's Section 8 housing vouchers have been able to find regular two-bedroom apartments for rents around $1,600 a month. These are better than average rental units that meet HUD's housing standards. The median rent of two-bedroom units in DC is about $1,400.

The evidence on cost-effectiveness argues strongly for phasing out project-based assistance in favor of tenant-based assistance. This would contribute greatly to poverty alleviation without spending more money by increasing the number of poor families that receive housing assistance.

Phasing out project-based assistance will contribute to poverty alleviation for another reason. Under the current system, the best units in new projects in the best locations have high market rents. They are much more desirable than the average rental unit. The worst units in the oldest projects in the worst locations have low market rents. Identical families living in the best and worst projects pay the same rent. Therefore, the current system provides enormous subsidies to some families and small subsidies to others in the same economic circumstances.

Equalizing these subsidies would contribute to poverty alleviation. Under the housing voucher program, identical households within the same housing market are offered the same assistance on the same conditions. Therefore, providing incremental housing assistance in the form of housing vouchers rather than subsidized housing projects would contribute to poverty alleviation by giving larger subsidies to the families that would have received the smallest subsidies in the absence of reform and smaller subsidies to similar families that would have received the largest subsidies.

These inequities have not been carefully documented but are obvious to all knowledgeable observers. A recent segment on *PBS NewsHour* revealed that $500,000 had been spent per apartment to build a housing project for the homeless in San Francisco.[11] This is expensive even by Bay Area standards. The median value of owner-occupied houses in the San Francisco metro area was $558,000, and the median household income of their occupants was $104,000. So this government program provided apartments to the poorest families that were almost as expensive as the houses occupied by the average homeowner.

Ensuring that the homeless occupy housing meeting reasonable minimum standards does not require anything like the amount of money spent on these units. More than 20 percent of owner-occupied houses in the San Francisco area sell for less than $300,000. Furthermore, almost half of the families in the area are renters whose median income is about $50,000. They live in much less expensive units than homeowners.

We do not need to build new units to house the homeless. They can be housed in satisfactory existing units at a much lower taxpayer cost. More than 6 percent of the dwelling units in the area were vacant at the time.

In Portland, Oregon, where the median value of owner-occupied houses was $249,000, $360,000 per apartment was spent to build another housing project for the homeless.[12] These cases are not anomalies. The HUD website is filled with photographs of such housing. The desire of the people involved in the current system to provide the best possible housing for their clients is understandable. However, this is not costless. Dollars spent on these high-cost projects are dollars not spent providing housing to more people.

Tenant-based assistance has other important advantages in addition to its greater equity and its much lower cost for providing equally desirable housing. For example, it allows recipients to choose housing that better suits their preferences and circumstances, such as living close to their jobs. This increases their well-being without increasing taxpayer cost.

In contrast to occupants of subsidized housing projects, voucher recipients have chosen to live in neighborhoods with lower poverty and crime rates. Scott Susin found that public housing tenants live in census tracts with poverty rates 8.8 percentage points higher than in the absence of assistance, tenants in HUD-subsidized privately owned projects live in tracts with poverty rates 2.6 percentage points higher, and voucher recipients live in tracts with poverty rates 2.3 percentage points lower.[13] Michael C. Lens, Ingrid Gould Ellen, and Katherine O'Regan found that occupants of tax-credit projects live in neighborhoods with crime rates about 30 percent higher than voucher recipients and only slightly lower than the crime rates in public housing neighborhoods.[14] Because voucher recipients have much more choice concerning the location of their housing, this suggests that subsidized housing projects are poorly located from the viewpoint of recipient preferences.

Voucher recipients have exercised this choice in a way that benefits their children. A widely cited, recent paper shows that better neighborhood environments lead to better adult outcomes for children in recipient households.[15] They have higher college attendance rates and labor earnings and are less likely to be single parents.

Before considering reforms of low-income housing policy, it is important to address a bit of folklore that has been influential in housing policy debates: that construction programs perform better than housing vouchers in tight housing markets. Todd Sinai and Joel Waldfogel show that additional housing vouchers result in a larger housing stock than the same number of newly built units in subsidized, privately owned housing projects.[16]

In light of other evidence, the most plausible explanations are that subsidized construction crowds out unsubsidized construction considerably and that the housing voucher program induces more recipients to live independently. The voucher program serves poorer households that are more likely to be doubled up in the absence of housing assistance. Crowding out is surely greatest in the tightest housing markets. In the absence of subsidized construction in these markets, unsubsidized construction would be high, and unemployment among construction workers would be low. Subsidized construction would divert workers from unsubsidized construction.

Furthermore, it is reasonable to believe tenant-based vouchers get families into satisfactory housing much faster than any construction program, even in the tightest housing markets. For example, the amount of time from when new vouchers are allocated to housing authorities to when they are used by voucher recipients is surely less than the amount of time from when new tax credits are allocated to state housing agencies to when tax-credit units are occupied.

Even though some households do not use the vouchers offered, housing authorities can put all, or almost all, their vouchers to use in less than a year in any market condition. They can fully use available vouchers by overissuing vouchers early in the year and then adjusting the recycling of the vouchers that are returned by families that leave the program late in the year. No production program can hope to match this speed in providing housing assistance to low-income households.

Proposed Reforms of Low-Income Housing Policies to Alleviate Poverty

The available evidence on program performance has clear implications for housing policy reform. To serve the interests of taxpayers who want to help low-income families with their housing and the poorest families that have not been offered housing assistance, Congress should shift the budget for low-income housing assistance from project-based to tenant-based housing assistance as soon as current contractual commitments permit and phase out active construction programs.

This section describes proposals for reform of low-income assistance that will alleviate poverty without spending more money. The reforms deal with all parts of the current system—active construction programs, existing privately owned housing projects, public housing, and the housing voucher program.

Active Subsidized Construction Programs. The Low-Income Housing Tax Credit (LIHTC) is the largest active construction program. It subsidizes the construction of more units each year than all other programs combined. LIHTC recently became the nation's largest low-income housing program, serving 2.4 million households, and it is the fastest growing. The tax credits themselves involved a tax expenditure of about $6 billion in 2015. However, these projects received additional development subsidies from state and local governments, usually funded through federal intergovernmental grants, accounting for one-third of total development subsidies.[17] Therefore, the total development subsidies were about $9 billion a year.

Furthermore, the GAO found that owners of tax-credit projects received subsidies in the form of project-based or tenant-based Section 8 assistance on behalf of 40 percent of their tenants.[18] The magnitude of these subsidies has never been documented. If their per-unit cost were equal to the per-unit cost of tenant-based housing vouchers in 2015, they would have added more than $8 billion a year to the cost of the tax-credit program. If so, the full cost of housing people in tax-credit projects would have been about $17 billion in 2015.

Unlike HUD's programs, the LIHTC is poorly targeted to the poorest households. Some tax credits are used to rehabilitate older housing projects built under HUD and US Department of Agriculture programs that continue to provide deep subsidies to their occupants. Other tax-credit units are occupied by families with portable Section 8 housing vouchers. The families in these units typically have very low earnings. However, the majority of occupants of tax-credit projects do not receive these deep subsidies related to their income. Their average income is more than twice the average for the occupants who receive the deep subsidies, and they are well above poverty thresholds.[19]

The poor targeting of its subsidies and the evidence on its cost-ineffectiveness argue strongly for the cessation of subsidies for additional LIHTC projects. Reducing new authorizations under the program by 10 to 20 percent each year would achieve this outcome in an orderly fashion. The money spent on this program would be better spent on expanding HUD's well-targeted and cost-effective Section 8 Housing Choice Voucher Program.

Because the congressional committees that oversee the two programs are different, this transfer of funds would be difficult to arrange. However, the committees that oversee the LIHTC could divert the reduced tax expenditures on the LIHTC to a refundable tax credit for the poorest low-income homeowners, thereby offsetting to some extent the anti-homeownership bias of the current system of low-income housing assistance. About 25 percent of all unassisted households in the lowest real-income decile are homeowners.[20] To avoid excess profits to sellers, it is extremely important that buyers are able to purchase from any seller.[21]

Existing Privately Owned Subsidized Projects. The second broad proposal to reform low-income housing policy in the interest of poverty alleviation is to not renew contracts with the owners of private subsidized projects. The initial agreements that led to building or substantially rehabilitating these projects called for their owners to provide housing that meets certain standards to households with particular characteristics at certain rents for a specified number of years. At the end of the use agreement, the government must decide on the terms of the new agreement, and the private parties must decide whether to participate on these terms. A substantial number of projects end their use agreements each year. When use agreements are not renewed, current occupants are provided with other housing assistance, almost always tenant-based vouchers.

Up to this point, housing policy has leaned heavily in the direction of providing owners with a sufficient subsidy to induce them to continue to serve the low-income households in their projects. We should not repeat these mistakes. Instead we should give their tenants portable vouchers and force the owners to compete for their business. The evidence on the cost-effectiveness of renewing use agreements versus tenant-based housing vouchers indicates that offering such vouchers would reduce the taxpayer cost of assisting these families. The savings could be used to assist additional families.

It is important to realize that for-profit sponsors will not agree to extend the use agreement unless this provides at least as much profit as operating in the unsubsidized market. Because these subsidies are provided to selected private suppliers, the market mechanism does not ensure that rents paid for the units will be driven down to market levels. If this is to be achieved at all, administrative mechanisms must be used. Administrative mechanisms can err in only one direction—providing excess profits. If the owner is offered a lower profit than in the unsubsidized market, the owner will leave the program. We should leave the job of getting value for the money spent to the people who have the greatest incentive to do so: namely, the recipients of housing assistance.

It is often argued that giving families that live in privately owned subsidized housing projects portable housing vouchers at the end of the use agreement will force them to move. This would not be the case if tenants are offered the same options as they are offered under the current system when the project's owner opts to leave the program. HUD will pay the market rent for the unit as long as the tenant wants to remain in it but offers the tenant the option of a regular housing voucher. This would enable the family to continue to live in its current unit without devoting more income to rent, and it would offer the family other options that it might prefer.

It is also argued that the failure to renew use agreements on privately owned subsidized projects reduces the number of affordable housing units. If the occupants of these projects are offered portable vouchers, this could not be further from the truth. When use agreements are extended, the only unit that is made affordable to an assisted family living in the project is its own unit. If that family is offered a portable voucher, many units become affordable to the family. Contrary to the arguments of lobbyists for project-based housing assistance, failing to renew use agreements on subsidized housing projects increases rather than decreases the stock of housing that is affordable to low-income households.

Public Housing. The public housing reform proposals seek to better use the funds and assets currently available to public housing authorities. They are designed to alleviate poverty by delivering better housing to tenants who remain in public housing, providing current public housing tenants with more choice concerning their housing, assisting additional households, and reducing the concentration of the poorest families in public housing projects. The proposals would require congressional action to change the restrictions on housing authorities, except possibly for those participating in HUD's Moving to Work Demonstration.

Currently, HUD provides public housing authorities with more than $6 billion each year in operating and modernization subsidies for their public housing projects. My proposal would give each housing authority the same amount of federal money as it would have gotten with the old system, so no authority would be able to object on the grounds that it would have less to spend on its clients. However, the proposal would alter greatly the restrictions on the use of this money and increase the total revenue of housing authorities.

The proposal requires every public housing authority to offer current tenants the option of a portable housing voucher or remaining in their current unit on the previous terms, unless the housing authority decides to demolish or sell its project. To ensure that housing authorities can pay for these vouchers with the money available, the generosity of the voucher subsidy would be set to use the housing authority's entire federal subsidy in the highly unlikely event that all public housing tenants accepted the vouchers. The generosity of these vouchers would almost always differ from the generosity of regular Section 8 vouchers, although the difference would be small in most cases.

Housing authorities would be allowed to sell any of their projects to the highest bidder with no restrictions on its future use. This would provide additional revenue to improve their remaining projects or provide vouchers to additional households. The requirement that these projects must be sold to the highest bidder maximizes the money available to help low-income families with their housing. It also avoids scandals associated with sweetheart deals.

Many housing authorities would surely choose to sell their worst projects. With uniform vouchers offered to families living in all of a housing authority's projects, it is reasonable to expect that the vouchers will be accepted by more tenants in the worst projects. These are the projects that would be the most expensive to renovate up to a specified quality level. They are the types of projects that have been demolished under the HOPE VI program and that Congress intended to voucher out under the 1998 Housing Act. By selling the public housing projects on which they would have spent the most money and providing their occupants with vouchers that have the same cost as the authority's average net expenditure on public housing units, the public housing authority would free up money to better maintain its remaining units or provide vouchers to additional households.

When a project is sold, the remaining tenants in that project would be offered the choice between vacant units in other public housing projects or a housing voucher, the standard procedure when projects are demolished or substantially rehabilitated. When public housing units are vacated by families that accept vouchers, the housing authority would offer the next family on the waiting list the option of occupying the unit or a portable housing voucher. If the family takes the voucher, the housing authority would be allowed to charge whatever rent the market will bear for the vacant unit. This would provide additional revenue to housing authorities without additional government subsidies.

To reduce poverty concentrations in public housing projects, Congress might want to eliminate the income-targeting rules for families that pay market rents for public housing units. Indeed, it might want to eliminate upper-income limits for these families. Under current regulations, at least 40 percent of new occupants must have extremely low incomes. Under the proposal, the new occupants will receive no public subsidy, and so income targeting would serve no public purpose.

Each year some former public housing tenants who had used the proposed vouchers to leave their public housing units would give up these vouchers for a variety of reasons. The money saved from their departure should be used to offer similar vouchers to other families eligible for housing assistance. The recycling of voucher funds would ensure that the tax money spent on public housing will continue to support at least the same number of families.

The preceding proposals would benefit many current public housing tenants without increasing taxpayer cost. The public housing tenants who accept vouchers would obviously be better off because they could have stayed in their current units on the old terms. They would move to housing meeting HUD's housing standards that better suits their preferences. Tenants who remain in public housing would benefit from better maintenance of their units.

The only public housing tenants who might be hurt by the proposal are tenants who want to remain in the projects that housing authorities decide to sell. Since it is impossible to justify renovating structures that reach a certain level of obsolescence and dilapidation, the initial opposition of a small minority of public housing tenants should not prevent benefits to the majority. Generally, public housing redevelopment has not required occupants' consent.

Given the difficulty of predicting all the consequences of such far-reaching changes, we should start with a controlled experiment involving innovative public housing authorities willing to implement these proposals for a randomly selected subset of their public housing projects. This experiment would produce evidence on the effects of the proposals, and it would provide useful information for modifying them to avoid unforeseen negative consequences and achieve better outcomes.

Housing Voucher Program. Even though HUD's Housing Choice Voucher Program is the country's most cost-effective and equitable low-income housing program, it too offers opportunities for reform in the interest of poverty alleviation. The Housing Choice Voucher Program provides large subsidies to its recipients while offering nothing to other families in similar circumstances.

In 2015, the national mean subsidy for a household with one adult, two children, and no countable income was almost $12,000. The poverty threshold for this family was about $20,000. A voucher subsidy of this magnitude enables its recipient to occupy a rental unit of about average desirability among two-bedroom units, that is, a unit with about the median market rent.

From the viewpoint of poverty alleviation correctly conceived, it is surely better to provide somewhat more modest housing to more of the poorest households rather than housing of this quality to a fortunate few. The current welfare system provides recipients of housing vouchers with resources well above the relevant poverty threshold, while leaving others without housing assistance well below it.

In the interest of ameliorating this inequity and reducing poverty without harming current recipients, new recipients could be offered less generous subsidies so that more households could be served with a given budget, and current voucher recipients could receive the generous subsidies that are offered by the current program. Because more than 10 percent of voucher recipients exit the program each year, this initiative will allow more families to be served each year without spending more money and will improve the program's equity. Eventually, all participants in the same economic circumstances would receive the same lower subsidy.

The new subsidy level could be chosen so that the voucher program could serve all of the poorest households that asked for assistance. At current subsidy levels, many more people want to participate than can be served with the existing budget. Reducing the voucher subsidy by the same amount for households at all income levels would make families currently eligible for subsidies less than this amount ineligible for voucher assistance. These are the currently eligible households with the largest incomes. This would free up money to provide vouchers to needier households that would not have been served by the current system.

By reducing the subsidies sufficiently, we would reach a point where all the poorest households that ask for assistance would get it. In a previous paper, I analyze the effect of alternative reforms of this type on who is served by the voucher program.[22] This reform would surely reduce evictions and homelessness, although these effects have not been studied.

Conclusion

The rapid growth of spending on entitlement programs for the elderly that will occur until they are substantially reformed will create pressure to reduce spending on programs such as low-income housing programs whose budgets are decided each year by Congress. In this situation, we should be focusing on how to get more from the money currently allocated to these programs.

Building new units is an extremely expensive way to provide better housing to low-income households, and subsidizing selected suppliers is especially expensive. Renting existing units that meet minimum standards is much cheaper. This also avoids providing recipients of low-income housing assistance with better housing than the poorest families ineligible for assistance. The proposed reforms will gradually move the system of low-income assistance toward more cost-effective approaches and enable us to provide housing assistance to millions of additional people without spending more money.

It is often argued that a shortage of affordable housing calls for subsidizing the construction of new units. This argument is seriously flawed. Almost all people are currently housed. If we think that their housing is too expensive (commonly called unaffordable), the cheapest solution is for the government to pay a part of the rent. The housing voucher program does that. This program also ensures that its participants live in units that meet minimum standards. Building new units is a much more expensive solution to the affordability problem.

Furthermore, constructing new units to house the homeless is not necessary or desirable. The number of people who are homeless is far less than the number of vacant units—indeed, far less than the number of vacant units renting for less than the median. In the entire country, there are only about 600,000 homeless people on a single night and more than 3.6 million vacant units available for rent. Even if all homeless people were single, they could be easily accommodated in vacant existing units, and that would be much less expensive than building new units for them. Furthermore, most of the 600,000 people who are homeless each night already have roofs over their heads in homeless shelters, which are also subsidized. The best provide good housing.

Reducing the substantial differences in subsidies across identical households that characterize the current system would contribute further to poverty alleviation. It would help fill the gap between poverty thresholds and the resources of the poorest households. The current system provides substantial subsidies to recipients while failing to offer housing assistance to many others who are equally poor. Even among the fortunate minority who are offered assistance, the variation in the subsidy across identical households living in subsidized housing projects is enormous. The best housing projects offered by a particular program are much more desirable than the worst, but tenants with the same characteristics pay the same rent for units in either. Because the most cost-effective program offers the same subsidy to identical recipients, the shift away from other programs toward it will focus more of the system's resources on the poorest families.

Notes

1. Edgar O. Olsen, "The Effect of Fundamental Housing Policy Reforms on Program Participation," University of Virginia, January 14, 2014, http://eoolsen.weebly.com/uploads/7/7/9/6/7796901/ehpfinaldraftjanuary2014coverabstracttextreferencetablesonlineappendices.pdf.

2. For a detailed overview of the current system of low-income housing assistance and a summary of the evidence, see Edgar O. Olsen, "Housing Programs for Low-Income Households," in *Means-Tested Transfer Programs in the U.S.*, ed. Robert Moffitt (Chicago: University of Chicago Press, 2003); and John C. Weicher, *Housing Policy at a Crossroads: The Why, How, and Who of Assistance Programs* (Washington, DC: AEI Press, 2012). For a more detailed account of the evidence, see Edgar O. Olsen and Jeff Zabel, "U.S. Housing Policy," in *Handbook of Regional and Urban Economics*, ed. Giles Duranton, J. Vernon Henderson, and William Strange, vol. 5 (Amsterdam: North-Holland, 2015).

3. Olsen and Zabel, "U.S. Housing Policy."

4. For a detailed summary of the evidence on the cost-effectiveness of low-income housing programs, see Edgar O. Olsen, "Getting More from Low-Income Housing Assistance," Brookings Institution, September 2008, http://www.brookings.edu/papers/2008/09_low_income_housing_olsen.aspx.

5. James E. Wallace et al., *Participation and Benefits in the Urban Section 8 Program: New Construction and Existing Housing*, vol. 1 and 2 (Cambridge, MA: Abt Associates, 1981).

6. Stephen K. Mayo et al., *Housing Allowances and Other Rental Assistance Programs—A Comparison Based on the Housing Allowance Demand Experiment, Part 2: Costs and Efficiency*, Abt Associates Inc., 1980.

7. Meryl Finkel et al., *Status of HUD-Insured (or Held) Multifamily Rental Housing in 1995: Final Report,* Abt Associates Inc., May 1999, Exhibit 5-1; Mark Shroder and Arthur Reiger, "Vouchers Versus Production Revisited," *Journal of Housing Research* 11, no. 1 (2000): 91–107; US General Accounting Office, *Federal Housing Programs: What They Cost and What They Provide,* July 18, 2001, http://www.gao.gov/products/GAO-01-901R; and US General Accounting Office, *Federal Housing Assistance: Comparing the Characteristics and Costs of Housing Programs,* January 31, 2002, http://www.gao.gov/products/GAO-02-76.

8. Mayo et al., *Housing Allowances and Other Rental Assistance Programs*; Wallace et al., *Participation and Benefits in the Urban Section 8 Program*; Mireille L. Leger and Stephen D. Kennedy, *Final Comprehensive Report of the Freestanding Housing Voucher Demonstration*, vol. 1 and 2 (Cambridge, MA: Abt Associates Inc., 1990); and ORC Macro, *Quality Control for Rental Assistance Subsidies Determination,* US Department of Housing and Urban Development, Office of Policy Development and Research, 2001, chap. 5.

9. For a summary of the evidence, see Olsen, "Getting More from Low-Income Housing Assistance," 14.

10. Aaron C. Davis and Jonathan O'Connell, "Shelter Plan May Benefit Mayor's Backers," *Washington Post*, March 17, 2016; and Fenit Nirappil, "Shelters' Cost Stun Some D.C. Lawmakers," *Washington Post*, March 18, 2016.

11. *PBS NewsHour,* aired October 9, 2013 (New York, MGM Television).

12. Peter Korn, "Police Threaten Complaint as Calls Mount at the Commons," *Portland Tribune,* January 9, 2014.

13. Scott Susin, "Longitudinal Outcomes of Subsidized Housing Recipients in Matched Survey and Administrative Data," *Cityscape* 8, no. 2 (2005): 207.

14. Michael C. Lens, Ingrid Gould Ellen, and Katherine O'Regan, "Do Vouchers Help Low-Income Households Live in Safer Neighborhoods? Evidence on the Housing Choice Voucher Program," *Cityscape* 13, no. 3 (2011): 135–59.

15. Raj Chetty, Nathaniel Hendren, and Lawrence F. Katz, "The Effects of Exposure to Better Neighborhoods on Children: New Evidence from the

Moving to Opportunity Experiment," *American Economic Review* 106, no. 4 (2016): 855–907.

16. Todd Sinai and Joel Waldfogel, "Do Low-Income Housing Subsidies Increase the Occupied Housing Stock?," *Journal of Public Economics* 89, no. 11–12 (2005): 2137–64.

17. Jean L. Cummings and Denise DiPasquale, "The Low-Income Housing Tax Credit: An Analysis of the First Ten Years," *Housing Policy Debate* 10, no. 1 (1999): 299.

18. US General Accounting Office, *Tax Credits: Opportunities to Improve Oversight of the Low-Income Housing Program*, 1997, 40.

19. Ibid., 146.

20. In determining a household's real income, this calculation adds an imputed return on home equity to the income of homeowners and accounts for differences in family size and composition and price levels across locations. Edgar O. Olsen, "Promoting Homeownership Among Low-Income Households," Urban Institute, August 20, 2007, Table 1, http://www.urban.org/UploadedPDF/411523_promoting_homeownership.pdf.

21. Edgar O. Olsen and Jens Ludwig, "The Performance and Legacy of Housing Policies," in *The Legacies of the War on Poverty*, ed. Martha Bailey and Sheldon Danziger (New York: Russell Sage Foundation, 2013), 218–21.

22. Olsen, "The Effect of Fundamental Housing Policy Reforms on Program Participation."

Child Welfare: In Search of Lasting Reform

MAURA CORRIGAN
American Enterprise Institute

Measured by federal expenditures, our nation's child welfare effort is relatively small. Ranked by the vulnerability of those it serves, it ranks near the top. Many people and institutions have failed children involved in child welfare—most importantly, the parents responsible for their nurture, safety, and well-being. The government cannot protect all children whose parents do not adequately care for them. And government cannot fully repair the damage to children caused by abuse or neglect. But the task of child welfare programs is to prevent harm to children as effectively as possible and to place children whose parents' rights have been terminated into safe, caring, and permanent homes. Given the long-standing and appropriate deference society gives to parents, and the potential consequences of a mistaken decision, child welfare professionals have a tough task.

I approach this issue from the perspectives of both a child welfare administrator and a judge, having heard child welfare cases as a judge, and later as a justice and chief justice of the Michigan Supreme Court. I left the supreme court to become the director of human services in Michigan, where my responsibilities included administration of child welfare programs. I managed 3,400 public child welfare workers and a $1.1 billion child welfare budget, principally funded by federal dollars. We received about 140,000 complaints of abuse and neglect each year, which required screening and assignment for investigation where appropriate. We had an average daily census of 13,000 children in foster care. About 3,000 children were adopted from foster care annually. Michigan then had the seventh-largest child welfare system in the country, measured by the number of children in care.

Our nation has made great strides in some aspects of child welfare. Far fewer children are in foster care and awaiting adoption than a decade ago, although the number of children rose modestly in 2013 and 2014.[1] Recognizing the trauma caused by removal, workers now try to keep children in their own homes while parents address their issues instead of seeking removal and placement in foster care. This is a good thing. Recruiting adoptive parents has substantially improved relative to need, as has support for those parents. The information systems used by child welfare programs have also improved. And most importantly, fewer children are being harmed.

Child welfare is one of the few policy areas in our nation that has generated bipartisan cooperation over a substantial period of time. Generally speaking, federal policymakers have tended to put aside their differences to advance legislation that they view as protecting vulnerable children.

But significant challenges remain. Current funding structures favor amelioration through the foster care system over prevention. Youth in foster care who age out of the system without a permanent home experience poor life outcomes. The short average tenure of state child welfare leaders and the high turnover of frontline workers impede sustained improvement. The smart use of data to quickly triage complaints for risk to child safety is not as widespread as it should be. The proliferation of federal requirements on practice and reporting that has accompanied federal funds impose substantial and, in some cases, counterproductive burdens on state agencies.

The recent Commission to Eliminate Child Abuse and Neglect Fatalities (CECANF) report notes that nearly 30 major federal programs in more than 20 agencies across three federal departments involve child safety and welfare.[2] Lack of coordination among congressional committees and lack of federal oversight on these crucial issues is a problem. And the federal courts' involvement in setting child welfare agency practice and goals can impede states' ability to exercise discretion in their programs, test new strategies, and direct resources toward care.

I faced these problems directly in Michigan. I am convinced that addressing these issues could substantially improve our child welfare programs over the long term.

The Basics of Child Welfare

Child welfare programs seek to prevent child abuse and neglect and to ensure that children have safe and permanent homes. States are responsible for these efforts, although the federal government has become increasingly involved over the past several decades. Child welfare programs are administered by the state and local child welfare agencies, generally conforming to federal requirements tied to their acceptance of federal funds. Federal funding for child welfare totals about $8 billion per year and is awarded to states through myriad grant formulas and eligibility rules. Because the states cannot afford to forgo federal funding, they assent to federal guidelines.

Child welfare programs' work typically starts with allegations of child abuse or neglect made to agencies and departments of state governments, tribes, and territories. These can come from anyone, but a substantial share comes from mandatory reporters: those required to report suspected abuse (e.g., medical professionals and teachers). In 2014, state and local agencies received 3.6 million calls or other referrals alleging abuse or neglect, which involved roughly 6.6 million children.[3]

Agencies decide whether complaints warrant investigation under a complex web of state and federal laws. If a report is deemed to need further investigation, a child protection worker does so. If the child's safety is at risk, the worker will seek removal of the child from the home through the courts. If safety is not an issue, the worker may decide, applying governing standards, to offer preventive services in the home to avoid future maltreatment.

A child who is removed from home may be placed with relatives or with nonrelatives in the foster care system. In 2014, nearly 415,000 children were in the custody of foster care systems.[4] In most cases, the goal was reunifying the child with parents. Under governing laws, parents have an opportunity to remedy the problems that lead to substantiated charges of abuse or neglect and improve their parenting behavior. If the parents do not improve, CPS workers will seek termination of parental rights in state courts, in accordance with federal and state standards.

Following termination of parental rights, children become eligible for adoption or permanent guardianship. In 2014, about 60,898 children were waiting to be adopted because their parents' rights had been terminated. Many do find adoptive homes—50,644 children were adopted with public child welfare agency involvement in 2014—but some do not.[5]

About 29 percent of children waiting to be adopted have resided in foster care placements for more than three years.[6] The foster care agencies move a majority of children among placements, including foster homes and institutions, and the average number of placement changes per stay was 3.2 as of 2008.[7] In 2014, more than 56,000 children in the current foster care population resided in residential institutions, such as a group home or institution.[8]

In 2014, about 22,000 young people "aged out" of foster care.[9] That is, they grew up in foster care as legal orphans after their parents' rights were terminated. The child welfare system failed these children. It did not find them a "forever family"—whether that was an adoptive home or guardianship—and these youth reached the maximum age for foster care without permanence.

Young people who age out of foster care face enormous odds. One longitudinal study found that nearly 25 percent of youth who aged out had no high school diploma or GED. By age 24, only 6 percent had obtained a two- or four-year college degree. Two-thirds of the young women became pregnant after leaving foster care, and 45 percent of the young men reported that they had been incarcerated. Only 48 percent reported being currently employed, and nearly a quarter reported that they had been homeless.[10] Substance abuse rates are higher than for peers with no history in the foster care system. Rates of homelessness are very high: one national survey of the currently homeless found that 27 percent were in foster care as minors.[11] Individuals who spend time in foster care as children are greatly overrepresented in our nation's prisons.[12]

Child welfare programs walk a delicate line respecting removal of children from their homes. On the one hand, removing a child from his home is traumatic, and multiple foster care placements can make things worse. On the other hand, a child's physical safety in the home is paramount.

The most horrifying cases in the nation's child welfare system involve child fatalities. A tragically high number of children die from abuse or neglect each year, both inside and outside the child welfare system. According to the federal government's National Child Abuse and Neglect Data System (NCANDS), 1,580 child fatalities resulted from abuse or neglect in 2014. These data may be questionable because states report child fatalities in different ways. Some researchers estimate that the actual number is closer to 3,000. The recent CECANF report states that four to eight children die every day from abuse and neglect in the United States. Approximately 75 percent of the victims are infants and children under three; a majority of these homicides are caused by a parent.[13]

Child welfare agencies assist in nearly every step of the processes needed to help keep children safe. They receive and investigate allegations and work with parents to remedy allegations deemed credible. They identify kin to care for children if the children must be removed from their home and provide financial assistance and support to these "kinship care" families. They recruit nonrelative foster care families for children who cannot return home or live with kin, match children in need of homes with foster families, and provide financial assistance and support to those families once a match is established. And they work to recruit adoptive parents for those in foster care who are not on track to return to their parents, match children with adoptive parents, and support those parents after the adoption.

These cases are frequently tragic. I recall one specific case in which a homeless mother of three, living in her car, died in another state. A Michigan man had been identified as the children's father, so the state in which she passed away sent the children to live with their father. He initiated a paternity test, and the results indicated that he was not the biological father of any of the children. So he turned the children over to the State of Michigan's foster care system.

The children were orphaned, their father unknown, and the agency had to pick up the pieces. These are the tragedies that child welfare workers face.

Federal Spending

Congress appropriated roughly $8 billion in 2015 for child welfare programs. This funding is spread across a host of programs, including many that are quite small. The bulk of these dollars ($7.1 billion in 2015) falls under Title IV-E of the Social Security Act. This title primarily reimburses states for a share of the costs they incur providing foster care and adoption assistance. Most IV-E funding in 2015 ($4.3 billion) was appropriated for payments to families who care for children in foster care and for program administration, and another $2.5 billion was dedicated to adoption assistance (financial assistance to families who adopt children with special needs who could not be placed after reasonable efforts to place them without assistance).[14]

States also direct to child welfare efforts a substantial share of federal funds that are not explicitly tied to child welfare. These include the Social Services Block Grant, Temporary Assistance for Needy Families (TANF), and Medicaid. Unlike the dedicated child welfare funding streams, states are not required to meet federal guidelines for their child welfare programs to apply this funding to their child welfare efforts. It is estimated that states apply as much as $5.3 billion from these sources annually toward their child welfare efforts.[15] States and localities are also contributors, of course. Combined, they typically spend a bit more on child welfare programs than does the federal government.

The Growing Federal Role in Child Welfare

Since the 1970s, the federal role in child welfare policy has expanded substantially. Over that time, Congress has passed more than 20 federal acts governing the substance and procedure of child protection, foster and kinship care, and adoption and guardianships. National standards now affect nearly all aspects of child welfare practice at the state and local levels. Most such statutes and rules address important concerns. On balance, they have improved the nation's care for vulnerable children. At the same time, the scope of activities for which states are de facto responsible by virtue of federal funding streams have grown dramatically.

The current array of federal child welfare programs got its start in 1935, when Congress provided limited funding in the Social Security Act. Reach expanded with the Aid to Families with Dependent Children (AFDC) program in 1961, which allowed states to use federal funds for foster care of children in AFDC-eligible families. The program was later expanded to include all states.

The Child Abuse Prevention and Treatment Act (CAPTA) was the first statute solely dedicated to child abuse and neglect. CAPTA provides modest federal funding to the states (about $100 million each year) and requires them to develop protocols to report, investigate, and protect children at risk of abuse and neglect as a condition of funding receipt. It also established strict confidentiality provisions.

Congress then enacted foster care and adoption assistance payments under the Adoption Assistance and Child Welfare Act of 1980 (AACWA) to support children adopted from foster care. This act compelled states to use "reasonable efforts" to preserve and maintain families and to reunify them if their children are removed from their custody. It also required state plans for case planning, relative placements, and permanency planning, which had to be approved by the DHHS.

In 1994 Congress established child and family services reviews (CFSRs) of state child welfare programs to ensure compliance with requirements in various federal funding programs. CFSRs review many indicators, with a focus on safety; permanency; and the physical, educational, and mental needs of children involved in those programs. Only four small states have passed these national benchmarks. A third round of state reviews is currently underway. States that fail to pass the reviews are required to file Program Improvement Plans to ameliorate the adverse findings; federal dollars are at risk for noncompliance or unsatisfactory implementation of the improvement plans.

In 1997, Congress passed the Adoption and Safe Families Act (ASFA) and amended the AACWA significantly, making the child's safety the paramount criterion in assessing child abuse and neglect. It placed time limits on parents to improve conditions that led to the child's removal, so as to provide for timely permanency, and required background checks for all foster and adoptive parents and for adults living in foster or adoptive homes, so as to protect children from harm at the hands of caregivers. The ASFA also provided bonuses for expeditiously moving adoption cases through state courts.

In 2012, Congress passed the Fostering Connections to Success and Adoption Improvement Act. Among other changes, it allowed youth to remain in foster care until age 21, with continued federal supports if states match those contributions. Fostering Connections increased opportunities for relatives to participate by mandating notice to relatives of a child's removal. It also authorized subsidized guardianships, extended adoption and guardianship assistance, and created educational rights for foster children to attend school—either to remain in their same school or, when a move is necessary, to obtain assistance for a prompt transfer to a new school.

And in 2014, Congress passed the Preventing Sex Trafficking and Strengthening of Families Act, requiring states to develop policies around children at risk of becoming sex-trafficking victims. It further required states to amend foster care licensing standards to allow foster families to provide developmentally appropriate extracurricular, enrichment, cultural, and social activities, and it required the same of group homes. Under this law, foster children 14 and older must receive and sign an advice of rights form (for example, rights to education, health, participation in court proceedings, and visitation).

This is just a sketch of federal developments in child welfare. But even from this, it is clear that the scope of activities for which states are responsible—provided that they accept federal funds—has expanded dramatically alongside increased federal support for those activities, as have the rules and requirements with which entities administering child welfare programs are expected to comply.

Successes in Child Welfare

By many important measures, child welfare has improved substantially. Most importantly, fewer children appear to be suffering harm. In 1990, child maltreatment rates were estimated to be 13.4 per 1,000 children in the country. After peaking at 15.3 in 1993, rates are now estimated to have fallen to 9.4 per 1,000 children, although up slightly from 2012.[16] These are substantial declines reflecting a primary goal of child welfare programs and policies, and they should be properly celebrated.

Additionally, fewer children are living in foster care—another big success. Complaints and the number of children in foster care have risen modestly over the past couple of years—a subject of much discussion in the child welfare arena—but still remain far below what they were just a decade ago.

Why? In part because fewer children are being removed from their homes. One of the greatest advances in child welfare practice is that child welfare professionals have become more cognizant of the trauma caused by removal. Nationally, they have minimized trauma when removal is necessary. More children are remaining with their own families following complaints, often with the help of preventive and supportive services to their families.

In 2005, 513,000 children were in foster care in the US.[17] Over the past decade, the number of children in care has decreased significantly—about 100,000 fewer children, or nearly a 20 percent reduction. As a result, payments to foster families to help defray the cost of caring for a child have fallen as well.

And efforts to increase adoptions have borne fruit—federal adoption assistance payments are on an upward trend. In 2005, 130,997 children awaited adoption; that number had fallen to 107,918 in 2014.[18] The number of children adopted has remained essentially stable over the past decade: 51,625 children were adopted with public child welfare agency involvement in 2005, while 50,644 were adopted with the involvement of public child welfare agencies in 2014.[19] This is good news against a backdrop of falling numbers of children in the system available for adoption. Of course, our goal should be that every waiting child finds a "forever family," that no child face the prospect of aging out of the system and the adversity that entails. Nonetheless, progress has been made.

And sometimes, boring improvements are also important improvements. Information systems fit that category. Agencies need to track cases and outcomes and respond quickly with as much information at their disposal as possible. Many agencies have substantially improved the systems they use for complaint intake, investigation, and case management. Of course, what agencies do with information matters. But from what I saw as an administrator, infrastructure capability enables success. We are far better off in this regard than we were two decades ago.

Overarching Challenges

While there are decreasing child maltreatment rates, fewer children in foster care, increasing federal adoption assistance, and more efficient child welfare agency structures, many challenges still hinder the continued improvement of the child welfare system. Three of the most pressing challenges include a federal financing structure that focuses too little on helping families stay together, an overreliance on consent decrees to reform child welfare agencies, and low workforce retention rates.

Federal Financing Structure. Federal funding in child welfare is focused on supporting the foster or adoptive families of children who have been removed from their parents. More than three-quarters of dedicated federal funding are appropriated to these two purposes, with two-thirds of that dedicated to supporting foster care placements. Support for those efforts is needed.

Based on what I saw as an administrator, however, the current financing approach is too ameliorative. Although practice has recognized the importance of keeping children in their families if the child's safety is not in jeopardy, and progress has been made on that front, federal funding structures have not fully caught up. The bulk of dedicated federal funding for child welfare is narrowly focused on reimbursing states for their efforts to maintain children in foster care arrangements. Funding is less focused on helping families stay safe and together in the first place or on permanence once parental rights are terminated.

A related issue is that states' eligibility for federal reimbursement of costs is based on the income criteria of the children involved in their programs—criteria set in 1996 in accordance with TANF eligibility guidelines through the Personal Responsibility and Work Opportunity Reconciliation Act. This was an outgrowth of child welfare's historical connection to the AFDC, which enabled states to claim reimbursement for foster care costs incurred by AFDC-eligible children who were removed from their homes. This may have made sense in 1996, but it does not make sense today.

State child welfare agencies have a responsibility to investigate claims of abuse and neglect, whatever the household income of the child in question, and respond in the child's best interest. And there is some concern that guaranteed federal funding for the care of poor children may result in unnecessary foster care for low-income children.

Child Welfare Class-Action Litigation. Class-action litigation has long been a thorn in the side of child welfare agencies. No agency is perfect, and horrifying lapses on the part of agencies continue to occur. Class-action suits are brought on behalf of those children whose federal statutory or constitutional rights have been violated while in state custody, with the underlying goal of driving child welfare agency reforms. For a variety of reasons, especially the negative publicity generated by a trial, these suits are often settled, and a consent decree is frequently a major component of the settlement. The decree often lays out a series of improvements to the child welfare system proposed by plaintiffs that the state agrees to undertake as part of the settlement. Progress is monitored and enforced by the federal courts.

These decrees are widespread. In 2005, the Child Welfare League of America documented child welfare class-action litigation in 32 states, with consent decrees in 30 states, including 26 decrees in federal courts.[20] Since then, 20 new decrees have gone into effect. The subjects fingered for improvement in the decrees touch nearly every area of child welfare practice, including:

- Reporting, investigating, and intake in child protection cases;

- Staffing, caseloads, training, and supervision of case workers;

- Information technology;

- Quality control; and

- Recruitment, retention, and licensing of foster parents, relatives, and group homes.

Operating under a consent decree substantially changes the emphasis and focus of an agency's efforts. I know this firsthand, having operated under one in Michigan.

Consent decrees hold states accountable for practices that result in violating rights guaranteed in the Constitution and federal statutes. Upholding these rights is, of course, vital, and consent decrees can be useful in this regard. But as currently practiced, they also present problems. Decrees often address concerns that extend far beyond vindication of federal rights. They have questionable returns on investment; they often lack sunset periods, existing in perpetuity; they are difficult to modify and update; their requirements are frequently beyond the ability of even high-performing programs to meet; and they divert state dollars away from services and toward payment of attorneys' fees and court monitors.[21]

The *Oklahoman* recently reported an example of diverting state tax dollars to plaintiffs' attorneys and court monitors. Oklahoma has been subject to a federal consent decree over its child welfare operations for the past four years. During that time the state has paid $5.6 million to court monitors, including three who charged $315/hour. Because of reduced state tax revenues, Oklahoma's Department of Human Services concurrently offered buyouts to 400 of its employees. The *Oklahoman* questioned whether children are really better off under this federal court decree.[22]

The requirements embedded in consent decrees can also be at odds with each other. Michigan's decree, for example, requires a certain percentage of children be placed in a permanent home within 12 months. It also requires a certain share of placements to be successful in the long term. Michigan has a strong record on permanency. But requiring the state to move more quickly is likely to result in poorer matches, dragging down the state's success on permanency. The decree also contains a distance requirement that most children be placed in homes that are geographically close to the home from which they were removed. This makes sense in theory, but good matches are difficult to make. It may be better for a child to be placed in a good home further away than a less optimal home 20 miles closer.

Ordinarily, child welfare professionals would decide their priorities. But in mandating measures for satisfying decrees, agencies and their leaders are hamstrung. Lack of prioritization and inadequate recognition of trade-offs are endemic to bureaucracies generally, and decrees can exacerbate those problems. Narrow and inflexible consent decrees can drive decisions that guard against legal action at the expense of a child's best interest, and they can hinder reforms.

New York City provides another good example of the problem. A consent decree prevented the city from adopting best practices, such as neighborhood-based services, that could have improved the child welfare system in the 1990s. Linda Gibbs, a former top aide to Mayor Michael Bloomberg, described her experience trying to address problems in the child welfare system as "a classic case of the adversarial nature of litigation creating stalemates that delay reform."[23]

Workforce Retention. Child welfare is hard work. Studies across the decades have grappled with the problem of employing and retaining frontline child welfare workers. I dealt with this problem in Michigan. According to the Annie E. Casey Foundation, 20 percent of the public child welfare workforce turns over every year; turnover in private child welfare agencies is 40 percent.[24]

Because long-term relationships in child welfare cases are almost always an asset to care—not to mention efficiency—turnover is more than a marker of employee satisfaction; it limits the quality of care that agencies provide. Studies have been remarkably consistent about the causes leading to departures of employees in such high numbers: high caseloads, staff shortages, and lack of adequate supervision and training.

Too little federal attention has been directed to the problem of worker retention. Yet in various performance-improvement plans submitted to DHHS regulators in response to CFSRs, 17 states described workforce-retention issues as barriers to implementing federal demands. Stabilizing each state's child welfare workforce is central to lasting reforms in child welfare. Certainly child welfare can be a resource black hole—no amount of resources will make child welfare programs perfect. But the status quo on retention suggests it is a problem.

The worker-retention issue starts at the top. Sustained senior leadership matters for change and affects agency workers' morale. Conventional wisdom holds that the tenure of a state executive branch child welfare leader is 18 months. A revolving door of state leadership presents yet another significant barrier to lasting change. In bureaucracies, incumbents resist change—especially when leadership changes frequently. Why should the bureaucracy change when new leadership will propose a new direction in 12 months? From both a service and agency change perspective, frontline and senior tenure in child welfare agencies demands serious attention.

Suggestions for Reform

These shortcomings should be addressed with reforms that align federal funding with our priorities, ensure consent decrees do not lead to unnecessary entanglements, improve the morale of workers on the frontlines, and better integrate predictive analytics tools into our efforts to keep children safe.

Federal Financing. Many in the child welfare community agree that the current federal financing system for child welfare should shift from a "damage control" model—in which federal funding flows primarily toward supporting services for foster children—toward one more attentive to keeping families together in the first place and moving children into permanent families as quickly as possible. This concept has received attention from leading legislators such as Sen. Orrin Hatch (R-UT) and Sen. Ron Wyden (D-OR), was highlighted in the CECANF report, and has been a point of focus for the Annie E. Casey Foundation and Casey Family Programs.

Federal financing reform has the potential to make a difference on these issues. It is worth considering how federal funding streams can more effectively incentivize states to focus on prevention and permanence, as opposed to amelioration. Take Title IV-E funding, for example. If a child meets eligibility criteria, the federal government reimburses a share of the costs of providing for that child's care—sometimes for a long period of time, and sometimes in less preferable settings. Essentially, the federal government gets what it pays for with Title IV-E: lots of foster care and little focus on prevention or permanence. Title IV-E's structure does not send strong signals to states regarding what is important.

To address this, the federal government could limit federal reimbursement for less preferable arrangements with weaker links to permanence (e.g., shelter or congregate care), placing additional pressure on states to find kin, foster families, and adoptive parents more quickly and encouraging a greater focus on prevention. Other measures aimed at incentivizing permanence could also be considered but should be tempered by the knowledge that a substantial majority of the foster caseload is, and is likely to continue to be, extremely difficult to place in a permanent home.

State agencies should also be provided increased flexibility in their application of federal child welfare dollars (specifically with Title IV-E), allowing them to direct federal funds toward activities aimed at keeping families together, recruiting and supporting kinship care and foster families, and recruiting and supporting adoptive parents with the goal of expeditious permanency. The restriction on a child's eligibility for federal reimbursement of foster care costs, based on AFDC limits, could also be revised to acknowledge that income is not the primary issue here—it is the safety and well-being of the child, whatever his family's income. One option worthy of consideration is eliminating the eligibility limit entirely and lowering federal reimbursement rates across the entire population of children to keep federal costs and state reimbursements flat.

Significant new reforms incorporating many of these ideas appear to be in progress. They could be some of the most consequential reforms of the past two decades. The current system is in some ways a funding source that provides states with little direction, and it should be changed.

Consent Decrees. Federal policymakers should examine class-action litigation with a critical eye. In our paper, *Rethinking Consent Decrees*, John Bursch and I suggest that Congress look again at legislation similar to Senator Lamar Alexander's Consent Decree Fairness Act and impose controls such as tying ongoing judicial review of decrees to the election process. This would eliminate the so-called "dead hand" problem—that is, the decree continues in existence for decades, far beyond the terms of office of those state actors who negotiated the decrees.

Such a reform would also tie such decrees to a violation of a federal right. It would preclude any consent decrees, or aspects of consent decrees, that do not remedy violations of federal statutory or constitutional rights. And it would bar adopting standards from federal funding carrots, such as the CFSRs, and relying on standards created by private organizations (e.g., caseload limits), which have no source in federally protected rights.

Any decree overseen by federal courts should be narrowly tailored to the violation of a federal right. Congress should place the burden of proof on plaintiffs to show that the decree's terms are necessary to prevent future violations of these rights. Such a reform would ensure that violated rights are appropriately recognized and remedied, without allowing consent decrees to introduce unnecessary entanglement in agency practice that is unrelated to the specific violation at issue. Consent decrees' effect on agency practice, resources, and child well-being is significant. Agencies should be held accountable, but an appropriate recognition of the importance of professional judgment, flexibility, and innovation must temper such efforts.

Workforce Retention. At the federal level, efforts to increase worker retention should start with a critical and comprehensive accounting of the rules and requirements placed on those at the state and local levels who are tasked with administering programs supported with federal funds. As decades of new programs have stacked atop one another, many with different rules and requirements, the child welfare system has become breathtakingly convoluted, landscaped by funding silos, and tangled up with exacting reporting requirements that seem to honor process for process' sake.

Child welfare agencies tasked with administering these programs, and their workers, are constantly on the defensive. Too often, in my experience, they are preoccupied with ensuring that they do not miss process minutiae, rather than being focused on the overarching goals of protecting children; securing permanent, caring homes for children removed from the custody of their parents; and supporting families in those efforts. This drags on morale and passion for their work.

A few examples of the questions such a review might ask are as follows. Is the requirement that each child placed in foster care be provided with a detailed notice of rights, and that this notice be signed, useful? Does it make sense for a 14-year-old to be required to review and sign a notice if the adults caring for these children are ultimately responsible and are well aware of their responsibilities as caregivers?

Does it make sense to have a hard pass/fail judgment on CFSRs? Michigan received a score of 99.35 on its recent CFSR and failed; the federal bar for passing is 99.39. Would it make more sense to evaluate agencies on a continuum that recognizes and rewards performance without being arbitrary?

A key driver of leadership turnover is negative media attention surrounding a child fatality, but many leaders believe CAPTA's confidentiality provisions bar them from responding to these reports and telling the agency's side of the story. Does this make sense? Would it be more desirable to empower leaders to defend their strategy and employees if that could be done without violating confidentiality or chilling the press, or would clearer guidance be helpful? To be sure, many requirements are useful and needed. But they should be carefully chosen.

Speaker of the House Paul Ryan has called for consolidation and flexibility in adult poverty programs. Child welfare would benefit from similar scrutiny—not to simplify the system for simplification's sake, but because it would likely improve leadership and line-worker morale and decrease turnover. Both of these are foundational to long-term success and change in this arena.

A broader examination of proper metrics should accompany this process because requirements and punishments have been added piecemeal with each development in federal policy. What top-line outcomes do we want to see? How will performance be rewarded or subpar performance punished? Are we comfortable giving states more freedom on process? I do not pretend to have all the answers to these questions. But I do know from personal experience that the current system is numbingly convoluted and needs a critical review of requirements before new mandates are added. Even putting aside resource questions, which are worthy of discussion, I am confident that substantial improvements could be made.

Predictive Analytics. By design, child welfare agencies are reactive. They receive allegations of abuse or neglect and respond to them. Some agencies do this more effectively and quickly than others. But with the development of new integrated data systems, child welfare agencies have the opportunity to proactively identify the cases in which child safety is at highest risk and address concerns more quickly. Good caseworkers are important, but insurance companies use complex models to evaluate risk-based decisions for a reason: they are generally better than humans.

Child welfare agencies have ample opportunities to incorporate such models in their services. Predictive analytics, which has been piloted with some success in Hillsborough County, Florida, uses past child welfare records to identify the risk factors most associated with child abuse and neglect fatalities. Caseworkers use this information to target their efforts to the riskiest cases. Using this model allowed the local child welfare program to almost entirely eliminate child abuse and neglect fatalities.

States and localities would do well to explore how they could integrate these predictive models into their practice. Federal policymakers should thoughtfully consider ways in which the federal government could help—perhaps by establishing a best-practices clearinghouse and offering technical assistance—without getting in the way. Predictive analytics is not a panacea, but it is a likely next frontier of improvement in child welfare programs.

Conclusion

Children involved in the child welfare system are among the most vulnerable in our society. We have made substantial progress in reducing the number of children in foster care and increasing adoptions to permanent homes. Many weaknesses remain—among them, frequent leadership changes in state and local programs, a dated federal financing scheme, high frontline worker turnover, poorly designed federal requirements that impede service and change, and federal courts overinvolved in policy and practice.

These issues are central to creating an environment conducive to long-term change in service of those broader goals. Efforts to better align federal funding with desired outcomes, rationalize and smartly reign in federal requirements in child welfare programs, limit the intrusion of federal courts into practices unrelated to specific constitutional or statutory violations, and intelligently support the experimentation and adoption of new predictive analytics tools would all be steps in the right direction.

Notes

1. US Department of Health and Human Services, Administration for Children and Families, Administration on Children, Youth, and Families, Children's Bureau, *Adoption and Foster Care Analysis and Reporting System (AFCARS) Reports*, various years, http://www.acf.hhs.gov/programs/cb/research-data-technology/statistics-research/afcars.

2. Commission to Eliminate Child Abuse and Neglect Fatalities, *Within Our Reach: A National Strategy to Eliminate Child Abuse and Neglect Fatalities*, 2016, https://www.acf.hhs.gov/sites/default/files/cb/cecanf_final_report.pdf.

3. US Department of Health and Human Services, Administration for Children and Families, Administration on Children, Youth, and Families, Children's Bureau, *Child Maltreatment*, January 25, 2016, http://www.acf.hhs.gov/programs/cb/research-data-technology/statistics-research/child-maltreatment.

4. US Department of Health and Human Services, Administration for Children and Families, Administration on Children, Youth, and Families, Children's Bureau, *Trends in Foster Care and Adoption: FY 2005–FY 2014*, 2015, https://www.acf.hhs.gov/sites/default/files/cb/trends_fostercare_adoption2014.pdf.

5. US Department of Health and Human Services, Administration for Children and Families, Administration on Children, Youth, and Families, Children's Bureau, "The AFCARS Report, No. 22," July 2015, http://www.acf.hhs.gov/sites/default/files/cb/afcarsreport22.pdf.

6. Ibid.

7. Casey Family Programs, "Foster Care by the Numbers," August 2010, http://www.fostercareandeducation.org/portals/0/dmx/2013%5C07%5Cfile_20130719_111354_oStS_0.pdf.

8. HHS Children's Bureau, "The AFCARS Report, No. 22."

9. Ibid.

10. Mark E. Courtney et al., *Midwest Evaluation of the Adult Functioning of Former Foster Youth: Outcomes at Ages 23 and 24* (Chicago: Chapin Hall at the University of Chicago, 2010), https://www.chapinhall.org/sites/default/files/Midwest_Study_Age_23_24.pdf.

11. Martha R. Burt et al., *Homelessness: Programs and the People They Serve: Findings of the National Survey of Homeless Assistance Providers and Clients*, Urban Institute, December 7, 1999, http://www.urban.org/research/publication/homelessness-programs-and-people-they-serve-findings-national-survey-homeless-assistance-providers-and-clients/view/full_report.

12. Sara McCarthy and Mark Gladstone, *State Survey of California Prisoners: What Percentage of the State's Polled Prison Inmates Were Once Foster Care Children?*, California Senate Office of Research, December 2011, http://

www.sor.govoffice3.com/vertical/Sites/{3BDD1595-792B-4D20-8D44-626EF05648C7}/uploads/Foster_Care_PDF_12-8-11.pdf.

13. Commission to Eliminate Child Abuse and Neglect Fatalities, *Within Our Reach*; and US Department of Health and Human Services, Administration for Children and Families, Administration on Children, Youth, and Families, Children's Bureau, *Child Abuse and Neglect Fatalities 2013: Statistics and Interventions*, April 2015, https://www.childwelfare.gov/pubPDFs/fatality.pdf.

14. Emilie Stoltzfus, *Child Welfare: An Overview of Federal Programs and Their Current Funding*, Congressional Research Service, January 23, 2015, https://www.fas.org/sgp/crs/misc/R43458.pdf.

15. Ibid.

16. US Department of Health and Human Services, Administration for Children and Families, Administration on Children, Youth, and Families, Children's Bureau, *10 Years of Reporting Child Maltreatment 1999*, 2001, http://archive.acf.hhs.gov/programs/cb/pubs/cm99/cm99.pdf; HHS Children's Bureau, *Child Maltreatment 2014*, 2016, http://www.acf.hhs.gov/sites/default/files/cb/cm2014.pdf; and Andrea J. Sedlak et al., *Fourth National Incidence Study of Child Abuse and Neglect (NIS-4)*, HHS Office of Planning, Research, and Evaluation and the Children's Bureau, http://www.acf.hhs.gov/sites/default/files/opre/nis4_report_congress_full_pdf_jan2010.pdf.

17. US Department of Health and Human Services, Administration for Children and Families, Administration on Children, Youth, and Families, Children's Bureau, "The AFCARS Report, No. 13," September 2006, http://www.acf.hhs.gov/sites/default/files/cb/afcarsreport13.pdf.

18. US Department of Health and Human Services, Administration for Children and Families, Administration on Children, Youth, and Families, Children's Bureau, "Children in Public Foster Care on September 30th of Each Year Who Are Waiting to Be Adopted FY 2005–FY 2014," http://www.acf.hhs.gov/sites/default/files/cb/children_waiting2014.pdf.

19. US Department of Health and Human Services, Administration for Children and Families, Administration on Children, Youth, and Families, Children's Bureau, "Adoptions of Children with Public Child Welfare Agency Involvement by State FY 2005–FY 2014," http://www.acf.hhs.gov/sites/default/files/cb/children_adopted2014.pdf.

20. Shay Bilchik and Howard Davidson, "Introduction," in *Child Welfare*

Consent Decrees: Analysis of Thirty-Five Court Actions from 1995 to 2005, by Amy Kosanovich, Rachel Molly Joseph, and Kira Hasbargen (Washington, DC, Child Welfare League of America, 2005), 2–4, http://www.acf.hhs.gov/sites/default/files/cb/cm2013.pdf.

21. For seminal work, see Ross Sandler and David Schoenbrod, *Democracy by Decree: What Happens When Courts Run Government* (Yale University Press, 2003).

22. Oklahoman Editorial Board, "Despite Optics, Spending by Oklahoma DHS Has Been Needed," *Oklahoman*, March 9, 2016, http://newsok.com/article/5483633.

23. Linda Gibbs, "New York City's Administration for Children's Services Reform Effort: When Solutions Are the Problem" in *For the Welfare of Children: Lessons Learned from Class Action Litigation*, eds. Judith Meltzer, Rachel Molly Joseph, and Andy Shookhoff (Washington, DC: Center for the Study of Social Policy, 2012), 125–28.

24. Annie E. Casey Foundation, *The Unsolved Challenge of System Reform: The Condition of the Frontline Human Services Workforce*, 2003.

Temporary Assistance for Needy Families

RON HASKINS

Brookings Institution

Few federal programs arouse the strong reactions elicited by the Temporary Assistance for Needy Families (TANF) program. Most Republicans regard the program as one of the most important achievements of Republican policy in recent decades because it fulfills the party's primary goal of helping, incentivizing, or cajoling poor welfare recipients to work. By contrast, some Democrats and most progressive advocates despise the program and think it fails in what they see as a welfare program's single most important function: providing benefits to destitute families. The goal of this chapter is to provide an overview of the TANF program, examine its association with changes in work and poverty since it was enacted in 1996, and review what are widely seen as the weaknesses of the program, along with possible solutions to some of these weaknesses.

Five Major Features of TANF

Although the TANF program has many complexities, its essence is captured by five features: a focus on ending entitlement, block grant, work requirements, time limits, and sanctions. Not only do these features mark a radical change from the old Aid to Families of Dependent Children (AFDC) program that TANF replaced, but they also distinguish TANF from every other federal means-tested program.

Entitlement. The most important change embodied by TANF is the end of entitlement. This is the TANF provision that most aggravated Democrats during the welfare-reform debate of 1995–96.[1] No wonder.

A key characteristic of AFDC and many other means-tested programs, such as Medicaid and the Supplemental Nutrition Assistance Program (SNAP; formerly Food Stamps), is that everyone who meets the program's qualifications has a legal right to the benefits. By contrast, many federal programs, such as housing and day care, have a fixed appropriation each year and are given to recipients on a first-come, first-serve basis, with many eligible families left out. During the welfare-reform fight in the mid-1990s and previously, Republicans were intent on implementing the principle that welfare recipients should not just sit back and get guaranteed benefits. Rather, to retain eligibility, they should have to actually work or prepare for work.

Even though President Franklin D. Roosevelt told Congress in 1935, the year he signed the Social Security Act that created AFDC, "we must and shall quit this business of relief,"[2] AFDC had become—or perhaps always was—more of a handout than a hand up. Far from quitting relief, over the years the federal government had surrounded AFDC with a host of other means-tested programs.

In 2012, the Congressional Research Service released a remarkable memorandum giving a brief overview of the benefits provided by 83 means-tested programs and summarizing federal—and state if the program included at least partial state financing—spending on each program. Total state and federal spending on these programs in 2011 was nearly $1.1 trillion in 2015 dollars.[3] Quitting the business of relief this is not. Given the proliferation of programs and spending, Republicans were intent on taking action to make it clear to recipients that at least one program (TANF) is a contingent program—able-bodied adults would not get cash unless they were working or making state-defined efforts to prepare for or look for work.

Block Grant. The federal government gives money to states in many ways. The block-grant method typically gives states abundant flexibility in using federal money to achieve goals specified in federal law.

TANF is a block grant that provides states with $16.5 billion each year. No allowances were made for inflation, thereby ensuring that the block grant's value in current dollars would decline over time. By

2015, the block grant's purchasing power had declined by around a third.[4]

The money is distributed among the states on a formula basis; the formula's main element is how much states had been spending on the AFDC program in the years before the legislation was enacted in 1996. Because of this funding formula, rich states that had high AFDC benefits, such as California and New York, receive approximately 6.2 times more money per child in poverty than poor states that had low AFDC benefits, such as Mississippi and Nevada ($2,216 per child for New York versus $357 per child for the latter two states).

States are authorized to spend the funds on four goals: (1) to support children from destitute families so they can be raised at home; (2) to help families achieve independence from welfare through work and marriage; (3) to increase the percentage of children being reared in married, two-parent families; and (4) to reduce nonmarital births.

A particular advantage of replacing AFDC with a block grant is that the incentives for state policy and practice are much more in line with the goal of helping people leave welfare. Under the AFDC entitlement, every time states added someone to the welfare rolls, the feds gave them an average of about $0.55 for each dollar they spent on benefits. Many AFDC critics saw this financing mechanism as providing states with a financial incentive to add people to the rolls. Similarly, for every person who left the rolls, sometimes because the state helped them find a job, the federal government reduced their payment by an average of $0.55 on the dollar.

By contrast, under the block grant, if the states add someone to the rolls, they must pay the entire cost out of their block grant. But if they help a recipient leave the rolls, they get to keep all the money that had been paying for that person's benefits. Thus, the block grant's structure gives states a financial incentive to help families leave the rolls. Of course, this financing system is subject to manipulation, a topic that I will discuss later.

Work Requirements. To make sure states get the message about work, TANF requires every state to design a work program. The definition of work is spelled out in great detail in the law so that states have to provide job-search assistance, training for work, work itself, or education or training on a limited basis.

When fully implemented, the law requires recipients to engage in work activities for 30 hours a week, and half the state's caseload had to meet the work requirement. If the states failed to do so, they were "fined" by having their block-grant allocation reduced. Education and training were restricted; individuals were allowed to count it toward the work requirement for a maximum of only one year, and only 30 percent of the state's work requirement could be fulfilled by recipients in education and training activities.

Time Limit. Another highly controversial feature of the welfare-reform law was the five-year time limit placed on benefit receipt for any given individual. From its appearance in House Republican proposals as early as 1991, the idea of time limits was a feature of every subsequent House Republican proposal, including the bill President Bill Clinton signed into law in 1996.[5] The concept of time limits is incompatible with the AFDC entitlement and embodies the basic idea of Republican welfare philosophy that welfare is not forever.

The version in the bill that passed Congress stipulated that individual families could not receive cash welfare for longer than five years. At that point, cash benefits would terminate. Poor parents would need to plan their lives so that once they had used cash welfare for five years, they could rely on another source of income, presumably earnings. The severity of this provision is considerably softened by a provision that allows states to continue benefits beyond the five-year limit for up to 20 percent of their caseload.

Sanctions. One way to overcome people's reluctance to aggressively prepare for and seek work is to impose sanctions on those who do not meet work requirements. The authors of the TANF program believed that sanctions were an important part of getting welfare recipients to work.[6] As a result, the law requires all states to reduce the welfare benefits of recipients who do not fully cooperate with work requirements. States are free to design their own system of sanctions, but it had to include benefit reductions.

Most states used a graduated system of benefit penalties, usually beginning with a loss of part of the benefit for a few months and then, if the recipient continues to violate the work requirement, moving to a loss of more benefits and for longer periods. By 2010, 36 of the 50 states had adopted policies that allowed them to eventually terminate the entire welfare check.[7]

Impacts of TANF on Work and Poverty

Virtually all policies produce positive and negative impacts. Too often, especially in political settings, Republicans and Democrats tend to overemphasize the success of policies they support and attack the shortcomings of policies they oppose. What is needed is a balanced appraisal that forthrightly reviews policies' successes and failures. This approach is especially important because using evidence to improve programs is a vital characteristic of the evidence-based culture both Republicans and Democrats say they support.

TANF, like all policies, has produced successes and failures. In this section, I deal with successes. Later I deal with the problems TANF has caused, at least in part.

The most important goal of TANF—both for the Republicans who wrote the legislation and for President Clinton who signed it, with support from half the Democrats in the House and Senate—was to promote work among low-income, single mothers who go on welfare or could be considered at risk for going on welfare. The claim of those who supported the 1996 welfare reforms was that many or most of the mothers who wound up on welfare could work.

As we have seen, an important purpose of the TANF reforms was to signal that welfare recipients and applicants would know from the beginning that they are required to work or prepare for work. They face a time limit and work requirements backed by sanctions that will reduce and could eliminate their cash benefit if they do not meet the work requirements. The signals could hardly be much clearer. But did they actually boost work among mothers on or at risk of going on welfare?

Figure 1. Employment-to-Population Ratio for Never-Married Mothers and All Women, 1980–2014

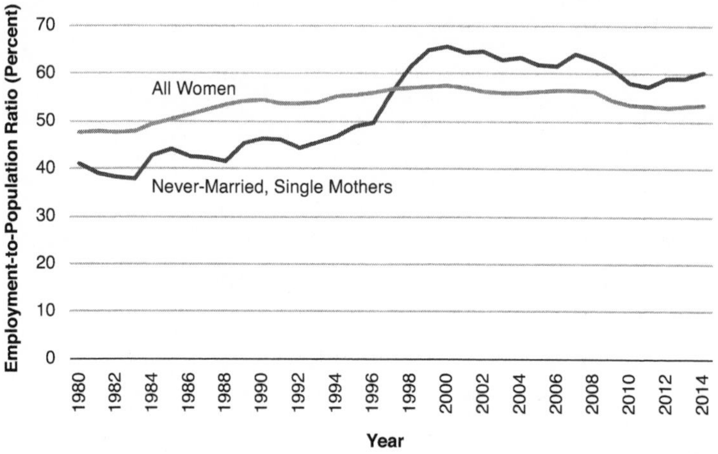

Source: CPS-IPUMS online tool and FRED data.

Figure 1 shows the employment-to-population ratios (EPRs) for never-married mothers, the group most likely to be poor and to go on welfare, as compared to all women. The EPR is a good measure for our purpose because it shows the percentage of all people in the group being analyzed who are working. Figure 1 shows that the EPR for never-married mothers had been well below the EPR of all women for many years. The ratios reversed position for the first time after the enactment of welfare reform.

We can get a good idea of the course of EPRs after welfare reform by comparing the average ratio of the five years before welfare reform (1991–95) with the average ratio of the five years following welfare reform (1997–2001). The former average was 46.4 percent; the latter was 62.6 percent—an increase of 35 percent. This may well be the biggest increase in work rates over a short period for any demographic group in American history.

The recessions of 2001 and 2007–09 reduced the EPR of never-married mothers—and nearly every other group. For

Figure 2. Poverty Rate for All Children, Female-Headed Family Households with Children Under 18, and Black Children, 1959–2014

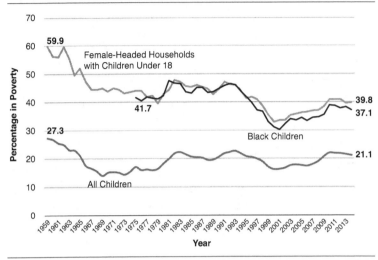

Source: US Census Bureau, Poverty Division, "CPS ASEC," Families Table 4 and People Table 3.

never-married mothers, the EPR declined from a high of 66 percent in 2000 to a low of 57 percent in 2011. But as the economy recovered from the Great Recession of 2007–09, the EPR began to move up again in 2012. The 60 percent rate for never-married mothers in 2014 is nearly 30 percent above the comparable rate in the five years before welfare reform.

The poverty rate is a second important measure of outcomes associated with TANF's influences.[8] Figure 2 shows the poverty rates for female-headed families with children, for all black children, and for all children. During the period of rapid increase in work by all single mothers and never-married mothers after the 1996 reforms, the poverty rate dropped sharply for female-headed families with children by 20 percent and for black children by 25 percent. Given that the poverty rate for female-headed families with children is just over five times the poverty rate of married-couple families, the nation must reduce the poverty rate among female-headed families with children to significantly decrease the nation's child poverty rate. This is precisely what happened during the years following welfare reform.

This analysis is not definitive because it is based on only correlations and not on scientific-evaluation designs. But I do not argue that welfare reform was the only factor at work here. Rather, most analysts attribute the increase in work and the decline in poverty shown in Figures 1 and 2 to three major factors: welfare reform; the increase in the earned income tax credit (EITC), which boosted the income of so many single mothers; and a hot economy that created a net increase of about 12 million new jobs between 1995 and 2000.[9] It is reasonable to argue that all these factors played a role in increasing the work rates among poor mothers on welfare and reducing the poverty rate for them and their children.[10]

A study by the Congressional Research Service shows that the decline in poverty in the two decades that followed welfare reform is largely attributable to deliberate policy of the federal government, both the TANF policy emphasizing work and programs such as the EITC that provided financial support for low-income working families. Throughout the 1980s, 1990s, and later, the federal government created or expanded a series of programs that provide income—often in-kind income such as food and medical care—to poor and low-income working families. Taken together, these programs might be called the nation's "work-support system" because all the programs provide cash or in-kind benefits to low-income working families. Not only did these work-support programs lift the families financially, but also they reduced the disincentive to work for mothers receiving public benefits before roughly the 1990s.

Figure 3 shows how the work-support system increases income and reduces poverty among low-income, working mothers. The top line shows the poverty rate among single-mother families based only on earnings. As would be expected, as work rates of these mothers increased beginning in the 1990s, the poverty rate based on earnings fell steadily until the recession of 2001. For the next 10 years, this poverty rate either held steady or increased, until falling again

Figure 3. Effect of Earnings, Transfers, and Taxes on the Poverty Rate of Households Headed by Single Mothers, 1987–2013

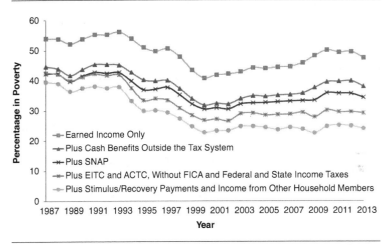

Source: Thomas Gabe, *Welfare, Work, and Poverty Status of Female-Headed Families with Children: 1987-2013*, Congressional Research Service, July 15, 2011.

starting in 2011 during the economic recovery from the Great Recession. The poverty rate based on earnings never fell below 42 percent; it was 48 percent in 2013 after three years of decline.

The four lines below the earnings poverty rate show that the various work-support programs substantially reduced the poverty rate in every year and was increasingly effective in reducing poverty at the end of the 25-plus-year period. It reduced poverty by less than 30 percent in 1987 but by 50 percent in 2013.

An interesting point highlighted by the chart is that as the poverty rate based on earnings increased steadily during the years following the recession of 2001, the post-transfer poverty rate held more or less steady. This outcome is probably caused by work-support benefits increasing as earnings declined for many mothers. In any case, the work-support system almost always reduces the poverty rate of single mothers and their children.

Table 1. Problems with TANF

Funds in the Block Grant Shrink Every Year. The original TANF block grant distributed $16.5 billion to states, but because funds in the block grant are not adjusted for inflation, the block grant loses value every year. So far, it has lost about one-third of its value.

Flawed Distribution Formula. Because the formula for distributing funds among states is based on state spending of federal funds on benefits in selected years before welfare reform was enacted in 1996, and because poorer states had lower benefits, the funding received by states from the block grant is inversely proportional to state per capita income; the federal TANF annual payments to New York and California, for example, are more than six times bigger on a per-child-in-poverty basis than annual payments to Mississippi and Nevada.

Questionable Use of Block-Grant Funds. States use the block grant for many purposes besides supporting work and paying a cash welfare benefit to poor families with children. In 2015 states spent about 40 percent of TANF funds on a variety of programs other than cash assistance and work programs.

Fewer Poor People Receive Cash Welfare. While states spend block-grant funds on a host of activities, many poor families with children who would have received cash assistance under the AFDC program do not receive cash assistance under TANF. For example, despite an increase in the number of families in poverty and deep poverty in Michigan, Michigan now pays out about 80 percent less in TANF assistance than before the 1996 reforms were enacted.

More Families with Children Are in Deep Poverty. In part because of fewer poor families receiving cash welfare, the number of families in deep poverty has increased substantially in recent years.

Caseload Reduction Credit. As an incentive to help families leave the welfare rolls, states were allowed to subtract the percentage by which they reduced their TANF caseload after 1995 from the 50 percent work requirement. For example, if a given state reduced its caseload by 40 percent, the percentage of the TANF caseload it would need to have in work activities was reduced from 50 percent to 50 percent minus 40 percent, or only 10 percent. The TANF caseload fell so rapidly in most states that between 1997 and 2011, between 20 and 30 states consistently had a work participation requirement of 0 percent. The Deficit Reduction Act of 2005 changed the base year for calculating the credit from 1995 to 2005, which tightened the requirement considerably, but many states still have a modest work requirement because of the caseload reduction credit.

Separate State Program. Creating a state program separate from TANF, not specifically authorized in the 1996 TANF legislation, can be used by states to avoid almost all the state requirements in the TANF law. For example, states can greatly reduce the number of recipients who must be in work programs by simply putting them in a separate state program paid for with state funds. State funds spent in this way can be counted toward the state maintenance-of-effort requirement in the TANF law.

Criticisms of TANF

Although TANF has played an important role in increasing work and reducing poverty among low-income mothers and their children, there are problems associated with the TANF program. Table 1 provides a list of the problems most frequently raised by the program's critics. Here I focus attention on two of the most serious: TANF's block-grant structure and the growing number of mothers and children mired at the bottom of the income distribution, often in dire poverty, most of whom appear to be eligible for but do not receive assistance from TANF.

Many problems shown in Table 1 are associated with one of the most sweeping of the 1996 reforms. Specifically, the legislation converted the AFDC entitlement program, in which the federal government reimbursed states for a portion of the cash benefits they paid to mothers, into a block grant, in which states now receive a fixed amount of money each year. The intent of the Republicans who designed this approach was to give states flexibility in their use of welfare funds and financial incentive to help mothers leave welfare because their federal funds would not fall when mothers left the rolls as they had under the reimbursement funding. Most Republicans appeared to think that states would spend part of their block-grant allocation to pay cash welfare and part to promote work by paying for child care, transportation, and similar work supports, as well as for job-search assistance, education, and training.

A recent detailed report from the Center on Budget and Policy Priorities (CBPP) summarizes how states spent TANF block-grant funds in 2014 and how much the 1996 law required states to spend from their own funds in a requirement called maintenance of effort (MOE).[11] In 2014 states spent only 26 percent of their total TANF and MOE funds on cash assistance. This figure is down from around 70 percent of spending on basic assistance in the years before the 1996 reforms. There is significant variation across states; 10 states spent less than 10 percent of their funds on basic assistance.

The second major category of spending the authors of welfare reform assumed states would pursue is work and supports related to work. The three categories of block-grant spending that could reasonably be counted as work or work-related are work-related activities and support, child care, and refundable tax credits. States spent 32 percent of their block grant and MOE funds on these three categories.

The combined 26 percent for basic assistance and 32 percent for work activities leaves a little more than 40 percent of block-grant spending in the average state for purposes that are not directly related to basic assistance or work. Not surprisingly, according to the CBPP, states are spending a "large and growing share" of their TANF and state MOE funds on child welfare, for which the federal government already gives states about $8 billion in separate funds, and "to replace existing state funds" in non-TANF programs.[12] Few if any of these state expenditures are illegal under the great flexibility TANF provides states, but such expenditures do not appear to be what Congress had in mind when states were given a block grant to facilitate flexible spending.

That state block-grant spending on basic assistance has declined so much is especially surprising in view of the number of families with children living in poverty. There is now a well-developed literature on "disconnected" mothers, those who do not have cash welfare or earnings.[13] This body of research shows that the number of disconnected mothers has more than doubled since 1996 and that more than 80 percent of these mothers and their children live in poverty. Research also shows that these mothers have multiple barriers to work, such as depression, disabled or chronically ill children, poor transportation, and living in an area with a depressed economy.[14]

Despite the multiple problems these mothers face, states are now much less likely to provide them with either cash welfare or help qualifying for or finding work than before welfare reform was enacted. In 1979, for example, for every 100 families in poverty, 82 families received AFDC; by contrast, in 2013 the comparable ratio was 26 families receiving TANF for every 100 families in poverty.[15]

Similarly, over the past 15 years or so, the Census Bureau's measure of deep poverty (poverty at or below half the poverty level or about $9,550 in 2015) has shown a troubling trend. Like the measure of poverty, in the years just after welfare reform, deep poverty fell. But starting with the recession of 2001, deep poverty rose or held steady in most years, gradually building up over time. Between 2000 and 2014, it rose from 4.5 percent to 6.6 percent, or by more than 45 percent. Not all those in deep poverty were disconnected mothers, but many were. Besides, the deep-poverty measure is a general indication that an increasing number of families and individuals at the bottom of the income distribution are experiencing serious economic distress.

Conservatives have responded to these figures on state spending and deep poverty with several arguments. First, a major problem with the Census Bureau's data on poverty and deep poverty is that abundant evidence now shows that when interviewed by the Census Bureau, people tend to seriously underreport the level of benefits they receive from government programs. A recent study by Bruce

Figure 4. Share of People in Deep Poverty

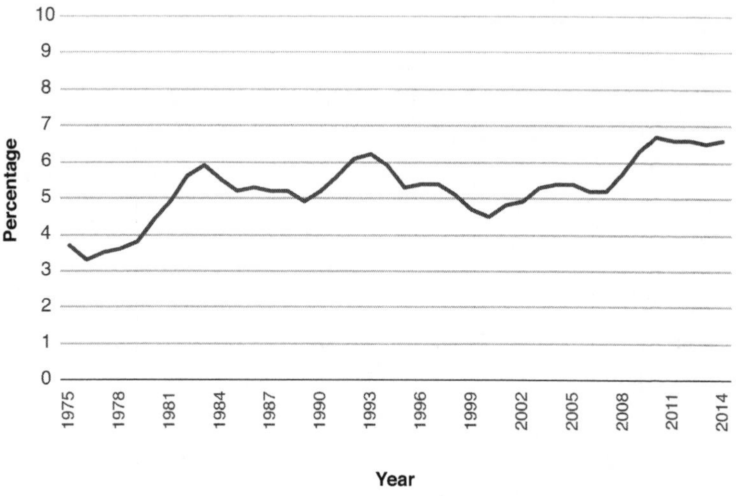

Source: Census Bureau, Poverty Table 22.

Meyer and Nikolas Mittag of the University of Chicago compares administrative data from New York State to survey data from the Census Bureau's Current Population Survey (CPS).[16] They find that "program receipt in the CPS is missed for over one-third of housing assistance recipients, 40 percent of food stamp recipients and 60 percent of TANF and General Assistance recipients."[17]

It follows that the estimates of poverty rates and deep-poverty rates cited earlier are probably too high because they are based on underreported TANF income. Any broader measure of poverty, such as the measure used in the CRS analysis that showed considerable progress against poverty, would be even more deeply flawed because these measures include public benefits other than cash, such as SNAP and housing, which are also underreported. An interesting implication from this work is that underreporting income on surveys may explain, at least in part, why poverty rates and poverty gaps based on income data are higher than poverty rates and gaps based on consumption data.[18]

In addition, conservatives argue that claiming that all "disconnected" mothers and children are destitute—or even "disconnected" from public benefits—is an exaggeration. All are eligible for SNAP, and the overwhelming majority actually receive it; and all the children and many if not most of the mothers are eligible for Medicaid. The children are also eligible for additional benefits, such as school lunch and the Special Supplemental Food Program for Women, Infants, and Children.

Possible Solutions

Even so, given their primary role in writing the 1996 reforms, it seems appropriate for Republicans to respond to the problem of declining assistance for poor mothers and children by helping states find ways to help these mothers hold jobs or ensure that, if they are meeting the state work requirement and trying to find work, they would remain eligible for cash assistance and actually receive it. One approach would be to ensure that troubled families receive casework from the social workers employed by the TANF program. With advice and encouragement from experienced caseworkers, some mothers may be able to stabilize their lives and take steps toward work.

States should devote some of the TANF resources they have been spending on other programs to help these mothers move toward self-sufficiency. To do so, they could strengthen the TANF program by initiating special caseworker training, perhaps supplemented by coaching; giving mothers small doses of job experience; improving the way they deal with barriers to work; and helping mothers who work get the work-support benefits for which they qualify, such as the EITC, Additional Child Tax Credit, SNAP, and child care. This last focus of state caseworkers is especially important because high-quality research shows that children from families leaving welfare with increased income from earnings and work supports had enhanced school achievement.[19]

A particularly robust example of the enhanced-casework approach is the Pathways program developed by Toby Herr and her colleagues at the Erikson Institute in Chicago.[20] The Pathways program features five types of activities: a supportive environment for mothers to discuss their day-to-day lives, including barriers to employment; choices about how the mothers can meet the Pathway monthly work or participation requirements; a sufficiently broad array of activities so that nearly all mothers can participate in an activity for which they experience success; assistance in moving to more complex activities that lead to employment; and recognition for incremental progress.

Few if any of the enhanced-casework programs have strong evidence of success from rigorous research designs. Helping mothers with multiple barriers to work move toward work and self-sufficiency will apparently require new and innovative programs. State and local social service and workforce agencies, perhaps working with nonprofit organizations, are in a good position to develop and test these programs.

For this reason, Congress should initiate a research program administered by the Departments of Health and Human Service (HHS) and Labor to work with state agencies that emphasize education, training, job search, counseling, and similar activities that lead to employment. Programs must enroll parents who are qualified for the state TANF program (both or either mothers and fathers) and must be evaluated by rigorous designs. The secretaries of HHS and Labor should be given a moderate annual sum of money, perhaps $500 million, to conduct these experiments for five years, with mandatory reports to Congress after two and five years.

In addition to other outcomes, the experiments must report enrollment and participation in the job-preparation programs, and outcomes should include employment, duration of employment, wages, and reasons for termination of employment for those who lose or leave their jobs. At least one experiment should include long-term follow-up of at least five years. States must agree to use the state workforce agency's employment records to track employment and earnings.

The nation needs effective employment programs for mothers with barriers to work to fulfill the promise of welfare reform. Unless the nation can develop successful programs of this type, a group of mothers and their children will likely remain at the bottom of the income distribution and in or near destitution.

Notes

1. Ron Haskins, *Work over Welfare: The Inside Story of the 1996 Welfare Reform Law* (Washington, DC: Brookings Institution Press, 2006).

2. Franklin Delano Roosevelt, "Second State of the Union Address," January 4, 1935, https://en.wikisource.org/wiki/Franklin_Delano_Roosevelt %27s_Second_State_of_the_Union_Address.

3. Congressional Research Service, *Spending for Federal Benefits and Services for People with Low Income, FY 2008-2011: An Update of Table B-1 from CRS Report R41625, Modified to Remove Programs for Veterans*, memorandum to the Committee on the Budget, US Senate, October 16, 2012, http://www.budget.senate.gov/republican/public/index.cfm/files/serve/?File_id=0f87b42d-f182-4b3d-8ae2-fa8ac8a8edad. For federal and state spending on programs for people with low income, see Committee on the Budget, US Senate Republicans, "Sessions Comments on Congressional Report Showing Welfare Is Single Largest Federal Expense," October 18, 2012, http://www.budget.senate.gov/republican/public/index.cfm/2012/10/sessions-comments-on-congressional-report-showing-welfare-is-single-largest-federal-expense.

4. Gene Falk, *Temporary Assistance for Needy Families (TANF): Financing Issues*, Congressional Research Service, September 2015, 13.

5. Haskins, *Work over Welfare*.

6. Ibid.

7. The $1.1 trillion figure includes approximately $4 billion in means-tested veterans benefits paid in FY 2009, which were excluded from the Congressional Research Service memorandum prepared for the Senate Budget Committee. Urban Institute, "Welfare Rules Database," http://wrd.urban.org/wrd/Query/query.cfm.

8. Scott Winship, "Welfare Reform Reduced Poverty and No One Can Contest It," Forbes, January 11, 2016, http://www.forbes.com/sites/scottwinship/2016/01/11/welfare-reform-reduced-poverty-and-no-one-can-contest-it/.

9. Author's calculations from US Department of Labor, Bureau of Labor Statistics, "Data Retrieval: Labor Force Statistics (CPS)," 2015, http://www.bls.gov/webapps/legacy/cpsatab9.htm.

10. Rebecca Blank and Ron Haskins, eds., *The New World of Welfare*

(Washington, DC: Brookings Institution Press, 2001).

11. Liz Schott, Ladonna Pavetti, and Ife Floyd, *How States Use Federal and State Funds Under the TANF Block Grant*, Center on Budget and Policy Priorities, October 2015.

12. Schott, Pavetti, and Floyd, *How States Use Federal and State Funds,* 3; and Emilie Stoltzfus, *Child Welfare: An Overview of Federal Programs and Their Current Funding,* Congressional Research Service, March 2016.

13. Rebecca M. Blank, *Helping Disconnected Single Mothers,* Brookings Institution, Center on Children and Families, 2007; Pamela J. Loprest, *Disconnected Families and TANF,* Urban Institute, 2011; and Ron Haskins, "TANF at Age 20: Work Still Works," *Journal of Policy Analysis and Management* 35, no. 1 (2016): 224–31.

14. Lesley J. Turner, Sheldon Danziger, and Kristin S. Seefeldt, "Failing the Transition from Welfare to Work: Women Chronically Disconnected from Employment and Cash Welfare," *Social Science Quarterly* 87, no. 2 (2006): 227–49.

15. Donna Pavetti, testimony before the Subcommittee on Human Resources, Ways and Means Committee, US House of Representatives, April 13, 2015.

16. Bruce D. Meyer and Nikolas Mittag, "Using Linked Survey and Administrative Data to Better Measure Income: Implications for Poverty, Program Effectiveness and Holes in the Safety Net" (working paper, National Bureau of Economic Research, October 2015).

17. Ibid, 1.

18. Bruce D. Meyer and James X. Sullivan, *Winning the War: Poverty from the Great Society to the Great Recession,* Brookings Institution, Fall 2012, 133–200; and Bruce D. Meyer and James X. Sullivan, "Consumption, Income, and Material Well-Being After Welfare Reform" (working paper, National Bureau of Economic Research, January 2006).

19. Pamela Morris et al., *How Welfare and Work Policies Affect Children: A Synthesis of Research,* MDRC, 2001.

20. Suzanne Wagner and Daria Zvetina, "Welfare Reform, the Next Phase," *Applied Research in Child Development,* no. 3 (Summer 2001).

The Supplemental Security Income Disabled Children Program: Improving Employment Outcomes in Adulthood

RICHARD V. BURKHAUSER
Cornell University

MARY C. DALY
*Federal Reserve Bank of San Francisco**

A core goal of US social policy is to promote equal *opportunity* for children to become self-sufficient adults. For children with disabilities, this goal is supported by targeted legislation. The Individuals with Disability Act (IDEA), passed in 2004, ensures access to a free and appropriate public education. The Americans with Disabilities Act (ADA), passed in 1990, ensures access to the built environment and to the labor market in adulthood.

Despite these supports, many children with disabilities fail to enter the labor market as adults. This shortfall is particularly apparent among low-income children receiving benefits from the Supplemental Security Income (SSI)-disabled children program. A majority of SSI-disabled children move directly onto the adult SSI program at age 18, and those who do not, work and earn less than their counterparts without disabilities.[1] These data raise the possibility that more should be done to assist children with

*The views expressed in this paper do not necessarily reflect the views of the management of the Federal Reserve Bank of San Francisco or of the Board of Governors of the Federal Reserve System. We thank Catherine van der List for exceptional research assistance.

disabilities living in low-income families and eligible for SSI.

In this chapter, we review the history of the SSI-disabled children program and argue that the program's goals, laid out nearly a half century ago, have fallen behind the modern view of people with disabilities embedded in IDEA and the ADA. We conclude that a fundamental change in the way we think about providing financial support for low-income children and youth with disabilities is warranted.

This new mindset would focus on investing in their human capital and giving them the best chance to be work-ready as adults. These changes will bring the SSI-disabled children program more in line with the tenets of self-sufficiency in IDEA and the ADA. We suggest that this is especially important given the rapid growth of the SSI-disabled children program since 1989.

History and Growth

The federal SSI program for disabled children provides cash benefits to low-income families with a disabled child.[2] When the program began in 1974, about 71,000 disabled children received benefits, and program expenditures totaled around $40 million. As Figure 1 shows, the program is far larger today. In 2014, about 1.3 million disabled children received benefits, and program costs were around $10.3 billion in 2015.[3]

Program growth increased most rapidly immediately following the 1990 Supreme Court decision in *Sullivan v. Zebley*, which greatly expanded disability eligibility criteria for children. Welfare reform in 1996 tightened eligibility standards and slightly reduced the rolls for one year. However, since that time, recipients and expenditures have steadily increased. Today, children are now twice as likely to reside in a household with some SSI income (6.9 percent) as in a household with some Temporary Assistance for Needy Families (TANF) income (3.4 percent).[4]

In principle, several factors could explain this growth. Since SSI is an income-tested welfare program, one possibility is that more families with a disabled child are meeting the income-eligibility

Figure 1. SSI-Disabled Children Caseload and Expenditures Growth

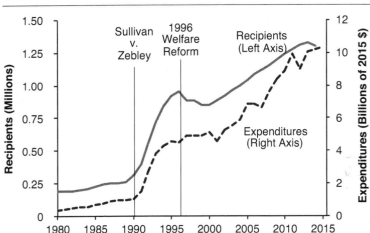

Source: Social Security Administration, "Annual Report of the Supplemental Security Income Program," 2015; and Social Security Administration, "SSI Annual Statistical Report, 2014," October 2015.

threshold. Another is that the underlying health of US children has deteriorated, increasing the number of children who meet the program's disability criteria.

In practice it is difficult to verify whether growth in the income-eligible population has contributed to caseload growth. The SSI means-test rules are complicated, and no reliable, publicly available data are available on how many children meet them. Hence, researchers must estimate the number of children who, if they were disabled, would be eligible for benefits.

One way to do this is to estimate the income-eligible population using the US poverty line. Figure 2 shows the results of this exercise. Our estimates are based on multiples of the US Census Bureau poverty line for a family of three, which was $19,078 in 2015. The top line shows caseloads as a fraction of all children below the US Census Bureau poverty line each year, indicating what the take-up rate would be if only families below the poverty line were income eligible.

Figure 2. Growth in Caseloads per 1,000 Eligible Children

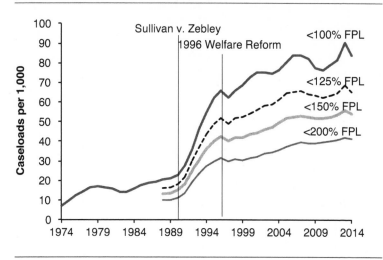

Note: "FPL" means federal poverty line.
Sources: Social Security Administration, "Annual Report of the Supplemental Security Income Program," 2015; US Census Bureau; and authors' calculations.

Since the maximum SSI income test level is likely to be above the poverty line for many families, we also compute what take-up rates would be if household income eligibility were set below 125 percent, 150 percent, and 200 percent of the poverty line.

Not surprisingly, estimates of the percentage of eligible children receiving SSI-disabled benefits in any given year vary with estimates of the income-eligible population. It is lowest for the most generous view of the size of the eligible population, 200 percent of the poverty line, and highest for the most conservative view, 100 percent of the poverty line. But no matter which income-eligibility estimate we use, the take-up rate has risen significantly over time. This pattern holds across all our measures of income eligibility, confirming that income-eligible population growth has not predominantly driven the rise in caseloads and expenditures.

Another possibility is that the underlying health of children explains program growth. Identifying such a trend is quite difficult.

Figure 3. Children Reporting Activity Limitations by Poverty Status

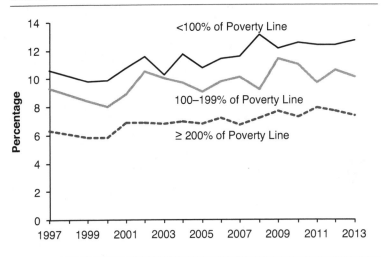

Note: Children are ages 5 to 17.
Sources: National Center for Health Statistics and authors' calculations.

However, the limited information on trends in child health and functional limitation suggest little change over time. Figure 3 shows the percentage of children ages 5 to 17 with an activity limitation reported by a parent according to poverty status. Functional limitations have changed little among any of these status groups, including those who may be income eligible. These data are limited, but they do not indicate that changes in child health explain the growth over time in the SSI-disabled children rolls.

If Not Income and Health, Then What?

When Congress originally enacted the SSI-disabled children program, it recognized the difficulty of applying the standards of the adult Social Security Disability Insurance program to children. Thus, Congress determined that a child should be considered disabled for program purposes if "he suffers from any medically determinable physical or mental impairment of comparable severity" to a disabling impairment in an adult. Between 1974 and 1989, the child disability determination process neither included functional assessment nor accounted for equivalents of adult vocational factors. The program experienced only modest growth and served children with severe physical and intellectual disabilities.

However, in 1990 the Supreme Court ruled in *Zebley* that a functional limitation component parallel to that in the adult program must be included in the initial disability determination process for children. In response, the Social Security Administration added two new bases for finding children eligible for benefits: functional equivalence, which was set at the medical-listing level of the disability determination process, and an individualized functional assessment, which was designed to parallel vocational assessment for adults. These assessments lowered the severity level required for children to be eligible for SSI benefits, allowing applicants who did not meet the medical-listing criterion to be found disabled if their impairments were severe enough to limit their ability to engage in age-appropriate activities, such as attending school.[5] In recent work, Mark Duggan, Melissa Kearney, and Stephanie Rennane argue that the most important factor causing SSI-disabled children program growth has been an expansion in the program's eligibility criteria.[6]

In 1996, as part of welfare reform, Congress revisited the definition of disability for children. It created new standards that were similar in spirit to those for adults but unique to children. Legislators intentionally tightened the eligibility criteria by raising the threshold for being functionally impaired and removing certain behavior-related limitations, such as maladaptive-behavior disorder, from the functional-listing criteria. Thus, the post-1996 standard represents a broader measure of disability than the one applied when the program began, but a narrower standard than the one used between 1990 and 1996. This reduced caseloads per 1,000 children across all our measures of the income-eligible population for one year. (See Figure 2.)

Changes in disability rules for children applying for SSI noticeably affected caseloads. But the way SSI administrators interpreted these rules also had an impact. Administrators found themselves interpreting more subjective eligibility criteria. The outcome can be seen in the percentage of SSI-disabled children awards for two categories: intellectual disability and other mental conditions. These represent extremes of the distribution between medically measurable and more subjectively determined conditions.

In 1983, approximately 37 percent of new beneficiaries qualified based on intellectual disability. Only 5 percent had other mental conditions. By 2003, more than half of new enrollees qualified based on other mental conditions, and that rose to around 57 percent in 2014.[7]

Welfare reform also contributed importantly to SSI-disabled children caseload growth among low-income families after 1996. Reform ended the Aid to Families with Dependent Children (AFDC) program, replacing it with TANF. TANF came with time limits and work requirements.

These reforms noticeably affected the SSI-disabled children program. The SSI program does not directly provide services to children with disabilities nor tie benefits to obtaining such services. It simply provides cash benefits to families with low incomes and a disabled child. In that sense, it is like AFDC or TANF, but with the additional stipulation that a family must include a child judged to have a disability.

Researchers have recognized that the populations served by TANF and the SSI-disabled children program overlap and have looked for evidence of program interactions. They have found that a low-income single mother who is also eligible for TANF heads the typical SSI-disabled children applicant family.

SSI-disabled children benefits are larger than TANF benefits and lack the TANF work requirement. Thus, single mothers have an incentive to apply for SSI-disabled children benefits. There is evidence that the greater the difference in benefits, the more likely they are to do so.[8] Moreover, in contrast with the old AFDC program, states have an incentive to move TANF families to the SSI-disabled children program. This allows them to shift costs from their TANF federal block grants to a fully federally funded program.[9]

In sum, the 1996 welfare reforms strictly limited low-income families' access to cash benefits and shifted more of the financial burden of support for such benefits onto the states. This created additional incentives for families with potentially eligible children to seek SSI-disabled children benefits, and it motivated states to help them. When these factors combined with relatively lower and more subjective eligibility standards, the SSI-disabled children program was poised to grow.

Unintended Consequences and Long-Term Costs

The data suggest that the rise in SSI-disabled children caseloads and costs are largely policy driven. Of course, this may not be a bad thing. While there are expenditure costs associated with providing benefits to low-income families via this program, it is a redistribution of income to a needy subgroup of poor and near-poor families. The problem is that additional costs associated with the redistribution, while unintended, have potential long-term impacts on recipients. For example, Jeffrey Hemmeter, Jacqueline Kauff, and David Wittenburg find that nearly two-thirds of SSI-disabled children beneficiaries move directly onto SSI-disabled adult rolls, with few attempting to work thereafter.[10]

Perhaps more concerning are results from research by Manasi Deshpande and Michael Levere looking at the adult earnings of former SSI-disabled children recipients. Deshpande finds that the marginal child recipient aging off the program, who is presumably most work-ready, earns only modestly more than those who remain on SSI benefits. Importantly, she also finds little increase in labor supply among these marginal former recipients over time, even into their mid-30s.[11] Similarly, Levere's results show that being an SSI recipient as a child reduces labor market earnings as an adult.[12]

One interpretation of these results is that graduates of the SSI-disabled children program are not being given the opportunities for success in adulthood that IDEA and the ADA intended. The average SSI child beneficiary moves directly to the adult SSI program and remains there throughout working life. Some beneficiaries have such severe disabilities that this outcome is inevitable. But others, especially those coming into the program under the less severe diagnosis permitted since the *Zebley* decision, might be able to hold a job with appropriate accommodation, training, and encouragement. In the context of our social and cultural commitment to include individuals with all types of disabilities in the labor market, the labor market outcomes for graduates of the primary support program for low-income children with disabilities are unacceptable.

Aligning Goals with Outcomes

The SSI-disabled children program's underlying goal is to allow low-income parents or guardians of children with disabilities to provide for them. Since the passage of IDEA and the ADA, our social commitment to children with disabilities has expanded to include preparing them for employment and self-sufficiency as adults, just like all other children. Measured against this goal, the SSI children program is failing. The question is what should be done about it.

While any proposal for change along these lines would be fundamental in its recognition that preparing SSI children for employment and self-sufficiency as adults is a core goal of the program, some proposals are more sweeping in scope than others.

In the incremental-change group are proposals to improve communication and coordination among families, schools, and the Social Security Administration (SSA) offices. At present, families primarily rely on their own networks to coordinate services.[13] Moreover, there is no formal transitional planning for SSI child recipients, meaning most are entering the redetermination point at age 18 without much knowledge of potential outcomes or plans for what to do, should they be denied.

In practice, communication can begin far earlier than age 18 and focus on helping parents learn about the potential employment opportunities for their children. For example, Wittenburg has proposed using the SSA Work Incentives Planning and Assistance program to proactively reach out to youth to develop, plan, and connect to other state services. He also suggests that for those who are able,

SSA should require SSI child recipients to meet with counselors to plan for the transition to self-sufficiency.[14] Tools such as the Youth Opportunity Guide, which gives youth an opportunity to compare scenarios with and without work over their lifetimes, could be used in these settings.[15]

More sweeping types of change would involve better incentivizing SSI child recipients and their families to invest in activities that promote work-readiness. For example, Wittenburg proposes waiving rules for reporting youth earnings to SSA and eliminating the implicit benefit tax on work.[16] The idea behind this proposal is to remove the burdens and fear associated with trying work. If youth are able to test their employability without fear of temporarily or permanently losing benefits, they can work more and discover if they need additional skills.

Along those lines, it seems reasonable to consider tying ongoing benefit receipt to school attendance, conditional on the ability to come to school. Since school is an obvious way to invest in work-readiness, requiring parents to hit attendance goals could improve outcomes.[17]

Most sweeping would be to rethink who is best able to administer an SSI-disabled children program whose primary goal is making its child beneficiaries work-ready as adults. In this vein, we have proposed moving jurisdiction of the SSI-disabled children program from the SSA to the states.[18] Unlike previous periods when SSI-like programs were in state hands, this devolution would, like TANF, hold states accountable to federal guidelines regarding outcomes of people with disabilities.

The federal government would continue to fund the program, but states would be able to use these funds to provide services, rather than cash, to children with disabilities. These services could be refined to match the specific needs of the local population and, most importantly, to improve these children's long-run ability to enter the labor force as adults, like all other children are encouraged to do. States would also be allowed to encourage greater work effort among the able-bodied parents of these children and greater work-related investments in the children themselves. Overall, moving the jurisdiction of the SSI-disabled children program to the states would better align states' incentives to their residents' needs, potentially resulting in investments in education, training, and accommodation necessary to enable children with disabilities to enter the workforce as adults.

Conclusion

To be effective, social policy must evolve with changes in understanding and knowledge. In the case of the SSI-disabled children program, the original mindset of protecting children and families from short-run financial hardship has failed to deliver on the more modern goals of preparing all children, even those with disabilities, for employment and self-sufficiency as adults. It is time for a fundamental change in that mindset to one that makes a core goal of the SSI-disabled children program the development of the skills necessary for them, as adults, to fully integrate into the economy and society.

Notes

1. The cost of providing even this low level of economic well-being to a growing number of young adults has raised concerns among policymakers and resulted in a large-scale attempt by the Social Security Administration to support work among these young adults. See Social Security Administration, *Annual Report of the Supplemental Security Income Program*, May 2006, https://www.ssa.gov/oact/ssir/SSI06/ssi2006.pdf; and John Martinez et al., *The Social Security Administration's Youth Transition Demonstration Projects: Implementation Lessons from the Original Projects*, Mathematica Policy Research Inc., February 22, 2010, https://www.ssa.gov/disabilityresearch/documents/YTD%20Special%20Process%20Report%202-22-2010.pdf/.

2. For a more detailed discussions of the history of the SSI-disabled children program see Mary C. Daly and Richard V. Burkhauser, "The Supplemental Security Income Program," in *Means Tested Transfer Programs in the United States*, ed. Robert Moffitt (Chicago, IL: University of Chicago Press, 2003), 79–140; Richard V. Burkhauser and Mary C. Daly, *The Declining Work and Welfare of People with Disabilities: What Went Wrong and a Strategy*

for Change (Washington, DC: AEI Press, 2011); and Edward D. Berkowitz and Larry DeWitt, *The Other Welfare: Supplemental Security Income and U.S. Social Policy* (Ithaca, New York: Cornell University Press, 2013).

3. Expenditure data are available through 2015; data on recipients are only available through 2014.

4. Mark Duggan, Melissa Kearney, and Stephanie Rennane, "The Supplemental Security Income Program," in *Means Tested Transfer Programs in the United States. Volume II*, ed. Robert Moffitt (Chicago, IL: University of Chicago Press, forthcoming).

5. Government Accounting Office, *Rapid Rise in Children on SSI Disability Rolls Follows New Regulations*, September 1994; and Government Accounting Office, *New Functional Assessments for Children Raise Eligibility Questions*, March 1995.

6. Mark Duggan, Melissa Kearney, and Stephanie Rennane, "The Supplemental Security Income Program."

7. See Social Security Administration, *SSI Annual Statistical Report, 2014*, October 2015, 130, Table 64, https://www.ssa.gov/policy/docs/statcomps/ssi_asr/.

8. See Bowen Garrett and Sherry Glied, "Does State AFDC Generosity Affect Child SSI Participation?," *Journal of Policy Analysis and Management* 19, no. 2 (2000): 275–95; Jeffrey D. Kubik, "Incentives for the Identification and Treatment of Children with Disabilities: The Supplemental Security Income Program," *Journal of Public Economics* 73 (1999): 187–215; and Michael Wiseman, "Supplemental Security Income for the Second Decade," prepared for conference, "Reducing Poverty and Economic Distress After ARRA: The Most Promising Approaches," Washington, DC, Urban Institute, 2010.

9. See Richard V. Burkhauser and Mary C. Daly, *The Declining Work and Welfare of People with Disabilities*; and Chana Joffe-Walt, "Unfit for Work: The Startling Rise of Disability in America," *Planet Money* on *This American Life*, National Public Radio, March 22, 2013.

10. Jeffrey Hemmeter, Jacqueline Kauff, and David C. Wittenburg, "Changing Circumstances: Experiences of Child SSI Recipients Before and After Their Age-18 Redetermination for Adult Benefits," *Journal of Vocational Rehabilitation* 30, no. 3 (2009): 201–21.

11. Manasi Deshpande, "Does Welfare Inhibit Success? The Long-Term

Effects of Removing Low-Income Youth from Disability Insurance," Massachusetts Institute of Technology, December 2014, http://economics.mit.edu/files/10156.

12. Michael Levere, "The Labor Market Consequences of Receiving Disability Benefits During Childhood," University of California, San Diego, 2015, http://econweb.ucsd.edu/~mlevere/pdfs/Levere_JMP.pdf.

13. Pamela Loprest and David C. Wittenburg, "Post-Transition Experiences of Former Child SSI Recipients," *Social Service Review* 81, no. 4 (2007): 583–608.

14. David Wittenburg, "Better Data, Incentives, and Coordination: Policy Options for Transition-Age Child SSI Recipients," presented at American Enterprise Institute and Brookings Institute Conference on Improving Outcomes for Children in the Supplemental Security Income Program, Washington, DC, December 2, 2014.

15. Phillip Armour et al., "Opportunity Guide for Youth with Disabilities: An Interactive Financial Literacy Tool," 2013 Mimeo. Tool available from authors upon request.

16. David Wittenburg, "Better Data, Incentives, and Coordination."

17. Importantly, part of the change in mindset around the SSI-disabled children program includes collecting and evaluating data on outcomes such as completed schooling, absenteeism, and so forth.

18. Richard V. Burkhauser and Mary C. Daly, *The Declining Work and Welfare of People with Disabilities*.

Child Care Assistance in the United States

ANGELA RACHIDI
American Enterprise Institute

Helping poor parents work is an important goal of our nation's social safety net. But to work, parents need child care. Paying for care can be difficult for workers with low incomes, and the inability to pay can lead to reduced or unstable employment.

Over time, several government programs have been created to address this challenge. But under the current system, many poor families do not receive child care assistance, and the assistance that is available may not align with the scheduling demands of today's labor market, which increasingly involve nonstandard work hours. A targeted expansion of the child and dependent care tax credit to poor families could increase employment and better meet the needs of poor, working families.

Government-funded child care assistance in its current form dates back to the 1970s. President Gerald Ford created the first federal program when he signed the Child and Dependent Care Credit into law in 1976. In his words, the tax credit was intended to help defray "expenses for household or dependent care services necessary for gainful employment."[1]

In 1990, President George H. W. Bush established the first direct-subsidy program for child care because he believed that helping low-income parents provide a safe environment for children while working was part of creating a "better America."[2] As part of the 2001 comprehensive tax reform, President George W. Bush expanded the Child and Dependent Care Credit to cover more child care costs for low- and moderate-income families and the Child Tax Credit to provide more tax relief to low-income, working families with children.[3]

Together, these efforts have created a system of government-supported child care for low- and moderate-income families.

However, a substantial share of poor, working families do not receive the assistance for which they are eligible. According to federal data, less than half of eligible poor families (those with family income below poverty level) receive child care assistance.[4] If eligible working families felt that they did not need it, this would not be a problem. Certainly some prefer that a spouse or relative care for the children at no cost. But evidence suggests that many poor families do not receive assistance because of insufficient program funding and that the current system is not well-suited to workers with nonstandard schedules who need informal care.

Why Should Government Fund
Child Care Assistance for Poor Families?

Child care assistance can be an important part of our nation's social safety net. It can increase employment for poor families and contribute to economic growth.

A lingering concern in today's economy is the relatively low labor force participation rate and its negative impact on economic output. In the average month in 2015, 62 percent of people age 16 and older were in the labor force, compared to 66 percent in 2007.[5] According to researchers at the Federal Reserve Board of Washington, DC, much of this decline is structural in nature (for example, an aging population), but not all of it, and government policies can help raise labor force participation among marginally attached workers.[6]

Even policy experts and economists who are generally cautious in their view of government's effectiveness have argued that child care assistance can increase employment and ultimately strengthen economic growth. Abby McCloskey, a former economic adviser to Jeb Bush's and Rick Perry's presidential campaigns, wrote in 2015, "In a country dealing with stalled economic growth, rising government debt, and low work-force participation, increasing rewards for work and reducing the barriers that make work difficult for mothers will encourage more women to participate in and con-tribute to the economy."[7] In 2014, AEI Resident Scholar Aparna Mathur and McCloskey argued that if America is to remain an eco-nomic powerhouse, all factors that hold women back in the labor market must be examined.[8]

A related concern that can be partially addressed by child care assistance is the high and increasing levels of nonwork among the poor, working-age population in America. US Census data show that 61.7 percent of working-age poor people in 2014 (according to the official definition of poverty) did not work at all in the prior year; in 1995, 50 percent of working-age poor people did not work.[9] The second most common reason among this population for not work-ing in 2014—behind illness or disability—was home and family responsibilities.[10] Encouraging more poor people to work by pro-viding child care assistance can improve their immediate economic situation and increase economic mobility over time.

Child care assistance for poor families also recognizes that the American economy, now global and increasingly technological, has left some workers behind. According to federal data, from 2000 to 2012, the real median income of families with children has stag-nated, while the real cost of child care has increased 20 percent.[11] Providing child care assistance to close this gap could substantially help poor families.

Others have proposed large expansions of child care assistance. In 2015, the Center for American Progress proposed a "high-quality child care tax credit" that expands government-provided child care assistance to low- and moderate-income working families, at a cost of up to $40 billion per year.[12] Publicly funded univer-sal pre-kindergarten for three- and four-year-olds has also gained national attention, at an estimated cost of $12 billion per year. Together, these proposals could cost as much as $60 billion per year in new federal spending. It is unclear whether such large and expansive efforts would have measureable gains for children, let alone whether it is politically feasible. But well-targeted efforts that increase child care assistance for poor families could increase employment and ultimately reduce poverty.

Benefits of Child Care Assistance

Research consistently shows that child care can be a problem for working families, especially unmarried or low-skilled mothers. In three separate studies of low-income working mothers from the early 2000s, problems with child care were found among approximately one-third of study participants.[13]

Not surprisingly, difficulties with child care can hinder employment.[14] Child care problems have been shown to eliminate employment altogether and to lower the number of months and hours worked.[15] Among low-income mothers, half of the women who experienced child care disruptions had to miss work as a result.[16]

Research also shows that child care costs can be a barrier to employment and that assistance can help mothers work, which is essential for many low-income families and supports broader economic growth.[17] Studies find that child care subsidies reduce out-of-pocket child care costs, and lower costs make employment more attractive.[18] Research finds a range of effects, but most suggest that child care assistance increases maternal employment anywhere from 5 to 21 percent among single mothers, depending on the subsidy's size.[19] Research has also linked receiving child care assistance to increased earnings and months worked.[20] For comparison, studies suggest that the earned income tax credit (EITC) increased employment among unmarried mothers by between 3 and 7 percentage points, which means child care assistance could affect employment more than the EITC does.[21]

The question of whether child care assistance leads to increased maternal employment is indisputable. However, questions remain about the general effects of child care on children. Research suggests that early and extensive nonparental child care can lead to elevated levels of externalizing behavior problems, along with possible negative effects on cognitive development.[22] While these findings are cause for concern, high-quality care in reasonable amounts has not been linked to poor outcomes. In addition, even among studies that have found negative outcomes, some positive effects for children from low-income households were found.[23] As such, negative child outcomes associated with child care, while important, should not be used to argue against child care assistance, especially in light of the positive benefits that employment can provide for families.

Child Care Assistance System in the United States

The current child care assistance system is complex. The main challenge is providing a system that values quality (health, safety, and child development), while also meeting the employment needs of poor families. The 2014 reauthorization of the Child Care Development Fund, the country's main child care assistance program, brought many needed quality improvements to the program, but it raises questions about whether a system focused on day care centers—which arguably is what the current system is becoming—can adequately meet the employment needs of most poor families. It also raises questions about whether the current system has adequate resources to support work for most poor parents and meet the development needs of children.

Government child care assistance for families in the United States involves four main programs: direct-subsidy programs administered through the Child Care Development Fund (CCDF) and the Temporary Assistance for Needy Families (TANF) Program, and tax-based assistance through the Child and Dependent Care Credit and flexible spending accounts. Early childhood programs, such as Head Start and universal pre-kindergarten, can also be considered part of the child care assistance system, but these programs are addressed in the Early Learning chapter in this volume.

Child Care Development Fund. The Personal Responsibility and Work Opportunity Act of 1996 consolidated existing child care assistance programs into one block-grant program—the CCDF—which provides states with funding to offer child care assistance to low-income families. It is administered by the federal government's Administration for Children and Families Office of Child Care, but because it is a block grant, states have flexibility to design and operate their own child care assistance program. The CCDF was reauthorized in 2014. Improvements to the program included an increased focus on health, safety, provider quality, and continuity of care.

The original CCDF was created to streamline the way states provided child care assistance at the time, but it is still complex. The CCDF pulls federal money from two programs—the TANF Child Care Block Grant and the Child Care Development Block Grant (CCDBG)—and the rules and regulations governing the use of these funds are specified by the legislation.[24] States are allowed to allocate up to 30 percent of their TANF block grant for CCDF subsidies, and the remaining funds are appropriated by Congress. CCDF block grants are distributed to states according to a formula included in the legislation.

Within certain federal parameters specified in the legislation, states have flexibility in determining who is eligible for child care assistance, the amount of assistance provided, and the amount of out-of-pocket expenses families must pay. Federal law allows subsidies to be used for formal and informal care (including relatives), but states have final discretion in deciding the types of providers that can be subsidized. The result is that some states provide subsidies for only formal care (for example, Massachusetts and Wisconsin).

Federal law has certain requirements around licensing and registering providers within states, with health, safety, and training requirements for providers, including background checks. The federal law also allows for exemptions to some of these requirements for certain providers (license-exempt providers), but all providers must follow health and safety requirements, except relative providers.

To be eligible for child care assistance through the CCDF, families must have income below 85 percent of the state median, have a child under 13 (or under 19 with special needs), and be working or in an approved work or education activity.[25] States are also required to prioritize children with special needs and families of very low income, and states often interpret this to mean that TANF families be given priority.[26]

The vast majority of child care assistance (90 percent) is offered through certificates or vouchers, in which individuals are given assistance to use with any licensed or registered provider. Vouchers tend to cover only a portion of the costs, and families must cover whatever is leftover. The remaining receive assistance through contracted care, in which the state contracts the care directly and places the child in a contracted slot. Only three states (California, Delaware, and Massachusetts) use contracted care for 40 percent or more of the children served.[27]

In total, the federal government and states spent $8.6 billion on child care assistance through the CCDF in FY 2013, with approximately one-third from the states.[28] The vast majority (80 percent) of expenditures was on direct services, meaning child care assistance provided directly to families, with the remaining spent on quality activities, administration functions, or other nondirect services.[29] These expenditures, primarily offered through vouchers, provided assistance for approximately 1.4 million children in the average month.

In 2014, the CCDF was reauthorized for the first time since its inception in 1996. Several important changes were made. An increased focus on health and safety was initiated, including requiring providers to conduct staff background checks and comply with annual monitoring inspections. These requirements also apply to license-exempt providers (typically informal child care providers not based in a day care center), but not to relative providers.

Other changes aimed to increase the stability of care for children and the availability of providers. CCDF reauthorization imposed a requirement that states must provide 12-month eligibility for children that accounts for the parent's temporary work status changes, as long as income remains under 85 percent of area median income. It also required that states follow standard payment practices, such as paying a provider for a slot rather than based on a number of hours. The purpose of these changes was to improve the quality of providers from a health and safety perspective, while also improving the stability and accessibility of care for children.

Temporary Assistance for Needy Families. Beyond the 30 percent of TANF block-grant funds that states can allocate to CCDF subsidies, states are also allowed to spend additional TANF block-grant money on child care directly.[30] However, recipients of child care assistance through TANF must meet TANF eligibility requirements, including income eligibility, which is similar to CCDF, and program participation requirements. TANF expenditures on child care are also subject to broader TANF rules, such as federal time limits.[31] This means that different rules apply to how CCDF funds can be used compared to TANF funds, and each state determines how to allocate funding depending on their specific needs.

For child care purposes, states can use federal TANF money or state money that they are required to spend for TANF purposes— that is, state maintenance of effort (MOE) funding.[32] In total, $3.4 billion of TANF block-grant money (not allocated to CCDF) was spent on child care in FY 2011 ($1.1 billion federal, $2.3 billion state MOE).[33] This represented 10.2 percent of TANF expenditures in that year.

Added to the $8.6 billion spent on child care assistance through the CCDF, roughly $11 billion is spent annually on child care assistance for low-income families through these two sources, although the financing mechanisms are complex, making it difficult to determine how much is actually spent directly on child care assistance. To put this into context, more than $60 billion was spent by the federal government on the EITC, $20 billion on the Child Tax Credit, and $76 billion on the Supplemental Nutrition Assistance Program (SNAP) in FY 2014.[34]

Child and Dependent Care Credit. Direct child care assistance for moderate- and high-income families is also provided through the tax system in the form of the Child and Dependent Care Credit and a dependent care flexible spending account. The tax credit covers 20 to 35 percent of child care expenditures when one (in the case of a single, custodial parent) or both parents are working or in school full time. It depends on the tax filers' adjusted gross income for tax purposes; it starts at 35 percent and is reduced starting at approximately $15,000 in annual income, but there is no income limit. The maximum amount of qualifying expenditures is $3,000 for one child and $6,000 for two or more children per year, which means 20 to 35 percent of these expenditures is provided as a credit. The

Child and Dependent Care Credit is not refundable, meaning that it only lessens taxes owed to the government. If there is no income tax liability, the credit is not provided, which is why it is not applicable to most poor families.

According to data from the Tax Policy Center, 6.4 million households received a child care tax credit in 2012 for a total of $3.4 billion.[35] The average tax credit was $538. However, less than 1 percent of total expenditures went to households with income in the bottom quintile because they typically have no tax liability.[36]

Flexible Spending Accounts (FSA). Employers can also provide flexible spending plans for child care expenses. Through an employer-sponsored flexible spending plan, the IRS allows up to $5,000 to be deducted from annual pay (pre-tax) to be used for qualifying child care expenditures. The total cost to the government was approximately $1.5 billion in FY 2012.[37] Children must be under 13 and parents must be working or actively looking for work to qualify. If two parents are in the households, both must be working, looking for work, or in school full time. Once the parent pays for child care, he or she can file a claim to get reimbursed for the child care cost from the FSA.

Similar to the Child and Dependent Care Credit, benefits through FSAs primarily go to moderate- and higher-income earners. This is because low-income earners are often not offered the FSA through their employer and because they would not benefit from the pre-tax deduction since they typically have no income tax liability. The same qualifying expenditures cannot be claimed against both the Child and Dependent Care Credit and FSAs, but families can use both programs if they have enough qualifying expenditures for both.

Child Tax Credit and Earned Income Tax Credit. Although the Child Tax Credit and the EITC are not directly related to child care expenses, both are intended to help cover the costs of raising children. However, because they are available to families no matter the child's age and whether they have child care expenses, these tax credits are generally not considered part of the child care assistance system.

Challenges Associated with the Current System

Combining the four main programs identified earlier (excluding early-learning programs, the Child Tax Credit, and the EITC) suggests that the government spends approximately $16 billion per year on child care assistance for families across income levels. It is difficult to know how many children are covered by these programs based on available data, but it is likely up to 10 million or more.

Even though CCDF reauthorization in 2014 made some important improvements, the system as a whole still faces two crucial challenges: (1) lack of assistance for many poor families and (2) limited options for families who need flexible (likely non-center-based) care. Failing to address these challenges means that existing child care assistance programs are not meeting their full potential and that opportunities to help more poor families strengthen their position in the labor market, as well as strengthen the economy more broadly, are lost.

More Assistance for Poor Families. Although CCDF reauthorization made several important changes, new requirements were not matched with funding increases. This likely means that fewer families will receive assistance as states attempt to meet the new requirements. While a 12-month certification period is good from a stability of care perspective, without additional funding, fewer families will receive assistance, even if families who get assistance receive it for longer.

Another concern is that the supply of providers who accept subsidies—especially those who offer informal, flexible care—will likely diminish because of the new health and safety requirements and annual monitoring inspections. While well-intentioned, these requirements may make it harder for small, informal providers to accept subsidies. In turn, this will make it harder for low-income families to use subsidies—even if they can get them—by reducing the already limited supply of providers.

Relatives are exempt from these new requirements, which makes relative care an option for nonstandard-hour workers. But according to federal data, 86 percent of children receiving a CCDF subsidy in

FY 2014 were in a regulated setting, and only two-thirds of those in an unregulated setting (13 percent) were cared for by a relative.[38] This means that 92 percent of existing providers will be subject to requirements, including annual monitoring visits. While the change is important from a health and safety perspective, it might unintentionally limit the availability of providers who accept subsidies from low-income families.

Already only 41 percent of poor working families receive child care assistance.[39] As CCDF reauthorization is implemented, this will likely be reduced even further. Without increased resources for child care assistance, the unintended consequence of quality improvements in CCDF-funded programs might be less employment among poor families.

Limited Options for Families with Nonstandard Work Hours. Another problem with the current system is that it provides limited options to families who need child care outside of normal business hours. As designed, CCDF subsides can be used for informal providers, including relatives, who might offer nonstandard-hour care. But in practice, some states do not allow informal care at all, and even if a state allows informal care to be subsidized, research shows that subsidies are much more likely to go to families using day care centers.[40] According to a recent analysis, this means that nonstandard-hour workers are less likely to receive child care assistance because they use day care centers less than their peers who work standard schedules.[41]

The most obvious reason why day care centers are more common among subsidy recipients is that a child care subsidy allows parents to afford a day care center. Another is that day care centers may help families secure a subsidy once the family expresses interest, which would exclude many nonstandard-hour workers who do not use day care centers. A more likely scenario is that state requirements may discourage some informal or family day cares from accepting subsidies, and this may also disproportionately hurt nonstandard-hour workers because they are more likely to use these types of providers because of their flexibility.

Small providers who might be more responsive to the needs of nonstandard-hour workers may not be able to meet the new requirements around training and annual monitoring visits. In addition, to make implementing the law easier for the states, states may choose to focus their attention on day care centers rather than encouraging small informal providers to accept subsidies.

All of this suggests that low-income working parents may need child care assistance that is offered outside of the direct-subsidy system. Enhancing existing tax credits for low-income families with young children is one way to provide additional child care resources and reduce economic hardship among poor families by promoting work.

Proposed Reforms

Expanding the Child and Dependent Care Credit for poor families (those below the official federal poverty level) with children under age five would provide more resources to poor families to cover child care costs and would better meet the needs of those who are unable to use day care centers, including many nonstandard-hour workers. Currently, the Child and Dependent Care Credit is not refundable, which means it provides no benefit to families who owe no income taxes. Making the credit refundable and increasing its amount to cover more qualifying child care costs for poor families—for example, 50 percent of qualifying costs instead of 35 percent and up to a maximum $5,000 per child—would provide more assistance for child care.

Expanding the Child and Dependent Care Credit, as opposed to other child-based tax credits, would ensure that the benefit goes to families with child care costs and does not overlap with the existing CCDF subsidies. For example, a poor family that receives a CCDF subsidy would be eligible for the Child and Dependent Care Credit for only out-of-pocket child care expenses that were not covered by the subsidy.

Using the tax system to distribute resources to help cover child care costs allows families the maximum level of choice and flexibility to find the child care provider that meets their needs. While the CCDF was originally passed because of the flexibility it seemingly provided, the reality is that many providers do not accept subsidies and states have discretion to exclude certain types of providers. This limits the amount of choice and flexibility that poor families have in the current direct-subsidy system. For example, 72 percent of children who receive a CCDF subsidy receive care from day care centers,[42] but among all children under five in a regular child care arrangement, only one-quarter are in day care centers.[43]

Based on existing estimates of children eligible for and receiving CCDF subsidies, approximately 1.5 to 1.75 million children under age five with family income below 150 percent of the federal poverty level are not receiving a CCDF subsidy and could be eligible for an expanded child care tax credit.[44] Assuming that each child received a maximum $5,000 credit, which most likely would not happen, the total cost could be between $7.5 and $9 billion.

Two problems would need to be addressed before using the tax system to distribute child care assistance more broadly. First, because tax credits currently are provided only once per year at tax time, efforts are needed to provide periodic payments, similar to the Affordable Care Act premium support provisions. Periodic payments could provide families with child care resources closer to the time they incur child care expenses. This involves estimating annual income and then receiving a quarterly payment from the IRS to reflect the estimated tax credit based on that income.

Second, improper payments related to refundable tax credits would need to be addressed. Studies have documented problems associated with improperly claiming the EITC and the refundable portion of the Child Tax Credit (the Additional Child Tax Credit).[45] Estimates suggest that as much as $15 billion of EITC payments are issued improperly.[46] Addressing this issue is crucial before expanding tax credits more broadly.

Conclusion

The current social safety net for poor families in America is largely conditioned on work. Cash assistance for work-able parents is mainly provided through the EITC and the Additional Child Tax

Credit, both of which require that a parent be working. This makes child care crucial.

But an effective child care assistance system is one that meets the needs of poor working families who need the help. Too many poor families cannot access child care subsidies at all—which might be made worse with implementation of CCDF reauthorization—and those who work nonstandard schedules may be at a particular disadvantage. Supplementing the existing direct-subsidy system with an expanded and refundable child care tax credit for poor families with young children will provide more child care resources for those who need it most and may be better suited to influence employment and reduce poverty than the existing system.

Some may argue that providing broader child care assistance will publicly subsidize child care that is either currently being privately provided (for example, relatives providing no-cost care) or being secured without government assistance. These are valid concerns. However, they must be balanced against the fact that some mothers may not work at all because they do not have resources for child care, or they may work less than they would otherwise because they have unstable or unreliable child care. Expanded access to child care assistance may strengthen the attachment to employment for poor parents and help them afford stable, better-quality care for their children.

Notes

1. S. Doc. No. 37-143 (March 20, 1997), https://www.gpo.gov/fdsys/pkg/CREC-1997-03-20/html/CREC-1997-03-20-pt1-PgS2651-3.htm.

2. George H. W. Bush, "President Bush on Child Care," January 31, 1990, http://www.ibiblio.org/pub/academic/political-science/speeches/bush.dir/b20.txt.

3. William G. Gale and Peter Orszag, *Bush Administration Tax Policy*, Tax Policy Center, September 13, 2014, http://www.taxpolicycenter.org/publications/bush-administration-tax-policy/full.

4. Nina Chien, *Estimates of Child Care Eligibility and Receipt for Fiscal Year 2012*, Office of the Assistant Secretary for Planning and Evaluation, Office of Human Services Policy, US Department of Health and Human Services,

November 2015.

5. Federal Reserve Economic Data (FRED), using data from the US Bureau of Labor Statistics.

6. Stephanie Aaronson et al., *Labor Force Participation: Recent Developments and Future Prospects*, Divisions of Research & Statistics and Monetary Affairs, Federal Reserve Board, September 2014.

7. Abby M. McCloskey, "Clearing the Way for Working Women," *National Affairs* 22 (Winter 2015), http://www.nationalaffairs.com/publications/detail/clearing-the-way-for-working-women.

8. Aparna Mathur and Abby McCloskey, *How to Improve Economic Opportunity for Women*, American Enterprise Institute, June 2014, http://www.aei.org/publication/how-to-improve-economic-opportunity-for-women/.

9. Angela Rachidi, *America's Work Problem: How Addressing the Reasons People Don't Work Can Reduce Poverty*, American Enterprise Institute, July 14, 2016, http://www.aei.org/publication/americas-work-problem-how-addressing-the-reasons-people-dont-work-can-reduce-poverty/.

10. Rachidi, *Poverty Is a Work Problem*.

11. See Katie Hamm and Carmel Martin, *A New Vision for Child Care in the United States*, Center for American Progress, September 2015, 4, Figure 1, https://cdn.americanprogress.org/wp-content/uploads/2015/08/31111043/Hamm-Childcare-report.pdf.

12. Ibid.

13. See Susan Hauan and Sarah Douglas, *Potential Employment Liabilities Among TANF Recipients: A Synthesis of Data from 6 State TANF Caseload Studies*, Office of the Assistant Secretary for Planning and Evaluation, US Department of Health and Human Services, October 2004; Elizabeth Oltmans Ananat and Robin Phinney, *Child Care as a Barrier to Employment*, Ford School of Public Policy, University of Michigan, January 2004, http://www.fordschool.umich.edu/research/poverty/pdf/ananatphinney.pdf; and Margaret L. Usdansky and Douglas A. Wolf, "When Child Care Breaks Down: Mothers' Experiences with Child Care Problems and Resulting Missed Work," *Journal of Family Issues* 29, no. 9 (2008): 1185–210.

14. Jean Kimmel and Lisa M. Powell, "Nonstandard Work and Child Care Choices of Married Mothers," *Eastern Economic Journal* 32, no. 3 (2006): 397–419.

15. See Hauan and Douglas, *Potential Employment Liabilities*; and Ananat

and Phinney, *Child Care as a Barrier to Employment.*

16. Usdansky and Wolf, "When Child Care Breaks Down."

17. W. Han and J. Waldfogel, "Child Care Costs and Women's Employment: A Comparison of Single and Married Mothers with Pre-School-Aged Children," *Social Science Quarterly* 82, no. 3 (2001): 552–68; and David M. Blau, "Child Care Subsidy Programs," in *Means-Tested Transfer Programs in the United States,* ed. Robert A. Moffitt (Chicago, IL: University of Chicago Press, 2003).

18. Julien O. Teitler, Nancy E. Reichman, and Lenna Nepomnyaschy, "A Balancing Act: Sources of Support, Child Care, and Hardship Among Unwed Mothers" (working paper, Columbia University School of Social Work, 2002); and Nicole D. Forry, "The Impact of Child Care Subsidies on Low-Income Single Parents: An Examination of Child Care Expenditures and Family Finances," *Journal of Family and Economic Issues* 30, no. 1 (2009): 43–54.

19. Han and Waldfogel, "Child Care Costs and Women's Employment"; Blau, "Child Care Subsidy Programs"; Erdal Tekin, "Child Care Subsidy Receipt, Employment, and Child Care Choices of Single Mothers," *Economics Letters* 89, no. 1 (October 2005): 1–6; and Haksoon Ahn, "Child Care Subsidy, Child Care Costs, and Employment of Low-Income Single Mothers," *Children and Youth Services Review* 34, no. 2 (2012): 379–87.

20. Sandra K. Danziger, Elizabeth Oltmans Ananat, and Kimberly G. Browning, "Childcare Subsidies and the Transition from Welfare to Work," *Family Relations* 53, no. 2 (2004): 219–28.

21. Bruce Meyer, "The Effects of the Earned Income Tax Credit and Recent Reforms" in *Tax Policy and the Economy* vol. 24, ed. Jeffrey R. Brown (Chicago: University of Chicago Press, 2010).

22. See Jay Belsky, "Effects of Child Care on Child Development: Give Parents Real Choice," Institute for the Study of Children, Families, and Social Issues, March 2009, http://www.mpsv.cz/files/clanky/6640/9_Jay_Belsky_EN.pdf; C. M. Herbst, "The Impact of Non-Parental Child Care on Child Development: Evidence from the Summer Participation 'Dip,'" *Journal of Public Economics* 105 (2013): 86–105; and Michael Baker, Jonathon Gruber, and Kevin Mulligan, "Non-Cognitive Deficits and Young Adult Outcomes: The Long-Run Impacts of a Universal Child Care Program" (working paper, National Bureau of Economic Research, 2015), http://

www.nber.org/papers/w21571.pdf.

23. Michael Kottelenberg and Lehrer Steven, "Do the Perils of Universal Child Care Depend on the Child's Age?" (working paper, Canadian Labour Market and Skills Researcher Network, March 2014), http://www. clsrn.econ.ubc.ca/workingpapers/CLSRN%20Working%20Paper%20no. %20132%20-%20Kottellenburg%20and%20Lehrer.pdf.

24. Blau, "Child Care Subsidy Programs."

25. Administration for Children and Families, Office of Child Care, *"FUN"damentals of CCDF Administration*, US Department of Health and Human Services, 2013, http://www.acf.hhs.gov/sites/default/files/occ/ fundamentals_of_ccdf_administration.pdf.

26. Ibid.; Sarah Minton, Christin Durham, and Linda Giannarelli, *The CCDF Policies Database Book of Tables: Key Cross-State Variations in CCDF Policies as of October 1, 2013*, Office of Planning, Research, and Evaluation, Administration for Children and Families, US Department of Health and Human Services, October 2014.

27. See Office of Child Care, Administration for Children and Families, "FY 2013 Final Data Table 2—Percent of Children Served by Payment Method," US Department of Health and Human Services, August 12, 2015, http://www.acf.hhs.gov/programs/occ/resource/fy-2013-final-data-table-2- percent-of-children-served-by-payment-method.

28. See Office of Child Care, Administration for Children and Families, "FY 2013 CCDF Table 4a—All Expenditures by State—Categorical Summary," US Department of Health and Human Services, September 30, 2015, http://www.acf.hhs.gov/programs/occ/resource/fy-2013-ccdf-table-4a.

29. See Office of Child Care, Administration for Children and Families, "CCDF Fiscal Year 2013 State Spending from All Appropriation Years," US Department of Health and Human Services, September 30, 2013, http://www.acf.hhs.gov/programs/occ/resource/ccdf-fiscal-year-2013- state-spending-from-all-appropriation-years.

30. For an explanation of child care assistance TANF expenditures, see Office of Family Assistance, Administration for Children and Families, "TANF Financial Data—FY 2011," US Department of Health and Human Services, August 1, 2012, http://www.acf.hhs.gov/programs/ofa/resource/ tanf-financial-data-fy-2011.

31. For a technical guide for understanding how child care assistance

is administered through TANF, see Rachel Schumacher and Mark Greenberg, "Using TANF for Child Care: A Technical Guide," Center for Law and Social Policy, http://www.clasp.org/resources-and-publications/publication-1/0075.pdf.

32. Under TANF rules, states are required to spend their own money on TANF-related services according to what they spent before PRWORA. This is called maintenance of effort (MOE) funding, and states can use MOE funds on child care.

33. See Office of Family Assistance, "TANF Financial Data—FY 2011."

34. See the Office of Management and Budget, "Historical Tables," Table 8.5, https://www.whitehouse.gov/omb/budget/Historicals.

35. Tax Policy Center, "Dependent Care Tax Credit: Number of Families and Amount of Credit, 1976–2013," December 13, 2015, http://www.taxpolicycenter.org/taxfacts/displayafact.cfm?DocID=180&Topic2id=30&Topic3id=39.

36. Tax Policy Center, *Briefing Book*, 2012, http://www.taxpolicycenter.org/briefing-book/key-elements/family/child-care-subsidies.cfm.

37. See White House Office of Management and Budget, *Analytical Perspectives: Budget of the US Government*, Fiscal Year 2014, 243–47, Table 16.1, https://www.whitehouse.gov/sites/default/files/omb/budget/fy2014/assets/spec.pdf.

38. Office of Child Care, Administration for Children and Families, *Characteristics of Families Served by Child Care and Development Fund (CCDF) Based on Preliminary FY 2014 Data*, US Department of Health and Human Services, October 22, 2015, http://www.acf.hhs.gov/programs/occ/resource/characteristics-of-families-served-by-child-care-and-development-fund-ccdf.

39. Chien, *Estimates of Child Care Eligibility and Receipt for Fiscal Year 2012*.

40. Tekin, "Child Care Subsidy Receipt"; Danielle A. Crosby, Lisa Gennetian, and Aletha C. Huston, "Child Care Assistance Policies Can Affect the Use of Center-Based Care for Children in Low-Income Families," *Applied Developmental Science* 9, no. 2 (2005): 86–106; Julia R. Henly, Elizabeth O. Ananat, and Sandra K. Danziger, "Nonstandard Work Schedules, Child Care Subsidies, and Child Care Arrangements" (working paper, University of Michigan Center for Poverty Studies, March 2006); and Anna D. Johnson, Rebecca M. Ryan, and Jeanne Brooks-Gunn, "Child-Care Subsidies:

Do They Impact the Quality of Care Children Experience?," *Child Development* 83, no. 4 (July/August 2012): 1444–61.

41. Angela Rachidi, "Child Care Assistance and Nonstandard Work Schedules," *Children and Youth Services Review* 65 (2016): 104–11.

42. Office of Child Care, *Characteristics of Families Served by Child Care and Development Fund.*

43. Lynda Laughlin, *Who's Minding the Kids: Child Care Arrangements: Spring 2011*, US Census Bureau, April 2013, 70–135.

44. See Chien, *Estimates of Child Care Eligibility and Receipt for Fiscal Year 2012*, Figure 1.

45. Treasury Inspector General for Tax Administration, *Existing Compliance Processes Will Not Reduce the Billions of Dollars in Improper Earned Income Tax Credit and Additional Child Tax Credit Payments*, September 29, 2014, https://www.treasury.gov/tigta/auditreports/2014reports/201440093fr.pdf.

46. Margot L. Crandall-Hollick, *The Earned Income Tax Credit (EITC): Administrative and Compliance Challenges*, Congressional Research Service, April 9, 2015.

WIC's Expanding Eligibility, Rather Than Enhanced Services

DOUGLAS J. BESHAROV
University of Maryland

DOUGLAS M. CALL
University of Maryland

The Special Supplemental Nutrition Program for Women, Infants, and Children (WIC) started as a two-year pilot program in 1972 and was made permanent in 1975. As Peter H. Rossi explained in *Feeding the Poor: Assessing Federal Food Aid*, "The main rationale for the WIC program is that significant numbers of poor pregnant and postpartum women, infants, and children have nutritional deficiencies that endanger the proper development of fetuses, infants, or children, leading to conditions such as prematurity, neonate mortality, low birth weight, slow development, and anemia."[1]

In 2014, WIC was an $8 billion program (about $6.2 billion in federal funding and about $1.8 billion through rebates from infant formula manufacturers),[2] which served about 8.2 million people, including 2 million infants, 4.3 million children ages one through four, and 2 million pregnant and postpartum mothers. Although WIC is a program of the US Department of Agriculture (USDA), most of its grantees are state health departments. Those state agencies, in turn, fund WIC services through local health-related agencies, such as health departments, hospitals, public health clinics, and community health centers.

Given WIC's purpose, benefits package, and putative eligibility rules, one would assume that its benefits would be targeted to the most needful Americans. But various formal and informal changes have liberalized eligibility criteria so that, according to the Census Bureau's Current Population Survey (CPS), in 2014, about 24 percent of WIC recipients lived in families with annual incomes above WIC's putative income cap of 185 percent of poverty, and about 8 percent in families with annual incomes at or above 300 percent of poverty.[3] In 2014, about 49 percent of all American infants were on WIC, and about 39 percent of postpartum and breastfeeding mothers received WIC benefits.[4]

We believe that the expenditures for these expansions in enrollment could have been much more effectively used to improve or intensify services for generally needier families. Aggravating the situation, WIC's rigid spending rules effectively prevent local programs from spending more than about 30 minutes with clients for nutrition education every six months and preclude enriching food packages with such items as iron supplements.

WIC Benefits

WIC serves seven groups of low-income women and children (see Table A1). As the USDA explains, "WIC was never intended to be a primary source of food, nor of general food assistance," except possibly for those young infants who are fed only formula.[5] That role is assigned to the Supplemental Nutrition Assistance Program (SNAP), previously Food Stamps, and other cash and noncash assistance programs. Instead, WIC seeks "to safeguard the health of low-income women, infants, and children up to age 5 who are at nutritional risk"[6] by providing "a package of supplemental foods, nutrition education, and health care referrals at no cost."[7]

WIC's monthly food packages contain such basics as milk or cheese, adult cereal, fruit juice, eggs, and peanut butter (or an equivalent legume product), worth on average about $45 per person/per month for women and children. Infants who are not "fully breastfed"[8] also receive iron-fortified formula, which brings the value of their package to about $124 per month.[9] Including the benefit for infants' mothers, the monthly value of the WIC package is about $175 for mothers with one child.[10]

WIC Food Packages: Monthly Contents and Values, 2014[11]

- Pregnant women and partially breastfeeding women (up to the infant's first birthday) receive milk, adult cereal, fruit juice, eggs, peanut butter (or an equivalent legume product), whole wheat bread, and a $10 cash voucher for fruits and vegetables, worth on average about $49.71.

- Non-breastfeeding postpartum women (up to six months after the end of the pregnancy) receive milk (in lesser quantities than breastfeeding women), adult cereal, fruit juice (in lesser quantities than breastfeeding women), eggs, and a $10 cash voucher for fruits and vegetables, worth on average about $38.58.

- Fully breastfeeding women (up to the infant's first birthday) receive milk, cheese, eggs, cereal, juice, peanut butter (or an equivalent legume product), tuna, and a $10 cash voucher for fruits and vegetables, worth on average about $53.37.

- Infants up to five months old receive iron-fortified formula. Six- to 12-month-old infants receive iron-fortified formula, infant cereal, baby-food fruits and vegetables, and (for breastfeeding infants only) baby-food meat. All infant packages are worth on average about $123.99 (at a cost of about $53.39 after the rebate).

- Children age one to four receive milk, adult cereal, fruit juice, eggs, peanut butter (or an equivalent legume product), whole wheat bread, and a $6 cash voucher for fruits and vegetables, worth on average about $40.10.

- Children or women with special dietary needs (that is, those who cannot consume food in the other packages for medically documented reasons) are supposed to receive tailored food packages,

(continued on the next page)

so the contents and value vary from person to person, but the packages generally include special forms of formula, cereal, and juice.

- Changes in these packages were adopted as an interim rule in December 2007 and become mandatory in 2009. The final rule was published in March 2014.[12]

Nutritional counseling is also a WIC benefit. Besides the fact that WIC provides a prescribed food package, its counseling services are what many think set it apart from SNAP, which is essentially a voucher (now in the form of a debit card) with which to obtain food. (In fact, most analysts consider SNAP to be a form of income support.)[13] WIC agencies, in contrast, are required to offer at least two nutritional education sessions on nutrition and health to all WIC participants during each certification period[14]—although they are normally no more than 15 minutes long and only once every three months.[15] For WIC recipients, these sessions are voluntary; the food package is not conditional on attendance.

At these sessions, staff advise parents on how to manage their own nutritional risks and those of their children, as well as encouraging breastfeeding.[16] As Abt Associates researchers describe: "Although WIC participants are not required to attend nutrition education, local WIC agencies often schedule nutrition counseling to coincide with food instrument issuance to encourage WIC clients to attend."[17]

Does WIC Work?

WIC's popularity stems from the widespread belief that research studies have proved that WIC "works."[18] Although some studies suggest real improvements in the diets and health of WIC recipients, the extensive benefits cited by some—including a widely repeated 3:1 benefit-cost ratio—are surely overstated, especially if one goes beyond WIC's prenatal program.[19]

Here are the updated conclusions, still applicable, from an earlier volume by the authors of this chapter.[20]

- Studies of WIC's impact are almost entirely nonexperimental; in other words, they are based on statistical analyses of program or survey data and, therefore, are subject to various threats to causal validity, including selection and simultaneity bias. Moreover, many of the most convincing studies are of limited applicability to assessing the current program because they are based on the program as it existed more than a decade ago and thus do not reflect the composition of the caseload today.

- WIC probably makes at least a small improvement in the diets and behaviors of some pregnant women, especially the most disadvantaged, and that improvement, in turn, may improve the birth outcomes for some infants. But these effects seem to be small and of limited policy significance.

- WIC probably increases the nutritional intake of some infants, especially those who would not have been breastfed, but for most groups, the health consequences of these increases are not clear. Moreover, WIC may reduce breastfeeding, which many believe can have negative health consequences.

- Overall, WIC probably makes little significant difference in the diets of all one- to four-year-olds in the program, but it may benefit some subgroups more noticeably, particularly those whose intake of nutrients might otherwise be inadequate.

- WIC has expanded beyond the truly disadvantaged, and its new participants are unlikely to need or benefit from the services it provides nearly as much.

- WIC is largely irrelevant to the most serious nutritional problem facing disadvantaged Americans: overweight and, too often, obesity.

- WIC does not result in the major cost savings that its advocates claim, and the overall program probably does not pass a basic benefit-cost test.

As those points suggest, research on WIC, when read in the most favorable light, provides some (and perhaps substantial) support for the proposition that WIC has significant social and policy effects on *particular* subgroups of participants. Little research identifies the makeup or identity of those subgroups, but they are likely the neediest families—the poorest of the poor. Rossi notes that this lack of focus on subgroups is one of the shortcomings of most current research.[21] That is what makes all the more concerning WIC's continuing eligibility expansion to families and households with higher incomes.

Eligibility and Enrollment

The main statutory rule for WIC eligibility is income at or below 185 percent of the federal poverty guidelines.[22] For simplicity, and in accord with common practice, this paper refers to income in relation to the "poverty line" or "poverty," rather than the more technically correct "poverty guidelines," "federal poverty level," or "FPL."[23] Because WIC uses the poverty guidelines rather than the poverty thresholds (as do most means-tested programs), for large households, program eligibility reaches far above the official poverty line (Table 1).

Officially, income is measured as the combined income "of related or nonrelated individuals who are living together as one economic unit."[24] This is a major issue in the expansion of WIC eligibility. Hence, throughout this paper, and depending on the context, we refer to both families and income-sharing households.

WIC eligibility can also be established adjunctively—that is, individuals are automatically eligible if they are receiving Medicaid, SNAP, TANF cash assistance, or certain other state-administered, means-tested programs, as long as these state programs have income-eligibility caps at or below 185 percent of poverty.[25] As

Table 1. WIC Income-Eligibility Guidelines in Contiguous United States, 2014–15

Persons in Family or Income-Sharing Household	185 Percent of Poverty Guidelines
1	$21,590
2	$29,101
3	$36,612
4	$44,123
5	$51,634
6	$59,145
7	$66,656
8	$74,167
For each additional individual, add:	$7,511

Note: The poverty guidelines for Hawaii and Alaska (each has its own) are higher than those for the contiguous United States. All numbers are in 2014 dollars.
Source: US Department of Agriculture, "WIC Income Eligibility Guidelines, 2014-2015," http://www.fns.usda.gov/sites/default/files/wic/FY2014-2015_WIC_IEGs_WEB.pdf.

described below, adjunctive (or "categorical") eligibility for the federal programs can result in income eligibility substantially above WIC's general income cutoff of 185 percent of poverty.

These relatively high income thresholds—in 2014–15, $36,612 for an income-sharing household of three and $51,634 for an income-sharing household of five[26]—are presumably meant to be mitigated by the additional requirement that applicants be found to be at "nutritional risk." Over the years, however, the criteria for determining nutritional risk have been watered down, and now just about all WIC applicants are deemed at-risk.[27]

For 2013 (the latest year for which eligibility estimates are available), the USDA's estimates of the percentages of each demographic group that were WIC eligible were as follows: 55 percent of all relevant demographic categories, 61 percent of infants, 56 percent of children age one to four, and 47 percent of pregnant and postpartum women.[28]

Our estimates are even higher. First, we believe that WIC agencies count only the income of subfamilies—not of all members of the household sharing food, as required by statute. Second, we estimate that more families and income-sharing households are categorically eligible for WIC because of the growth in other government programs. Hence, for 2013, we estimate that *between 71 and 81 percent of all American infants were WIC eligible*, with similar increases for WIC's other demographic categories.

This percentage may continue to increase as states continue to raise Medicaid income-eligibility caps, which automatically increases the number of adjunctively eligible families and income-sharing households. For example, we estimate that if the 2016 state Medicaid income-eligibility caps are applied to the 2013 infant population, then the number of adjunctively eligible infants in 2013 would have been about 55 percent higher.[29]

The fact that half of all American infants receive benefits from the program is especially striking. These high rates of eligibility and enrollment are partly explained by the fact that families and income-sharing households with young children have lower incomes than the general population and are an increasing portion of the population. But enrollment is also rising when measured as a percentage of the families with annual incomes above 185 percent of poverty. In 2014, there were 17 percent more WIC infants than infants in families with annual incomes below 185 percent of poverty. In fact, according to the Census Bureau's CPS, in 2014, about 21 percent of WIC infants lived in families with annual incomes above 200 percent of poverty (for a family of three, about $39,904), and about 8 percent lived in families with annual incomes above 300 percent of poverty (for a family of three, about $59,370).[30]

Despite a long-term increase in WIC enrollment, enrollment has declined more recently. Between 2009 and 2014, WIC enrollment fell from about 9.2 million to about 8.2 million. This decline appears, at least in part, to be the result of the declining number of births over this same period of time, resulting in a smaller population of possible eligible participants for WIC.[31] Some analysts think that some of the decline may also have been caused by how some states and localities responded to reductions in appropriations between 2011 and 2014 (a reduction of about $1.1 billion). According to Richard Lucas, deputy administrator for policy support at the Food and Nutrition

Figure 1. Ratio of WIC Recipients to Persons in Households Below 185 Percent of Poverty

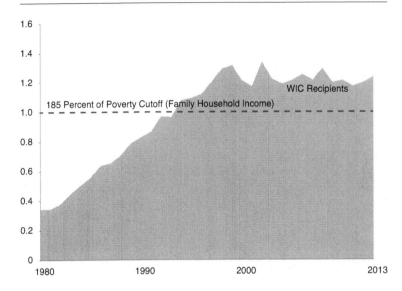

Sources: Author's calculations based on data from the following sources: US Department of Agriculture, Food and Nutrition Service, Office of Policy Support, *WIC Program Average Monthly Participation by Calendar Year*, 2015; University of Maryland, "Poverty Analysis and Tabulation Tool," Welfare Reform Academy, 2007; David Betson et al., *National and State-Level Estimates of Special Supplemental Nutrition Program for Women, Infants, and Children (WIC) Eligibles and Program Reach, 2000–2009: Final Report*, Urban Institute, December 2011, http://www.fns.usda.gov/sites/default/files/WICEligibles2000-2009Vol1.pdf; Michael Martinez-Schiferl et al., *National and State-Level Estimates of Special Supplemental Nutrition Program for Women, Infants, and Children (WIC) Eligibles and Program Reach, 2010: Final Report*, Urban Institute, January 2013, http://www.fns.usda.gov/sites/default/files/WICEligibles2010Vol1.pdf; Erika Huber and David Betson, *National and State-Level Estimates of Special Supplemental Nutrition Program for Women, Infants, and Children (WIC) Eligibles and Program Reach, 2011: Final Report*, US Department of Agriculture, March 2014; Paul Johnson et al., *National and State-Level Estimates of Special Supplemental Nutrition Program for Women, Infants, and Children (WIC) Eligibles and Program Reach, 2012: Final Report*, US Department of Agriculture, January 2015; and Paul Johnson et al., *National and State-Level Estimates of Special Supplemental Nutrition Program for Women, Infants, and Children (WIC) Eligibles and Program Reach, 2013: Final Report*, US Department of Agriculture, January 2016.

Service, some states closed WIC sites, which may have dampened applications for the program.[32]

Definitional Liberalization

The growth in WIC's eligibility and enrollment is substantially the product of liberalized interpretations of eligibility rules by WIC staff and officials at all levels of government, as well as formal congressional action (extending the length of WIC certification periods for children) and inaction (failing to cap income eligibility for WIC recipients who are adjunctively eligible). This section identifies the factors behind this liberalization and makes recommendations about what to do about them.

The major definitional elements that were loosened in WIC are similar in other means-tested programs. The WIC program has the added vagueness of the "nutritional risk" requirement, which has been interpreted away, as also discussed below.

Subfamily Income Versus Shared Household Income. To determine income eligibility, WIC agencies are supposed to count the entire household's income—if it is shared as one economic unit. Many agencies do not do so, however, and instead count the income of only the nuclear family, leaving out other sources of household income—for example, grandparents, siblings, and boyfriends.[33]

Using the CPS, in 2014, when the entire income of the family was counted, 46 percent of WIC recipients in related subfamilies lived in families with incomes at or above 185 percent of poverty; 21 percent in families with annual incomes between 200 percent and 299 percent of poverty, and 20 percent in families at or above 300 percent of poverty.[34] The failure to count all the household's income could, by itself, expand eligibility over the base of those with annual incomes below 185 percent of poverty by about 20 percent.[35]

Current Income Versus Income That "More Accurately Reflects the Family's Status." Because incomes can rise and fall throughout the year, WIC agencies are allowed to choose among annual, monthly, or weekly income. USDA regulations allow (but do not mandate) states to require that agencies select the period that "more accurately reflects the family's status."[36] Most WIC agencies, however, simply seem to use the lowest income, whatever it is, to maximize eligibility. Because only current income is counted, WIC ignores the *higher*, long-term (and truer) income of some families.

For example, in instances of unemployment, WIC regulations mandate that state and local WIC agencies count current income.[37] In instances of temporary illness or when a mother takes time off to have a baby, USDA regulations give state and local WIC agencies discretion in determining whether they will count current income or income that "best fits the family's situation," which most often results in the selection of current income.

In the 1990s, an additional 47 to 74 percent of pregnant women became eligible for this reason (between about 350,000 and 460,000 women).[38] According to Anne Gordon, Kimball Lewis, and Larry Radbill, these newly eligible women "were more educated, were more likely to live with the father, were more likely to be white, and had fewer children than those who were income-eligible during pregnancy."[39] Similarly, Alison Jacknowitz and Laura Tiehan used the Early Childhood Longitudinal Study, Birth Cohort (ECLS-B) to analyze the differences between mothers who enrolled in WIC in the prenatal period and those who enrolled in the postnatal period. They found that women who delayed enrolling had higher education levels, had higher household income, and were more likely to be employed before they gave birth.[40]

This failure to use the most appropriate income period could, by itself, expand eligibility over the base of those with annual incomes below 185 percent of poverty by about 20 percent.[41]

Certification Periods Versus Income Changes (Especially During Pregnancy). Once found income-eligible, successful applicants do not have their income eligibility recertified for six months or more (up to one year for infants and children)—even if incomes rise enough during that "certification period" to make them otherwise ineligible.

WIC's current 6- and 12-month certification periods could, by themselves, expand eligibility over the base of those with annual incomes below 185 percent of poverty by as much as 30 percent.[42] (Legislation currently pending in the Senate proposes that WIC certification periods for children be extended to two years.)[43]

Expanded Adjunctive Eligibility Versus Income Caps. Eligibility for WIC is also established adjunctively (in some other programs called "categorically")—that is, it is automatically granted to members of families and income-sharing households who are receiving[44] Medicaid, SNAP, or TANF cash assistance (if they can "provide documentation of receipt of assistance").[45] When this provision was added to the law, income eligibility for these programs was set below 185 percent of poverty. Hence, the original purpose of adjunctive eligibility was simply to facilitate the enrollment process, not to expand eligibility. However, recent legislative changes to Medicaid and the State Children's Health Insurance Program (SCHIP) authorized states to raise income limits for those programs to above 185 percent of poverty (and, in many states, above 300 percent of poverty), making adjunctively eligible a potential source of substantially enlarged WIC eligibility.

Between 2002 and 2014, according to the Congressional Budget Office, the estimated number of children receiving Medicaid increased from about 23 million to about 36 million, an increase of about 57 percent.[46] As more states increase Medicaid income-eligibility caps, the number of children on Medicaid will continue to rise, thereby increasing WIC eligibility. We estimate that if the 2016 state Medicaid income-eligibility caps were to be applied to the 2013 estimates of the number of infants who were adjunctively eligibility through Medicaid (the latest year for which data are available), the number would increase by 55 percent from about 442,000 to about 655,000.[47]

Under current Medicaid eligibility rules, adjunctive eligibility could, by itself, expand eligibility over the base of those with annual incomes below 185 percent of poverty by as much as 40 percent. And, barring legislative change, there is no limit to how much WIC eligibility can expand—via further increases in Medicaid and SCHIP income eligibility.

Nutritional Risk Assumed. In addition to being income-eligible or adjunctively eligible, WIC applicants are supposed to be at "nutritional risk." It appears, however, that this proviso has little practical impact on eligibility determinations. In a widely noted practice, WIC agencies find almost all applicants to be at nutritional risk.[48] This broad application of the definition of actual nutritional risk could, by itself, expand eligibility by as much as 25 percent.[49]

Poor Targeting and Horizontal Inequity

Why should we care about WIC's expansion beyond its putative income limit? Certainly, 185 percent of poverty is not a magic line. Those just above the line are not significantly better off than those just below it.

First, the way in which eligibility has been liberalized is deeply unfair to those families and income-sharing households whose incomes are just above 185 percent of poverty. The three main factors that have raised eligibility do not simply increase the level of WIC's income cap—they leapfrog eligibility to families and income-sharing households with significantly higher incomes.

Second is the long-standing unfairness that results from ignoring various forms of cash and noncash assistance (but counting other forms of income) in determining income.[50] This includes, for example, cash assistance such as the earned income tax credit (an average of about $3,000 per household with children)[51]; noncash assistance such as SNAP (an average of more than $3,000 per household)[52]; and housing assistance (an average of about $7,675 per household).[53] Most of these programs have almost universal coverage, so that the unfairness is somewhat limited. Housing assistance, however, reaches less than one-third of these eligible,[54] so its beneficiaries are much better off than some families and income-sharing households denied WIC because their incomes are slightly above 185 percent of poverty.

More fundamentally, this kind of hidden and priority-distorting expansion of eligibility—whether in WIC or any other means-tested programs—undercuts sound program planning. The addition of so many somewhat-better-off families and income-sharing households makes WIC less able to focus on the deep-seated nutritional and social needs of the most disadvantaged families and income-sharing households. Instead of enriching the services WIC can deliver to those below the income threshold, the funds that have been added to the program were used to expand coverage to higher-income families and income-sharing households.

Recommendations

This paper documents how the liberalization of WIC eligibility rules has substantially increased eligibility and enrollment. We believe that WIC would be most effective if its resources were targeted on those families and income-sharing households most in need of its services, including spending less on those better off financially and more on those in greater need. That would be the best way to make it more successful in meeting its prime goals.[55]

This analysis, however, should be important even for those who want to see WIC enrollments increased. Even those who want expansions in WIC eligibility and recipiency should be troubled by the haphazard and unequal expansions this report documents. Because eligibility depends on varying state and local policies concerning the income unit, period, and limits for Medicaid and SCHIP, the current program is plagued with substantial horizontal and vertical inequity in who receives benefits.

In our 2009 report, we made recommendations for the USDA to instruct state and local agencies on income measurement and to guide eligibility determination.[56] In 2013, the USDA issued a policy memorandum that provided clarification to states on the definition of the economic unit and "current income." We think this is a positive step and encourage the USDA to make the following steps:

1. USDA regulations should mandate careful attention to eligibility determinations.

2. USDA regulations should use a term such as "family and income-sharing household" and not just "family" to describe the income unit for WIC, and WIC agencies should use the income of the family and income-sharing household, not just the sub-family of parent and child, to determine income eligibility.

3. Adjunctive eligibility through Medicaid (directly or through SCHIP) and SNAP should be capped.

4. WIC's now meaningless test of "nutritional risk" should be dropped from eligibility determinations, or perhaps used as a means for directing program resources.

5. State and local WIC agencies should have a more direct financial stake in the proper governance of their programs, including the eligibility determinations.

This review of WIC's eligibility and enrollment practices illustrates how, when means-tested programs are not restrained by legal, financial, or political forces, they can expand beyond their putative income-eligibility limits. Sometimes, such expansions do nothing but add recipients to the program. Too often, though, as in the case of WIC, the addition of less-needy recipients diverts the program from its essential purpose, undermines sound program planning, creates significant horizontal inequities, and at least in a small way, puts pressure on other, less politically popular programs.

All means-tested programs would benefit from a similar examination. Hence, the larger lesson from this paper's analysis is that policymakers, administrators, and the public need a better understanding of the nature and application of income-eligibility rules across the panoply of means-tested programs. Details matter. As we have seen, identifiable variations in how and when to measure income can shift eligibility for large numbers of families.

Appendix

Table A1. WIC Eligibility at a Glance

Element	Formal or Original Rule	Implementation
Categories of Eligible Persons	*Pregnant women* up to entire pregnancy *Infants* up to age one *Children* age one to four *Breastfeeding women* up to one year *Postpartum women* up to six months after end of pregnancy	
Income Eligibility	Eligibility is set between 100 percent and 185 percent of the poverty level, at the state's option.	
Maximum Income Level	All states have set maximum eligibility at 185 percent of the federal poverty guidelines, unless the applicant is adjunctively eligible.	The expansion of Medicaid eligibility has inadvertently raised income limits in several states.
Income Unit	A unit is defined as households "of related or nonrelated individuals who are living together as one economic unit." Unborn children are counted as household members for determining income threshold.	Often, only members of the subfamily and their income are counted.
Income Period	Income is defined as income during the past 12 months or current income, whichever "more accurately reflects the family's status." However, "persons from families with adult members who are unemployed shall be eligible based on income during the period of unemployment if the loss of income causes the current rate of income to be less than" the income guidelines.	Usually, the lowest income is chosen, regardless of whether it "more accurately reflects the family's status."

Included Income	Gross cash income before deductions for income taxes, employees' social security taxes, insurance premiums, bonds, and so forth are included.	Income verification can be lax.
Excluded Income	Excluded income includes non-cash benefits (such as SNAP and housing benefits), military housing allowances, low-income energy assistance, and Title IV student financial aid. Also excluded are reimbursements for work expenses such as travel or meals.	
Earnings Disregards	None	
Asset Tests	None	
Adjunctive Eligibility (Sometimes Called "Categorical" or "Automatic" Eligibility)	Applicants are automatically eligible if they receive Medicaid, SNAP, or TANF cash assistance or are certified as eligible by the program. Medicaid enrollment also confers adjunctive eligibility on other eligible members of the household. At the state agency's option, this includes those eligible to participate in other state-administered programs, so long as this eligibility is based on income at or below 185 percent of poverty. The applicant must still be at nutritional risk.	
Nutritional Risk	Applicants must be at "nutritional risk," as determined by a WIC clinic or health professional.	Few applicants fail to qualify under at least one category of nutritional risk.

Priorities for Services	Services are prioritized in the following order: 1. Pregnant or breastfeeding women and infants with evident medical problems who demonstrate the need for supplemental foods 2. Infants whose mothers had medical problems during pregnancy who demonstrated the need for supplemental foods or whose mothers were program participants 3. Children with medical problems who demonstrate the need for supplemental foods 4. Infants or pregnant or breastfeeding women at nutritional risk because of an inadequate dietary pattern 5. Children at nutritional risk because of an inadequate dietary pattern 6. Postpartum women with any nutritional risk 7. Individuals certified for WIC solely due to homeless or migrant status and current WIC participants who could have medical or dietary problems without WIC	Following the order is seldom necessary due to funding increases in the 1990s.
Recerti-fication Periods		
Basic Rules	*Pregnant women* are certified for the duration of their pregnancies and up to the last day of the month in which the infant becomes six weeks old or the pregnancy ends.	

	Postpartum women are certified up to the last day of the sixth month after the baby is born or the pregnancy ends.	
	Breastfeeding women are certified approximately every six months. (The state agency may permit local agencies to certify a breastfeeding woman up to the last day of the month in which her infant turns one year old, or until the woman ceases breastfeeding, whichever occurs first.)	
	Infants are certified approximately every six months. (The state agency may permit its local agencies to certify an infant under six months of age up to the last day of the month in which the infant turns one year old, provided the quality and accessibility of health care services are not diminished.)	
	Children are certified approximately every six months, ending with the last day of the month in which a child reaches age five. (The state agency may permit local agencies to certify a child for up to one year.)	
State Agency Options	As noted above, state agencies may authorize local agencies to increase certification periods to up to six months for infants and breastfeeding mothers and one year for children.	Thirty states have opted to certify children for one year.
	They may also authorize local agencies to use shorter certification periods than noted above "on a case-by-case basis," as long as guidance is provided to local agencies.	

	Longer or shorter periods of up to 30 days may be granted when there are scheduling difficulties. State and local agencies may require recipients to report changes in their income during the certification period.	
Verification Requirements	State agencies must require proof of family or shared-household income or of identity, residency, pregnancy, and adjunctive eligibility.	States usually require proof of income through pay stubs, employer statements, or W-2 forms. Documentation is needed for pregnancy unless visually apparent.
Time Limits for Receiving Benefits	There are none while eligible because of pregnancy, post-pregnancy status, or child's age.	
Other Requirements	Applicants must reside in the state in which they are applying (except for Indian State agencies). Applicants must be physically present at certification.	

Source: Authors.

Notes

1. Peter H. Rossi, *Feeding the Poor: Assessing Federal Food Aid* (Washington, DC: AEI Press, 1998), 44–45.

2. Because of rounding, the total exceeds the sum of the subtotals. Unless otherwise indicated, all dollar amounts in this paper are in 2014 dollars.

3. To account for nonresponse to questions about WIC receipt in the CPS, the Census Bureau will impute WIC receipt based on characteristics indicating that a nonresponder is likely to be receiving WIC. For this paper, because of concerns about the Census Bureau's imputation strategy, we do not include data for families with imputed WIC receipt. If we had, the income distribution of WIC recipients is that, in 2014, about 26 percent of WIC recipients lived in families with annual incomes above WIC's putative income cap of 185 percent of poverty and about 11 percent in families with annual incomes over 300 percent of poverty.

4. Author's calculations based on data from the US Department of Agriculture, Food and Nutrition Service, Office of Policy Support, *WIC Program Average Monthly Participation by Calendar Year*, 2015; and Brady E. Hamilton et al., "Births: Preliminary Data for 2014," *National Vital Statistics Reports* 64, no. 6 (June 2015).

5. US Department of Agriculture, Food and Nutrition Service, "Special Supplemental Nutrition Program for Women, Infants and Children (WIC): Revisions in the WIC Food Packages," 7 CFR § 246.2 (2015), http://www.fns.usda.gov/sites/default/files/wicfoodpkginterimrulepdf.pdf.

6. US Department of Health and Human Services, "About WIC," http://www.fns.usda.gov/wic/about-wic.

7. Victor Oliveira, *The Food Assistance Landscape: FY 2014 Annual Report*, US Department of Agriculture, March 2015, 2, http://www.ers.usda.gov/media/1806461/eib137.pdf.

8. Nancy Burstein et al., *WIC Participant and Program Characteristics: Food Package Report*, US Department of Agriculture, November 2014, 9, http://www.fns.usda.gov/sites/default/files/ops/PC2012.pdf.

9. Ibid.; and Tracy Vericker, Chen Zhen, and Shawn Karns, *Fiscal Year 2010: WIC Food Cost Report*, US Department of Agriculture, August 2013, http://www.fns.usda.gov/sites/default/files/WICFoodCost2010_0.pdf.

10. Burstein et al., *WIC Participant and Program Characteristics*; and Vericker, Zhen, and Karns, *Fiscal Year 2010*.

11. Nancy Burstein et al., *WIC Participant and Program Characteristics: Food Package Report*, US Department of Agriculture, November 2014, http://www.fns.usda.gov/sites/default/files/ops/PC2012.pdf; and Tracy Vericker, Chen Zhen, and Shawn Karns, *Fiscal Year 2010: WIC Food Cost Report*, US Department of Agriculture, August 2013, http://www.fns.usda.gov/sites/default/files/WICFoodCost2010_0.pdf.

12. "Special Supplemental Nutrition Program for Women, Infants and Children (WIC): Revisions in the WIC Food Packages; Final Rule," *Federal Register* 79, no. 42 (March 4, 2014): 12274–300, http://www.fns.usda.gov/sites/default/files/03-04-14_WIC-Food-Packages-Final-Rule.pdf.

13. See, for example, James C. Ohls and Harold Beebout, *The Food Stamp Program: Design Tradeoffs, Policy, and Impacts* (Washington, DC: Urban Institute Press, 1993).

14. US Department of Agriculture, Food and Nutrition Service, *Nutrition Education and Promotion: The Role of FNS in Helping Low-Income Families Make Healthier Eating and Lifestyle Choices: A Report to Congress*, March 2010, http://www.fns.usda.gov/sites/default/files/NutritionEdRTC.pdf.

15. The only reliable information we can find on this topic dates back over a decade, but we have no reason to think it has changed. "Control group participants received the usual 10 minutes of dietary counseling during bimonthly clinic visits to pick up WIC vouchers." See Douglas J. Besharov and Peter Germanis, *Rethinking WIC: An Evaluation of the Women, Infants, and Children Program* (Washington, DC: AEI Press, 2001), 14–15; and Carol Olander, *Nutrition Education and the Role of Dosage*, US Department of Agriculture, June 2007, 3, http://www.fns.usda.gov/sites/default/files/LitReview_Dosage.pdf. "The average WIC recipient received approximately less than 20 minutes of nutrition education twice every six months." See US General Accounting Office, *Nutrition Education: USDA Provides Multiple Services Through Multiple Programs, But Stronger Linkages Among Efforts Are Needed*, April 2004, http://www.fns.usda.gov/wic/resources/MultiplePrograms.pdf.

16. Besharov and Germanis, *Rethinking WIC*, 14–15.

17. Bonnie Randall et al., *WIC Nutrition Education Demonstration Study: Prenatal Intervention*, US Department of Agriculture, March 2001, vii–viii and 1–2, http://www.fns.usda.gov/sites/default/files/WICNutEdPrenatal.pdf.

18. Steven Carlson and Zoë Neuberger, *WIC Works: Addressing the Nutrition and Health Needs of Low-Income Families for 40 Years*, Center on Budget and Policy Priorities, May 2015, http://www.cbpp.org/sites/default/files/atoms/files/5-4-15fa.pdf. See generally Besharov and Germanis, *Rethinking WIC.*

19. Besharov and Germanis, *Rethinking WIC.*

20. Ibid.

21. "Currently available evaluation studies place too much emphasis on central tendencies—means and medians—and do not give enough attention to measures of the distributions of responses and differentials among subgroups." See Rossi, *Feeding the Poor.*

22. The WIC statute requires the secretary to establish income eligibility standards for the states to apply for those at nutritional risk in families "with an income that is less than the maximum income limit prescribed under section 9(b) of the Richard B. Russell National School Lunch Act for free and reduced price meals." Child Nutrition Act of 1966, 42 USC § 1786, https://www.law.cornell.edu/uscode/text/42/1786. In turn, the National School Lunch Act provides that, for any given year, they "shall be 185 percent of the applicable family size income levels contained in the nonfarm income poverty guidelines prescribed by the Office of Management and Budget, as adjusted annually in accordance with subparagraph (B)." Richard B. Russell National School Lunch Act, Pub. L. No. 113-79 (February 7, 2014), http://www.fns.usda.gov/sites/default/files/NSLA.pdf. See also US Department of Agriculture, Food and Nutrition Service, "WIC Program Regulations," 7 CFR § 246.2 (2015), http://www.fns.usda.gov/sites/default/files/wic/WICRegulations-7CFR246.pdf.

23. The federal poverty guidelines, issued each year by the Department of Health and Human Services, are a simplified version of the federal poverty thresholds and are used primarily for administrative purposes (such as determining eligibility for certain programs), whereas the thresholds are used for statistical purposes (such as calculating a poverty rate). The guidelines are based solely on family size (which is calculated as a weighted average of the corresponding family size in the thresholds, rounded to multiples of $10), while the thresholds are based on both total family size and the number of children under 18 in the family. In addition, the guidelines have different sets of figures for Alaska and Hawaii (which the thresholds do not) and do not distinguish between elderly and nonelderly individuals (which

the thresholds do for family units of one or two persons). Finally, the guidelines for a given year are issued in February of that same year (but are based on the thresholds of the previous year), while the thresholds for a given year are issued in August of the next year. See US Department of Health and Human Services, "Frequently Asked Questions Related to the Poverty Guidelines and Poverty," http://aspe.hhs.gov/poverty/faq.cfm#differences.

24. "WIC Program Regulations," 7 CFR § 246.2 (2015).

25. Ibid.

26. Throughout this paper, we use as the income unit "family income"—that is, the income of "a group of two people or more (one of whom is the householder) related by birth, marriage, or adoption and residing together." But, as I point out in relevant places, WIC eligibility is keyed to the income of income-sharing households—that is, "a household maintained by a householder who is in a family, and includes any unrelated people (unrelated subfamily members and/or secondary individuals) who may be residing there"—which, at the median, is about 2 percent higher. See US Census Bureau, "Current Population Survey (CPS): Definitions and Explanations," http://www.census.gov/cps/about/cpsdef.html; author's calculations from Carmen DeNavas-Watt and Bernadette D. Proctor, *Income and Poverty in the United States: 2013*, US Census Bureau, September 2014, https://www.census.gov/content/dam/Census/library/publications/2014/demo/p60-249.pdf; and US Census Bureau, "Historical Income Tables—Families: Table F-6. Regions—Families (All Races) by Median and Mean Income: 1953 to 2013," http://www.census.gov/hhes/www/income/data/historical/families/2013/f06AR.xls.

27. Institute of Medicine, *Dietary Risk Assessment in the WIC Program* (Washington, DC: National Academies Press, 2002).

28. Author's calculations based on data from Brady E. Hamilton et al., "Births: Preliminary Data for 2014," *National Vital Statistics Reports* 64, no. 6 (June 2015); US Census Bureau, "Annual Estimates of the Resident Population by Single Year of Age and Sex for the United States: April 1, 2010 to July 1, 2014," http://factfinder.census.gov/faces/tableservices/jsf/pages/productview.xhtml?src=bkmk; and USDA, *WIC Program Average Monthly Participation by Calendar Year*.

29. Authors' calculations using US Census Bureau, "Current Population Survey."

30. Author's calculations based on US Census Bureau, DataFerrett,

"Current Population Survey, Annual Social and Economic (ASEC) Supplement," March 2016.

31. Compared to 2009, in 2010–14, the number of infants in each year, on average, was about 166,000 lower, and the number of children ages 1–4 in each year was, on average, about one million lower.

32. Richard Lucas (US Department of Agriculture, Food and Nutrition Service), email message to authors, April 6, 2016.

33. US Government Accountability Office, *WIC Program: Improved Oversight of Income Eligibility Determination Needed*, February 2013, 17–18.

34. Authors' calculations from US Census Bureau, "Current Population Survey."

35. This is an independent effect and could be smaller when present in combination with the other practices discussed in this paper.

36. "WIC Program Regulations," 7 CFR § 246.2 (2015).

37. "However, persons from families with adult members who are unemployed shall be eligible based on income during the period of unemployment if the loss of income causes the current rate of income to be less than the State or local agency's income guidelines for Program eligibility." See "WIC Program Regulations," 7 CFR § 246.2 (2015).

38. Anne Gordon, Kimball Lewis, and Larry Radbill, *Income Variability Among Families with Pregnant Women, Infants, or Young Children* (Princeton, NJ: Mathematica Policy Research Inc., 1997); and Aaron S. Yelowitz, "Income Variability and WIC Eligibility: Evidence from the SIPP" (working paper, National Bureau of Economic Research, 2002).

39. Gordon, Lewis, and Radbill, *Income Variability Among Families*, xv.

40. Alison Jacknowitz and Laura Tiehan, "Transitions into and out of the WIC Program: A Cause for Concern?," *Social Science Review* 83, no. 2 (2009): 151–83.

41. This is an independent effect and could be smaller when present in combination with the other practices discussed in this paper.

42. This is an independent effect and could be smaller when present in combination with the other practices discussed in this paper.

43. Improving Child Nutrition Integrity and Access Act of 2016, S., 114th Cong., 2nd sess., http://www.agriculture.senate.gov/imo/media/doc/WEI16005.pdf.

44. Although the statute uses the word "receiving," WIC regulations do

not require applicants to actually be receiving assistance, as long as they have been "certified eligible to receive assistance" under the programs. See "WIC Program Regulations," 7 CFR § 246.2 (2015). The certification is made by the Medicaid, SNAP, or TANF programs, not WIC. Zoë Neuberger (Center on Budget and Policy Priorities), email message to author, June 29, 2007. Presumably, the difference is de minimis, and most researchers estimate adjunctive eligibility on the basis of being "enrolled in" or being "participants" in the Medicaid, SNAP, or TANF programs. See Michele Ver Ploeg and David Betson, eds., *Estimating Eligibility and Participation for the WIC Program: Final Report* (Washington, DC: National Academies Press, 2003), 50; and Marianne Bitler and Janet Currie, "Medicaid at Birth, WIC Take-Up, and Children's Outcomes" (discussion paper, Institute for Research on Poverty, University of Wisconsin–Madison, August 2004), 2, http://www.irp.wisc.edu/publications/dps/pdfs/dp128604.pdf.

45. Child Nutrition Act of 1966, 42 USC § 1786. The receipt of TANF nonassistance does not confer adjunctive eligibility, as described below.

46. John Holohan and Bowen Garrett, *Rising Unemployment and Medicaid*, Urban Institute, October 2001, http://www.urban.org/uploadedPDF/410306_HPOnline_1.pdf; and Congressional Budget Office, "Fact Sheet for CBO's April 2014 Baseline: Medicaid," http://www.cbo.gov/sites/default/files/cbofiles/attachments/44204-2014-04-Medicaid.pdf.

47. Author's calculations from Paul Johnson et al., *National and State-Level Estimates of Special Supplemental Nutrition Program for Women, Infants, and Children (WIC) Eligibles and Program Reach, 2013: Final Report*, US Department of Agriculture, January 2016; and US Census Bureau, "Annual Estimates of the Resident Population by Single Year of Age and Sex for the United States, States, and Puerto Rico Commonwealth: April 1, 2010 to July 1, 2014," http://factfinder2.census.gov/bkmk/table/1.0/en/PEP/2014/PEPSYASEX.

48. US Department of Agriculture, Food and Nutrition Service, *WIC Policy Memorandum 98–9, Revision 8: 401 Failure to Meet Dietary Guideline for Americans*, March 2005.

49. This is an independent effect and could be smaller when present in combination with the other practices discussed in this paper.

50. According to the WIC regulations: "Income for the purposes of this part means gross cash income before deductions for income taxes,

employees' social security taxes, insurance premiums, bonds, etc. Income includes the following—(A) Monetary compensation for services, including wages, salary, commissions, or fees; (B) Net income from farm and nonfarm self-employment; (C) Social Security benefits; (D) Dividends or interest on savings or bonds, income from estates or trusts, or net rental income; (E) Public assistance or welfare payments; (F) Unemployment compensation; (G) Government civilian employee or military retirement or pensions or veterans' payments; (H) Private pensions or annuities; (I) Alimony or child support payments; (J) Regular contributions from persons not living in the household; (K) Net royalties; and (L) Other cash income. Other cash income includes, but is not limited to, cash amounts received or withdrawn from any source including savings, investments, trust accounts and other resources which are readily available to the family." States may exclude the following kinds of income: in-kind housing and other benefits, loans, military housing, school meals payments, LIHEAP, federal student financial assistance (including Pell Grants), and child care vouchers. "WIC Program Regulations," 7 CFR § 246.2 (2015).

51. Center on Budget and Policy Priorities, *Policy Basics: The Earned Income Tax Credit*, January 2015, http://www.cbpp.org/research/policy-basics-the-earned-income-tax-credit.

52. Center on Budget and Policy Priorities, *SNAP Helps Struggling Families Put Food on the Table*, January 2015, http://www.cbpp.org/research/food-assistance/chart-book-snap-helps-struggling-families-put-food-on-the-table.

53. Center on Budget and Policy Priorities, *Fact Sheet: The Housing Choice Voucher Program*, 2015, http://www.cbpp.org/sites/default/files/atoms/files/3-10-14hous-factsheets_us.pdf.

54. G. Thomas Kingsley, *Federal Housing Assistance and Welfare Reform: Unchartered Territory*, Urban Institute, December 1997, http://www.urban.org/publications/308023.html.

55. See Besharov and Germanis, *Rethinking WIC*.

56. Douglas J. Besharov and Douglas M. Call, *The Expansion of WIC Eligibility and Enrollment: Good Intentions, Uncontrolled Local Discretion, and Compliant Federal Officials*, American Enterprise Institute, March 2009, https://www.aei.org/wp-content/uploads/2011/10/WIC-090304.pdf.

Improving Our Federal Response to Homelessness

KEVIN C. CORINTH
American Enterprise Institute

Homeless assistance programs constitute the safety net of last resort for individuals and families who have fallen through all the cracks. As a result of extreme poverty, depleted support from relatives, and ineffective help from other safety-net programs, the homeless are unable to meet their basic housing needs. For many individuals, mental illness and substance abuse are linked to homelessness as well. It is essential that our programs catch the vulnerable populations that may otherwise go without shelter and provide the services necessary to lift them back up.

This chapter first describes who the homeless are, distinguishing between the single adults with high rates of substance abuse and mental illness, who frequently sleep on the streets, and the families, who most often are found in shelters. Then it summarizes our major federal efforts to confront homelessness. Finally, it offers recommendations to better prioritize assistance to the most vulnerable and, at the same time, provide more flexibility to local communities to try innovative ideas and boost program performance.

Who Are the Homeless?

Homelessness, as defined by the US Department of Housing and Urban Development (HUD), includes people who sleep in (1) places not intended for human habitation, such as parks, abandoned buildings, sidewalks, and vehicles; (2) emergency shelters, which provide

Figure 1. Sheltered and Unsheltered Status for Homeless Families and Single Adults

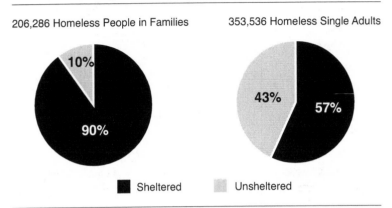

206,286 Homeless People in Families

353,536 Homeless Single Adults

■ Sheltered   Unsheltered

Note: Families include at least one adult and one child. Single adults are not accompanied by children. Excluded from both figures are 4,886 homeless children under the age of 18 who are unaccompanied by adults.
Source: US Department of Housing and Urban Development, "CoC Homeless Populations and Subpopulations Report," 2015, https://www.hudexchange.info/manage-a-program/coc-homeless-populations-and-subpopulations-reports/.

nightly or short-term stays; and (3) transitional housing programs, which provide stays for 6 to 24 months.[1] On a single night, just over 170,000 people are found sleeping in unsheltered locations, while close to 400,000 people are found in shelters (emergency shelters and transitional housing).[2] That implies that 1 in 1,849 Americans are found on the streets and 1 in 819 Americans are found in a homeless shelter at a single point in time. Over the course of an entire year, 1 in 214 Americans will sleep in a shelter on at least one night.[3] Homelessness is serious but not common, and for most, it does not last long.

In understanding who experiences homelessness and what that experience is like, it is important to distinguish between single adults and families. While 43 percent of homeless single adults are found on the street, only 10 percent of homeless families are found in unsheltered locations (see Figure 1).[4] Furthermore, shelters for single adults are much more likely to have shared sleeping arrangements without the ability to come and go, while families more often receive private rooms for extended periods of time.

Homeless single adults and families also differ substantially in their personal characteristics. Among single individuals accessing shelter throughout the year, 71 percent are male, 75 percent are over the age of 30, and 47 percent have a disabling condition (e.g., a substance abuse problem or severe mental illness).[5] Among adults in families, 78 percent are female, 53 percent are at or below the age of 30, and 21 percent have a disabling condition. Among children in families, 51 percent are below the age of six.[6] In broad terms then, single adults experiencing homelessness tend to be middle-aged men who often have an addiction or a severe mental illness, while the typical homeless family is a single mother with young children.

Our Federal Homelessness Programs

Programs to assist the homeless are funded by federal, state, and local governments, as well as private sources. The federal government alone funds 15 separate programs across 8 different agencies, with the bulk of funding administered by HUD, the Department of Veterans Affairs (VA), and the Department of Health and Human Services (HHS). Altogether, the federal government spent $4.2 billion on these programs in 2014 (see Figure 2).

The largest and most influential of the federal programs is HUD's Homeless Assistance Grants program, which allocated $2.1 billion dollars to local communities in 2014.[7] This represents 50 percent of all federal funds spent on homelessness programs overall and 75 percent of all funds not specifically dedicated to veterans. Table 1 summarizes the interventions funded in part by HUD.

Emergency shelter is the safety net of last resort for people who find they have nowhere else to sleep. It is noteworthy then that only 12 percent of HUD's homelessness budget can potentially be used for emergency shelter, with a portion of those funds used for other interventions as well.[8] As a result, emergency shelters are largely funded by local governments and private sources.

Figure 2. Federal Spending on Homelessness Assistance by Agency, FY 2014 (in Millions $)

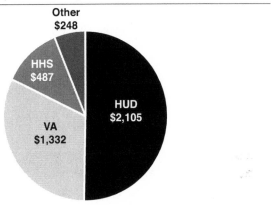

Source: Libby Perl et al., *Homelessness: Targeted Federal Programs and Recent Legislation*, Congressional Research Service (RL30442), May 6, 2015, https://www.fas.org/sgp/crs/misc/RL30442.pdf.

The majority of HUD's budget is used for longer-term, service-rich interventions. Transitional housing provides time-limited housing and supportive services intended to help people overcome problems and achieve self-sufficiency. Permanent supportive housing provides indefinite housing paired with supportive services for people with disabling conditions such as severe mental illness or substance abuse problems.

Other less intensive interventions funded by HUD include rapid re-housing and homelessness prevention. Rapid re-housing provides short- or medium-term rental subsidies along with case management to individuals or families soon after they become homeless. The intervention is intended to provide only the housing assistance and services needed to avert costly stays in shelter and prevent the recipient from returning to homelessness. Homelessness prevention is generally short-term financial assistance that helps families remain in their current housing.

These interventions are typically carried out by nonprofit service providers, which for the most part apply for HUD funding through

Table 1. Homelessness Interventions Funded in Part by the US Department of Housing and Urban Development

Intervention	Adult Beds	Family Beds	Description
Emergency Shelter	128,575	133,007	Short-term shelter (in congregate facilities, dormitory style arrangements, motels, or apartments) that often provides supportive services
Transitional Housing	74,868	83,693	Medium-term housing programs that provide supportive services that help people achieve self-sufficiency
Permanent Supportive Housing	199,327	119,194	Permanent housing programs that provide supportive services to people with severe mental illness, substance problems, or other disabling conditions
Rapid Re-Housing	15,433	44,861	Short- or medium-term rental assistance to quickly re-house people entering homelessness, accompanied by case management
Prevention	N/A	N/A	One-time financial assistance for people facing imminent threat of homelessness
Outreach	N/A	N/A	Seeking out and building relationships with people sleeping on the street to provide access to other services

Note: Beds for child-only households and safe haven beds are excluded from the table. Source: US Department of Housing and Urban Development, Office of Community Planning and Development, *The 2015 Annual Homeless Assessment Report (AHAR) to Congress: Part 1, Point-in-Time Estimates of Homelessness*, November 2015, https://www.hudexchange.info/resources/documents/2015-AHAR-Part-1.pdf.

local Continuums of Care (CoCs). Each CoC represents a specific geographic area (a city, county, or collection of counties), and its board includes representatives of local service providers, government officials, and at least one currently or formerly homeless individual. CoCs collect and rank funding applications, conduct annual counts of their homeless populations, maintain data systems that track individuals and families across participating service providers, and monitor the performance of providers.[9] HUD also requires CoCs to allocate interventions to people using coordinated entry systems that prioritize the most intensive interventions to the most vulnerable people and less intensive interventions to those with fewer needs.[10]

While CoCs have significant autonomy to determine how funds are allocated across providers, HUD rewards CoCs that target particular subpopulations and use certain types of interventions. In recent years, HUD has encouraged CoCs (via higher scores on applications and thus more funding) to offer permanent supportive housing to the chronically homeless—individuals or families who have been homeless for the past year or four separate times during the past three years and who have a disabling condition.[11]

As a result, the national inventory of permanent supportive housing has increased by 69 percent since 2007.[12] With these units, service providers are rewarded for employing a Housing First approach—providing housing and services without requirements that people maintain sobriety or engage with treatment.[13] For people who do not require intensive services, HUD encourages CoCs to offer rapid re-housing in lieu of extended stays in emergency shelter or transitional housing.[14]

Agencies besides HUD have smaller homelessness budgets. The VA distributes $1.3 billion across six programs for transitional housing, health care, and supportive services for homeless veterans. HHS distributes $487 million across four programs for health care and youth-specific programming. Other agencies that distribute small amounts of funding include the Department of Homeland Security ($120 million), the Department of Education ($65 million), the Department of Labor ($38 million), and the Department of Justice ($25 million).[15]

Lastly, a special agency called the Interagency Council on Homelessness is charged with coordinating the collective federal response to homelessness. In 2010, the council released a strategic plan known as Opening Doors, which sought to end homelessness in a decade.[16] Specifically, it set out to end homelessness among veterans and the chronically homeless by 2015 and among families by 2020. The word "end" is used loosely, however. The original plan called these goals "aspirational," and an amended plan in 2015 clarifies that ending homelessness means preventing it "whenever possible" and otherwise making it a "rare, brief, and non-recurring experience."[17] Nonetheless, the rhetoric in combination with HUD funding priorities may have been instrumental in driving large increases in permanent supportive housing and investment in housing and services for veterans over the past several years.

While the federal government plays an extremely important role in assisting the homeless, state, local, and private efforts are important as well. There is tremendous variation across the country in the availability and quality of local efforts. For example, New York City is one of the few places in the country to offer immediate shelter to all residents who need it as a legal right, and for families, shelter often means a private apartment unit. Perhaps as a result, 22 percent of all homeless families in the country are found in New York City alone.[18] Other cities often have waiting lists for shelters without legally mandated minimum quality standards and have much lower rates of family homelessness.[19]

Local variation in service quality not only complicates federal efforts but also brings to light a more fundamental problem; better options for the homeless increase the number of people who will take them up, including many who would have otherwise been housed. This means that services must be targeted carefully and must avoid promising benefits that are more generous than is necessary.

How to Improve Our Efforts

Our system of homelessness programs constitutes the final safety net for people who have no place else to go. It is a failure of that system when vulnerable human beings nonetheless sleep on our streets. While counts of the homeless have fallen since beginning in earnest in 2007, recent work suggests that much of that reduction may be due more to changes in methodologies and the quality of street counts than to how many homeless people there actually are.[20] Meanwhile, a number of major cities have reportedly seen recent spikes in the numbers sleeping on the street, leading several to declare a homelessness state of emergency.[21] Rather than double down on plans to end homelessness with old solutions, we should invest in innovative ideas that push progress forward, while ensuring that resources are prioritized to the people who need them most.

Better homelessness policy starts with making a fundamental distinction—homeless families are different than homeless single adults, and they require wholly different policy responses. Homeless families generally live in private rooms in shelters. They most often need temporary housing assistance to get back on their feet. Homeless single adults generally sleep on the street or in congregate shelters, and they often suffer from severe mental illness or substance abuse problems. They are more likely to require longer-term, service-rich interventions.

It makes little sense to lump these groups together. It is important that federal funds are intentionally allocated to each group separately and that they support the package of interventions best suited to each group. Solutions for each group are discussed next.

Single Adults. The federal government should have a strong, proactive response for homeless single adults. This group includes the most vulnerable individuals within the homeless population—individuals who suffer from severe mental illness or chronic addiction and who live on the streets as a way of life. Acting alone, localities have strong incentives to avoid the most vulnerable, perhaps in hopes that they move somewhere else, rather than bring them in to provide the expensive services they often need. But simply increasing federal funding will not solve the problem. The federal government must insist that funds are prioritized to the most vulnerable and that service providers achieve the best possible results with the resources they receive.

Fortunately, significant progress has been made on prioritization. HUD requires communities to implement coordinated entry systems that assess the needs of individuals experiencing homelessness and prioritize them based on vulnerability. But HUD has not fully embraced coordinated entry. Driven by a goal of ending chronic homelessness, HUD rewards CoCs for targeting permanent supportive housing to chronically homeless individuals.

Chronic status is a crude distinction that should be abandoned as long as CoCs are using a vetted coordinated entry process for allocating assistance. An individual with a severe mental illness and a co-occurring addiction problem who has been homeless for 11 months is not considered chronically homeless, but this individual may be much more vulnerable and in greater need of supportive housing than a chronically homeless individual who has been homeless for more than a year but solely has an addiction problem.

Even perfect prioritization is not sufficient, however, if the people who are most vulnerable do not actually use the services they are offered. HUD should take a more proactive role in ensuring that CoCs successfully bring in the most vulnerable. This may in part mean increasing funding for high-quality outreach efforts. But it also means finding ways to hold CoCs accountable for outreach quality.

For example, CoCs could be required to submit a list of all individuals encountered sleeping on the street who suffer from severe mental illness or a chronic addiction problem, ordered by their vulnerability. The CoC would then be required to explain why any individuals are still sleeping on the street if they were deemed more vulnerable than others who were actually brought into supportive housing.

Better prioritization and outreach is only half the battle for single adults, however. More attention must be paid to increasing the quality of services themselves. If service providers can more effectively address underlying problems such as addiction or family disconnection, or if they can help clients receive treatment needed to improve their mental health, clients can more quickly be transitioned out of supportive housing programs and into private living environments with family or on their own, freeing up resources for future people in need. These outcomes are also inherently valuable.

Unfortunately, HUD has stifled innovation by focusing more on encouraging specific service models than on service-provider performance. In particular, HUD encourages service providers to adhere to a Housing First approach, which does not require sobriety or treatment for clients to maintain housing. This approach is not inherently bad, and it may be the best one for some individuals. But it has not been shown to be superior to other models in reducing substance abuse or improving mental health; it may even be less effective than certain models that have yet to undergo rigorous testing with randomized controlled trials.[22]

A better way to unleash innovation is to focus on performance.[23] Service providers should be offered substantial flexibility in their service models, but they should be held accountable for their performance in helping their clients achieve desired outcomes. Performance measures should take into account the vulnerability of clients served so as not to punish service providers for accepting hard-to-serve individuals. This approach requires a renewed commitment to collecting high-quality data so that individual outcomes can be reliably tracked.

Over the past decade, HUD has taken the important step of requiring CoCs to establish data systems that track individuals through homeless assistance programs. But even better data are needed to monitor broader outcomes of individuals, including records from hospitals, emergency rooms, detox centers, mental health facilities, and jails. These records can indicate the costly use of other public services, as well as problems associated with poor mental health, addiction, and unstable living situations. HUD should offer additional support and flexibility to CoCs to build these broader data systems and evaluate service providers on performance measures.

Larger-scale innovation that altogether rethinks how homeless services are provided should be encouraged as well. For example, I discuss in a recent proposal how homelessness policy could be reoriented around smartphones and big data.[24] Homeless individuals could be given free smartphones and full service plans in return for providing daily information on their sleeping locations, health status, and other outcomes. Research could be revolutionized with access to detailed, longitudinal data on an otherwise hidden population. Innovative interventions could be delivered to individuals via smartphones, and using randomized controlled trials, their effects could more easily be tracked. Statistical algorithms could help homeless individuals make data-based choices about service use and other major decisions. Newly created Homeless Innovation Centers staffed by data scientists and homelessness experts could be charged with dynamically creating unique packages of interventions for each homeless individual, in conjunction with implementing a dynamic research agenda. Flexibility from other federal restrictions could be offered for CoCs wishing to experiment with this or other innovative ideas.

Families. A strong federal response to homelessness among families is less necessary than that needed for single adults. Families rarely sleep on the streets, and they almost never do so as a way of life. Family shelters are not highly desirable places in which to live, but they usually offer families private rooms without forcing them to leave in the morning, as is more often the case with single adults. As a result, the number of homeless families in a community depends largely on whether quality shelter is actually made available. Rather than keep families off the streets, shelters are more likely to keep families out of doubled-up situations that may or may not be problematic. Nonetheless, the federal government has an important role to play in empowering communities to provide an efficient housing safety net for families.

Prioritization of families for the appropriate intervention is just as necessary for families as it is for single adults. Diverting families who have safe places to stay with relatives or who can be better served by mainstream programs is a necessity if resources are to be available for families who otherwise face unsafe housing situations, especially in unsheltered environments. Meanwhile, service-intense interventions should be reserved for families who would actually benefit from them. HUD already requires that CoCs use coordinated entry systems but again impedes efficient prioritization by artificially prioritizing chronically homeless families.

The actual interventions offered to homeless families should primarily emphasize helping families to quickly regain housing. Toward this end, HUD has encouraged CoCs to increasingly rely on rapid re-housing, which by providing temporary rental assistance, can be a cost-effective way to help families get back on their feet. But HUD should also encourage CoCs to experiment with modified ways of offering rapid re-housing assistance that could better increase self-sufficiency without major cost increases.

For example, families could be allowed to share housing (or "double up") with others, with cost savings used to provide the family financial incentives for maintaining employment. HUD could also allow CoCs to experiment with providing greater autonomy to caseworkers assigned to families in rapid re-housing. Caseworkers could, for instance, require job-seeking activities or set expectations for other steps that would bolster self-sufficiency.[25]

At the same time that HUD has encouraged CoCs to invest more heavily in rapid re-housing, it has also discouraged investment in transitional housing. Given that transitional housing is expensive and its effectiveness is uncertain, this is a sensible decision.[26] However, if CoCs implement reliable methods of identifying specific transitional housing programs that achieve better outcomes than other forms of assistance, HUD should offer federal resources to such programs as well. Finally, HUD should continue to fund homelessness-prevention assistance, but it should remain cautious given the inherent difficulty in predicting which families would otherwise enter shelters.

Conclusion

Our homeless assistance programs are supposed to act as the final safety net for people who would otherwise have no other place to go. It is a failure then when, despite the billions of dollars spent by the federal government alone on programs for the homeless, tens of thousands of people with severe mental illness and chronic substance abuse problems live on the streets. Meanwhile, homeless families do not typically face life on the streets, but it is important to provide efficient assistance to those who otherwise would be housed in unsafe environments. Federal and local government must do better.

Better federal policy for single adults requires fully embracing coordinated entry systems, holding communities accountable for actually serving the most vulnerable living on the streets, and rewarding service providers for their performance in helping clients achieve a broad set of outcomes. At the same time, the federal government should provide more flexibility to localities to meet these objectives in innovative ways, rather than stifle innovation with blunt political goals. For homeless families, a full commitment to coordinated entry and experimentation with cost-effective variants of rapid re-housing assistance is needed. Ultimately, improving our homelessness policies requires clear thinking about who needs what, accountability for results, and a culture of innovation.

Notes

1. The official definition is in reality more complex than this. It can be found in 42 USC § 11302(a).

2. US Department of Housing and Urban Development, Office of Community Planning and Development, *The 2015 Annual Homeless Assessment Report (AHAR) to Congress: Part 1, Point-in-Time Estimates of Homelessness*, November 2015, https://www.hudexchange.info/resources/documents/2015-AHAR-Part-1.pdf.

3. US Department of Housing and Urban Development, Office of Community Planning and Development, *The 2014 Annual Homeless Assessment Report (AHAR) to Congress: Part 2, Estimates of Homelessness*, November 2015, https://www.hudexchange.info/onecpd/assets/File/2014-AHAR-Part-2.pdf.

4. US Department of Housing and Urban Development, *The 2015 Annual Homeless Assessment Report (AHAR) to Congress: Part 1*.

5. US Department of Housing and Urban Development, *The 2014 Annual Homeless Assessment Report (AHAR) to Congress: Part 2*.

6. Ibid.

7. Libby Perl et al., *Homelessness: Targeted Federal Programs and Recent*

Legislation, Congressional Research Service, May 6, 2015, https://www.fas.org/sgp/crs/misc/RL30442.pdf.

8. US Department of Housing and Urban Development, Office of Community Planning and Development, "Emergency Solutions Grants (ESG) Program," https://www.hudexchange.info/resources/documents/EmergencySolutionsGrantsProgramFactSheet.pdf.

9. Continuum of Care Planning Activities, 24 CFR 578.39 (April 2013).

10. Continuum of Care Planning Activities, 24 CFR 578.7 (April 2013).

11. US Department of Housing and Urban Development, Office of Community Planning and Development, "Notice of Funding Availability for the 2015 Continuum of Care Program Competition," September 17, 2015.

12. US Department of Housing and Urban Development, *The 2015 Annual Homeless Assessment Report (AHAR) to Congress: Part 1*.

13. US Department of Housing and Urban Development, "Notice of Funding Availability for the 2015 Continuum of Care Program Competition."

14. Ibid.

15. Perl et al., *Homelessness*.

16. United States Interagency Council on Homelessness, *Opening Doors: Federal Strategic Plan to Prevent and End Homelessness*, 2010.

17. United States Interagency Council on Homelessness, *Opening Doors: Federal Strategic Plan to Prevent and End Homelessness as Amended in 2015*, 2015.

18. US Department of Housing and Urban Development, "2007-2015 Point-in-Time Estimates by CoC," November 2015, https://www.hudexchange.info/resource/4832/2015-ahar-part-1-pit-estimates-of-homelessness/.

19. For additional discussion on right-to-shelter policies and homeless counts, see Kevin C. Corinth, "Ending Homelessness: More Housing or Fewer Shelters?," American Enterprise Institute, November 2015, http://www.aei.org/publication/ending-homelessness-more-housing-or-fewer-shelters/.

20. Kevin C. Corinth, "Street Homelessness: A Disappearing Act?," American Enterprise Institute, June 24, 2015, https://www.aei.org/publication/street-homelessness-a-disappearing-act.

21. For more details regarding homeless states of emergency, see National Alliance to End Homelessness, "Homelessness: A State of Emergency: Do

Local Decisions Have National Implications?," February 2016, http://www.endhomelessness.org/page/-/files/Homelessness_A%20State%20of%20Emergency_2.pdf.

22. See Kevin C. Corinth, "Pay for Performance: A New Solution for Vulnerable Homeless Adults," American Enterprise Institute, April 2016.

23. Ibid.

24. Kevin C. Corinth, "Smartphones for the Homeless: Taking Big Data to the Streets," American Enterprise Institute, April 11, 2016, http://www.aei.org/publication/a-tech-revolution-for-the-homeless.

25. Some of these ideas are discussed further in Kevin C. Corinth, "What Should We Do About Homeless Families? Comments on the Family Options Study," American Enterprise Institute, August 13, 2015, http://www.aei.org/publication/what-should-we-do-about-homeless-families-comments-on-the-family-options-study.

26. Daniel Gubits et al., *Family Options Study: Short-Term Impacts of Housing and Services Interventions for Homeless Families*, US Department of Housing and Urban Development, Office of Policy Development and Research, July 2015, https://www.huduser.gov/portal/portal/sites/default/files/pdf/FamilyOptionsStudy_final.pdf.

Federal Early Childhood Care and Education Programs: Advancing Opportunity Through Early Learning

KATHARINE B. STEVENS
American Enterprise Institute

[We aim] to lighten the burdens of children, to set their feet upon surer paths to health and well-being and happiness. . . .

Let no one believe that these are questions which should not stir a nation; that they are below the dignity of statesmen or governments. If we could have but one generation of properly born, trained, educated, and healthy children, a thousand other problems of government would vanish.

—President Herbert Hoover, 1930
Address to the White House Conference on Child Health and Protection

The poor life prospects for children born into disadvantage in America are increasingly recognized as an urgent national concern. More than a third of children born into the bottom fifth of the income distribution remain there as adults, while just 41 percent make it into the middle quintile or above. For children in single-parent homes, opportunity is especially lacking: 50 percent of children in the bottom quintile raised by never-married mothers remain there as adults, compared to just 17 percent of children raised by continuously married parents.[1] The circumstances that an

American child is born into determine too much about his chances to succeed in life.

Since the War on Poverty was declared in 1965, America has relied on public education as the primary strategy for breaking the cycle of intergenerational poverty and advancing equal opportunity for all children. Over the past several decades, spending on the country's schools has escalated dramatically toward that end. Federal, state, and local governments spent a total of $636 billion on K–12 education in 2013–14.[2] Public expenditures per student have doubled since the mid-1970s, reaching an average of more than $12,000 per student in 2012–13.[3]

A good education is key to social mobility and self-advancement. Yet it has become increasingly clear that K–12 schooling is falling short as our nation's primary engine of opportunity and human capital development. Three-quarters of low-income fourth graders and 80 percent of low-income eighth graders score below proficient in both reading and math on the National Assessment of Education Progress (NAEP). Seventeen-year-olds' reading and math scores have remained flat for almost half a century (see Figure 1).[4] Less than 40 percent of high school seniors scored at college- and career-ready levels on the 2015 NAEP exam, and just 5 percent of black students who took the ACT exam in 2013 were ready for college.[5] The bottom line is that two trillion public dollars and decades of efforts to improve schools have produced little progress in the economic and social well-being of America's neediest citizens. Children born poor today are just as likely to stay poor as they were 45 years ago.[6]

Recent reform initiatives, such as expanding school choice, have been gaining momentum and show some encouraging results. But progress is slow, and millions of children are left behind every year. In addition to continuing these efforts, we need to pursue new approaches to build our nation's human capital and ensure that all children have an equal chance to realize their full potential. High-quality child care that helps the country's youngest, most disadvantaged children get a good start while enabling their parents to work is an especially promising strategy. Done right, it

Figure 1. Total Public Spending on K–12 (in 2015 Dollars) and Achievement of 17-Year-Olds on the National Assessment of Education Progress (NAEP)

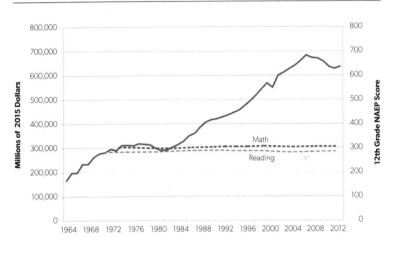

Source: National Center for Education Statistics.

provides a powerful approach to breaking the cycle of intergenerational poverty and advancing opportunity for two generations simultaneously.

Gaps Emerge Early

While we have long counted on K–12 schools to give children a strong start, often the schools' biggest task is to compensate for a weak start that handicaps many children long before they enter kindergarten. Developmental gaps between advantaged and disadvantaged children have been observed among children as young as nine months.[7] By 18 months, toddlers from low-income families can already be several months behind their more advantaged peers in language development.[8] By age three, children with college-educated parents have vocabularies as much as three times larger than those whose parents did not complete high school.[9] These gaps continue to widen: fewer than half of poor five-year-olds are ready for kinder-garten, and some are up to two years behind their peers.[10]

In other words, many children enter school unprepared to suc-ceed, and subsequent schooling largely fails to remediate those gaps.[11] Indeed, K–12 schools often amplify, rather than diminish, the consequences of early disadvantage. Achievement gaps between advantaged and disadvantaged children widen as they progress through school, and over the past quarter century, widening gaps have been growing even larger.[12]

The Lifelong Importance of Children's First Years

A rapidly expanding body of research indicates that one cause of this problem is that we have greatly underestimated the importance of children's preschool years. Extraordinary development occurs from conception to age five, laying the foundation for lifelong health, intellectual ability, emotional well-being, and social functioning. In just the first 1,000 days, a child grows from a helpless infant to a running, jumping, climbing preschooler. And, although less visible, children's early cognitive, social, and emotional development mir-rors this dramatic physical growth.

Human brains are not fully born—they are built, through the interactive influences of children's genes and early experiences. An infant's brain has about 100 billion brain cells, roughly the same number as an adult brain, but with many fewer connections between cells. In the first years of life, the brain's neural network expands exponentially, from around 2,500 connections per neuron at birth to about 15,000 connections between ages two and three, with rapid growth continuing into early elementary school (see Figure 2). Those new connections—called synapses—"wire" the structure of a young child's brain in response to the child's environment, driven almost entirely by his interactions with parents and other caretakers.

The developing brain is an integrated organ; emotional, social, and cognitive capacities are interconnected and interdependent. Foundational development begins at birth, peaks in the first few years of life, and is cumulative. Healthy development at any stage

Figure 2. Development of Synapses in the Human Brain Between Birth and Age Six

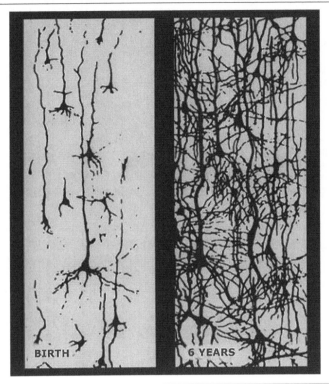

Source: J. LeRoy Conel, *The Postnatal Development of the Human Cerebral Cortex* (Cambridge, MA: Harvard University Press, 1959).

depends on healthy development in the previous stage as more complex neural connections and skills build on earlier, simpler ones. Neuroscientists from Harvard University's Center on the Developing Child underscore, "Early experiences determine whether a child's developing brain architecture provides a strong or weak foundation for all future learning, behavior, and health."[13]

The bottom line is that a solid early foundation, constructed in the first years of life, is crucial to a child's opportunity to fulfill his potential. While children's physical development unfolds naturally given adequate nutrition and physical freedom, their cognitive, social, and emotional development is driven by time- and attention-intensive adult nurture and care. From birth, back-and-forth, language-rich communication in the context of secure, loving relationships with adult caregivers literally builds the architecture of children's brains. Just as a plant's growth depends on sufficient water and light, children's development depends on hour-to-hour, day-to-day interactions with caring, responsive adults.

So for better or for worse, the early experiences of babies and young children have a profound, lasting impact on the rest of their lives. Young children raised in nurturing, supportive families learn and develop well. But when children's early environments—whether at home or elsewhere—are unsupportive or even damaging, it can compromise their development and jeopardize their chances for success in school and beyond.

Large numbers of young children in the United States are affected by interrelated factors that put them at particular risk, such as poverty, single motherhood, and low parental education. Of the 20 million children under age five, 23 percent of all children, 34 percent of Hispanic children, and 43 percent of African American children are living in poverty.[14] Almost half of all babies are born to women on Medicaid.[15] Among poor children under age six, 65 percent live with a single parent, and 42 percent have a mother who lacks a high school degree.[16] For many of these children, K–12 schooling—even starting in pre-K—is simply too little too late.

A New Strategy

Children do not choose their families. Yet they often pay a steep, lifelong price for being born into circumstances that fail to provide the early experiences promoting later academic, social, and economic success. Longer-term solutions to strengthening families, such as reducing single parenthood and increasing parental education and skills, are crucial.[17] At the same time, helping disadvantaged babies born today is equally significant in breaking the intergenerational cycle of poverty and family fragility.

Instead of continuing to rely on shopworn, often ineffective school-centered approaches, we need new strategies to improve the life chances of our youngest citizens. While parents bear the primary responsibility for their young children's upbringing, early care and learning programs that support vulnerable families in nurturing and developing their children hold great untapped potential to increase poor children's chances for success. By shifting the focus to reducing early gaps rather than remediating ever-worsening problems through K–12 schooling, early childhood programs target the very foundation of educational opportunity, providing an upstream approach that can help low-income children avoid falling behind before they even start school.

Reforming Federal Early Care and Education Programs

As the long-term impact of children's earliest years becomes increasingly clear, it has also become clear that federal early childhood programs are in urgent need of reform. Since 1935, the federal government has supported early care and education for poor children to promote their healthy development and give them a better chance to succeed. But the policymaking legacy of the past 80 years is a haphazard array of uncoordinated programs, shaped by outdated science and entrenched political interests, and long driven by addressing unintended consequences of previous policies rather than core goals.

The federal government now funds dozens of small programs providing services to children from birth through age five, but the preponderance of federal funds—$17.2 billion—is spent on three major programs: Head Start at $9.2 billion, the Child Care Development Fund (CCDF) at $5.4 billion, and child care expenditures from Temporary Assistance for Needy Families (TANF) at $2.6 billion annually.[18] All three programs fund poor children's participation in early care and education, and all originated in efforts to promote children's healthy development.[19] Yet today, they are disconnected from one another and lack coherent purpose. At the state and local levels, integrating disparate federal funding streams—each constrained by its own administration, rules, and monitoring frameworks—with growing city- and state-funded early childhood initiatives is difficult at best and often impossible.

At the heart of the current policy dysfunction lies a counterproductive conceptual split between custodial care and early education. While child care is recognized as an essential work support for adults, it also has a crucial impact on children during the most consequential phase of human development. Indeed, the commonly made distinction between "care" and "education" in early childhood is a false one, reflecting a fundamental misunderstanding of early learning and development.

We now know that young children are continuously and rapidly learning, wherever they are and from whomever they are with, starting at birth. So while we have long thought of "school" as where children learn, the reality is that every environment—whether home, school, or child care—is a learning environment for young children. The only question is the quality of that environment and whether it promotes or impedes children's learning.

This has crucial implications for federal policy. Head Start has long been emphasized as the federal government's primary early education program. But because children often spend many more hours in child care, starting much earlier in their lives, child care can actually have a much greater impact on their development. That is, child care is early education, no matter what we call the program or the funding stream.

In fact, child care is unique among early childhood programs precisely because it serves multiple purposes. Unlike any other federal program, it lies at the intersection of three paths to reduce poverty and expand opportunity: increasing work, supporting vulnerable families, and laying the crucial groundwork for children's later school and life success.[20] By promoting the complementary aims of adult responsibility and self-sufficiency on the one hand, and healthy child development on the other, child care offers a valuable strategy for two-generation human capital development in America's most disadvantaged communities. Yet Head Start, CCDF, and TANF all fall short of realizing the significant potential of this dual-generation approach to help needy families move ahead.

Head Start. Head Start has dominated the federal early childhood landscape for decades as the federal government's preschool program for poor children. Founded in 1965 as a centerpiece of President Lyndon B. Johnson's War on Poverty, Head Start reflects the then-emerging emphasis on schooling as the means to advance poor children. A half century later, it remains the largest and most visible federal early childhood program, with a total 2016 budget of $9.2 billion and spaces for almost 800,000 preschoolers in about 56,000 classrooms and 2,100 homes nationwide.[21] Early Head Start, a much smaller arm of the program, aims to support the healthy development of low-income infants and toddlers through home visiting and center-based care, with spaces for about 170,000 infants, toddlers, and pregnant women annually.[22]

While science has borne out Head Start's long-standing focus on the importance of early childhood development, the program's implementation quality is uneven across the country[23] and burdened by a half century of accumulated federal rules and regulations.[24] Perhaps Head Start's biggest shortcoming, however, is that it does not meet the needs of low-income working families: most Head Start programs run just three and a half hours per day for 128 days per year. Only 9 percent of center-based slots provide services for a full workday, year-round.[25]

Child Care Development Fund and Temporary Assistance for Needy Families. CCDF and TANF are the two major federal child care subsidy programs, aimed primarily at supporting low-income adults' participation in the labor market by helping them pay for child care.[26] In 2014, the programs together provided almost $8 billion in child care subsidies.

With a total federal budget of $5.4 billion, CCDF served an average of 1.4 million children per month in 2014. Fifty-six percent (784,000) were under age five and in out-of-home care an average of 37 hours per week.[27] TANF spent $2.6 billion federal dollars on child care subsidies in 2014; however, the program does not require detailed state reporting on families provided with TANF-funded child care, so the number of children served is not known.[28]

Although CCDF and TANF are now primarily focused on promoting adult work, they grew out of an early-20th-century effort to advance the development of disadvantaged children. The initial iteration of these programs, Aid to Dependent Children (ADC), was the federal government's first early childhood program, enacted in 1935. ADC's goal was to allow poor mothers to exit the workforce and care for their young children at home, aiming to ensure children's "health in mind and body," in President Herbert Hoover's words, and thus open "the door of opportunity" for every child.[29]

As the 20th century wore on, however, ADC evolved into Aid to Families with Dependent Children, expanding its scope to explicitly include support for adults. Adult welfare rolls exploded, and policy focus gradually shifted from children's early development to the financial self-sufficiency of adults. Through welfare reform passed in 1996, today's CCDF and TANF programs were established, framing child care as a work support for adults while deemphasizing its role in children's early development.[30]

Since then, efforts to strengthen federal early childhood policy have largely been confined to tinkering with these three existing funding streams. Useful improvements have been made over the past several years, but current, long-established programs do not provide the best means for accomplishing our fundamental goals.[31] We need new thinking to make substantial headway in improving the lives and life chances of poor children.

Moving Forward: A Better Approach

Family and child well-being are inextricably linked. Today's federal care and education programs for poor children from birth through age four must have two purposes: supporting parents' work in a modern, 24/7 economy and advancing children's healthy growth and learning. Those two aims are complementary, equally important strategies for building human capital in disadvantaged communities.

For most of history, early human development has been accomplished through full-time maternal care. But when low-income mothers of young children have to work outside the home to support their children financially, they cannot provide the time-intensive nurturing and care that is as necessary as material security for children's adequate development. A work-based safety net can unintentionally harm children, families, and society if it means that disadvantaged children are spending a large proportion of their most crucial developmental years in inadequate, counterproductive settings. While conditioning the social safety net on work improves children's financial security and helps adults move ahead, the gaps left for children's early development must also be addressed to advance the ultimate aim of ensuring opportunity for all.

The best path forward for federal early childhood programs is to realign them around a child care focus, strengthening whole families by simultaneously supporting healthy child development and adult work. Here are three principles to guide a dual-generation approach targeted at those most at risk.

Child care advances children by fostering their learning and development. Among children under age six, 65 percent of children overall and three in four African American children have all residential parents in the workforce.[32] Almost 11 million American children under five are now in out-of-home care, for an average of 36 hours a week.[33] So while children's home environment has the greatest impact, the second-most influential environment for many young children is child care.

Indeed, child care, long seen as an important safety net program to support parental work, has an equally important function as public education—investing in young children's human capital so they can grow into healthy, happy, and productive adults. Our current public school system emerged at a time when mothers remained at home to care full time for their young children, building the foundation necessary for children's success in school. However, as increasing numbers of low-income parents are working full time outside the home, the public role in supporting children's early learning and development becomes much more significant. Rather than trying to remediate early educational disadvantage in K–12 schools, it makes more sense to reduce that disadvantage by helping parents lay a strong foundation in the first place.

The Abecedarian Project provides an outstanding example of high-quality, educational child care. A well-known model pre-school program run in North Carolina from 1972 to 1985, it served poor children 50 hours a week for five years, starting just after birth and continuing until they entered kindergarten while their mothers finished school and found employment. A rigorous study carried out over the past half century has shown extraordinarily positive, long-term social and economic outcomes—far stronger than those of any Head Start or pre-K program studied—demonstrating child care's potential efficacy in advancing the well-being of poor children.[34]

Child care advances adults by supporting and rewarding work. Child care of any kind supports parental work. Yet while child care subsidies have been shown to increase work, research also shows that they can harm young children's academic, social, and emotional development if used to pay for poor-quality care.[35] And if subsidies are inadequate to purchase high-quality care, they can also fall short in promoting work because some parents may be reluctant to jeopardize their children's developmental well-being as a trade-off for improving their financial security.

At the same time, high-quality, educational child care can both incentivize and reward—as well as support—work. Parents care deeply about their children, and many may be additionally motivated to work if employment provides access to good early learning programs, empowering them to further their children's developmental and financial well-being simultaneously. Coupling work with high-quality child care honors the dignity of parent-hood, promoting self-sufficiency while helping parents lay the early groundwork that enables their children to have a better future than their own.

Child care advances family well-being by supporting children and working parents together. A focus on adult work to the exclusion of child development leaves out half the family equation. While having self-sufficient, working parents can benefit children by providing increased income and positive role models, it can also detract from child and family well-being by leaving less time for young children and increasing parental stress.[36]

High-quality child care can fill in gaps left when parents do not have enough time or social capital to invest sufficiently in their children's development. It can strengthen parents' child-rearing skills.[37] And it can both compensate for the effects of parental stress on children, while also removing some of that stress because parents know their children are in a stable, high-quality environment that supports their development. Done correctly, child care advances whole families, helping two generations at the same time and amplifying the impact on each.

A Crucial Role for Federal Leadership

Unlike K–12, early childhood care and education largely remains a decentralized, market-based sector, making it an ideal arena for innovation. Yet pressures for counterproductive regulation and centralized control have been growing rapidly. The federal government plays a large role in public spending on care and education programs for children under five and is well positioned to provide prudent leadership at this pivotal moment for the field.

What is needed now is countering the misguided push for pre-K, facilitating state and local experimentation to align federal funding around advancing families, and promoting rigorous research and innovation that increases our knowledge about what works best for children and families.

Counter the misguided push for pre-K. An increasing number of states, both red and blue, are committed to boosting investment in the well-being of disadvantaged young children. Powerful coalitions of K–12 stakeholders are seizing this opportunity to push for expanding pre-K nationwide.[38] The number of states with publicly funded pre-K programs has increased from 10 to 45 since 1980, and state spending on pre-K has risen from $2.4 billion in 2002 to almost $7 billion in 2016.[39]

But tacking a pre-K grade onto ofen-underperforming public schools is the wrong strategy for supporting vulnerable children and their families. A few hours a day of school for four-year-olds neither serves working parents nor adequately meets the developmental needs of many at-risk children. And pre-K expansion often precludes state spending on more effective early childhood approaches. As states continue to make crucial decisions about new early childhood investments, the federal government can play a timely and invaluable role by highlighting—and even incentivizing—smarter ways to invest in the most disadvantaged children and their families.

Promote alignment of federal funding streams at the state level around the dual goals of child development and adult work. The best way for the federal government to advance good early childhood policy is to support the work of leading, innovative states, allowing them to break down government silos and focus on the needs of children and families rather than the demands of bureaucracy.

One promising strategy is for the federal government to experiment with a competitive program that offers waivers enabling leading states to align early care and education dollars around the dual goals of advancing healthy child development and supporting adult work.[40] Using this approach, states could propose five-year pilot projects that increase access to high-quality early learning programs for disadvantaged children from birth through age four and, simultaneously, serve the needs of low-income working parents.

Approved states would be given flexibility to combine their state dollars with CCDF, TANF, and Head Start funds into a single pool, all subject to high, evidence-based standards of quality, established and enforced by the state. Means-tested scholarships would be provided directly to poor and low-income parents to use at the state-approved program of their choice. Providers that meet defined state guidelines—whether public, private, nonprofit, for-profit, center-based, home-based, Head Start, or religious providers—would be eligible

Minnesota's Early Learning Scholarship Program

Minnesota's Early Learning Scholarship program provides a good model of a market-based, choice-driven approach. The program provides scholarships to poor and low-income families to pay for early care and education at a broad range of state-approved providers.

With support from the business and philanthropic sectors, the state of Minnesota operates Parent Aware, a system that rates the quality of early education providers on a scale of one to four stars. Parent Aware helps parents choose the best place for their child by providing accessible, user-friendly information on providers' locations, characteristics, and quality.

Providers must participate in Parent Aware to qualify for the state's approved-provider network and be eligible to receive scholarship dollars. Over time, providers are required to meet a three- or four-star level to participate and are thus incentivized to raise quality to remain in the network and better attract parents.[41]

for scholarship payments, stressing value for children and families rather than federal funding stream or tax status.

The goal would be to support states in building market-based, choice-driven early childhood systems. These systems would increase the supply of reliable, high-quality early care and education programs that accommodate parents' work schedules, while ensuring that parents have sufficient information and means to make optimal decisions for their children.

This approach eliminates the counterproductive distinction between custodial and developmental settings and incentivizes state innovation and experimentation around how best to serve poor children and working parents. It makes states and programs accountable to parents as the final decision makers for their children. And it empowers parents to choose what is best for their family's well-being and their child's healthy development.

Advance research and innovation. Finally, we badly need better knowledge about what works in early learning programs for children from birth to five, both to improve current approaches and inform future action. The federal government has an essential role to play by supporting research on program effectiveness and investing in smaller-scale demonstration projects to test new approaches. Rigorous evaluation should be required of all programs, both established and experimental.

An Early Learning Research Program—modeled on the successful federal Small Business Innovation Research program for technology—could fund the development and testing of entrepreneurial, field-initiated ideas in multiple areas of early learning.[42] An online Federal Clearinghouse on Early Learning could disseminate evidence on existing initiatives, highlight best practices to inform smart policymaking, and spark new thinking on persistent problems.

Conclusion

The first 60 months are the most crucial developmental period of a child's life. The cognitive, social, and emotional growth that occurs from birth to age five lays the essential groundwork for all future learning and success. And too many children enter kindergarten so far behind that they can never catch up. Improving the well-being of America's youngest, most vulnerable children is crucial to both their life chances and the success of our country as a whole.

Federal early childhood programs play a key role in addressing inequality of opportunity and lack of economic mobility for disadvantaged children. Targeting investment to children's earliest years is sensible policy because it aims to build a strong foundation in the first place rather than trying to fix expensive, preventable problems down the line. Too often, though, our thinking is limited by what currently exists, not driven by what we are actually trying to accomplish. We need new strategies to accomplish our core aim: promoting the well-being of poor children so they can grow into healthy, happy, productive citizens.

The best path forward is to align funding around advancing disadvantaged families through a two-generation human capital development strategy that simultaneously enables adult work and supports young children's learning and development. By amplifying the impact of currently siloed programs and reducing regulatory and fiscal barriers to innovation, this solution-oriented, whole-family approach will increase states' capacity to support strong families and give America's least-advantaged children a fair chance at a good life.

Notes

1. Richard V. Reeves, *Saving Horatio Alger: Equality, Opportunity, and the American Dream*, Brookings Institution, August 20, 2014, http://www. brookings.edu/research/essays/2014/saving-horatio-alger#.

2. US Department of Education, "Summary of Expenditures for Public Elementary and Secondary Education and Other Related Programs, by Purpose: Selected Years, 1919-20 through 2013-14," 2016, https://nces.ed. gov/programs/digest/d16/tables/dt16_236.10.asp.

3. National Center for Education Statistics, "Gross Domestic Product per Capita and Public and Private Expenditures per Full-Time-Equivalent (FTE) Student, by Level of Education and Country: Selected Years, 2005 Through 2012," 2015, http://nces.ed.gov/programs/digest/d15/tables/dt15_605.10.asp.

4. Coalition for Evidence-Based Policy, "Evidence-Based Reform: Key to Major Gains in Education, Poverty Reduction, Crime Prevention, and Other Areas of Social Policy," http://coalition4evidence.org/mission-activities/.

5. ACT Inc., *The Condition of College & Career Readiness 2015*, 2015, http://www.act.org/content/act/en/research/condition-of-college-and-career-readiness-report-2015.html.

6. Raj Chetty et al., "Is the United States Still a Land of Opportunity? Recent Trends in Intergenerational Mobility" (working paper, National Bureau of Economic Research, 2014), http://www.nber.org/papers/w19844.

7. Tamara Halle et al., *Disparities in Early Learning and Development: Lessons from the Early Childhood Longitudinal Study—Birth Cohort (ECLS-B)*, Child Trends, June 2009, www.childtrends.org/wp-content/uploads/2013/05/2009-52DisparitiesELExecSumm.pdf.

8. Anne Fernald, Virginia A. Marchman, and Adriana Weisleder, "SES Differences in Language Processing Skill and Vocabulary Are Evident at 18 Months," *Developmental Science* 16, no. 2 (2013): 234–48.

9. Betty Hart and Todd R. Risley, "The Early Catastrophe: The 30 Million Word Gap by Age 3," *American Educator* 27, no. 1 (2003): 4–9, http://www.aft.org//sites/default/files/periodicals/TheEarlyCatastrophe.pdf. Vocabulary at age three predicts reading skills in third grade. In turn, third-grade reading skills are a strong predictor of long-term school and life outcomes. A 2009 study, for example, found that about 16 percent of children who were not reading proficiently by the end of third grade failed to complete high school—a dropout rate four times higher than that of proficient readers. Among children who were not reading proficiently at the end of third grade and were poor for at least one year, 26 percent failed to graduate from high school. In contrast, 89 percent of poor children who were reading on grade level by third grade graduated by age 19. Donald J. Hernandez, *Double Jeopardy: How Third Grade Reading Skills and Poverty Influence High School Graduation*, Annie E. Casey Foundation, April 2011, http://www.aecf.org/m/resourcedoc/AECF-DoubleJeopardy-2012-Full.pdf. Similarly, failure to complete high school strongly predicts unemployment, incarceration, and single motherhood. More than half (54 percent) of all high school dropouts and more than two-thirds (69 percent) of African American dropouts age 16 to 24 were unemployed in 2008. Nearly 1 in 10 male dropouts and one in four African American male dropouts age 16 to 24 were incarcerated on any given day in 2006–07. Female dropouts of that age were six times as likely to have given birth as peers who were college students or four-year-college graduates. Almost 23 percent were single mothers. Andrew Sum et al., *The Consequences of Dropping Out of High School: Joblessness and Jailing for High School Dropouts and the High Cost for Taxpayers*, Center for Labor Market Statistics, October 1, 2009, http://www.prisonpolicy.org/scans/The_Consequences_of_Dropping_Out_of_High_School.pdf.

10. Julia B. Isaacs, *Starting School at a Disadvantage: The School Readiness of Poor Children*, Brookings Institution, March 19, 2012, http://www.brookings.edu/research/starting-school-at-a-disadvantage-the-school-readiness-of-poor-children/.

11. David M. Quinn, "Kindergarten Black–White Test Score Gaps: Re-Examining the Roles of Socioeconomic Status and School Quality with

New Data," *Sociology of Education* 88, no. 2 (2015): 120–39, http://www.asanet.org/sites/default/files/savvy/journals/soe/Apr15SOEFeature.pdf; and Lisa G. Klein and Jane Knitzer, *Promoting Effective Early Learning: What Every Policymaker and Educator Should Know*, National Center for Children in Poverty, January 2007, http://www.nccp.org/publications/pub_695.html.

12. John K. McNamara, Mary Scissons, and Naomi Gutknecth, "A Longitudinal Study of Kindergarten Children at Risk for Reading Disabilities," *Journal of Learning Disabilities* 44, no. 5 (September/October 2011): 421–30; and Sean F. Reardon, "The Widening Academic Achievement Gap Between the Rich and the Poor," *Community Investments* 24, no. 2 (Summer 2012): 19–39, http://www.frbsf.org/community-development/files/CI_Summer2012_Reardon.pdf.

13. Harvard University Center on the Developing Child, *A Science-Based Framework for Early Childhood Policy*, August 2007, http://developingchild.harvard.edu/resources/a-science-based-framework-for-early-childhood-policy/.

14. The US Census Bureau has estimated that the undercount of children under age five is about one million children. United States Census Bureau, *The Undercount of Young Children*, February 2014, https://www.census.gov/content/dam/Census/library/working-papers/2014/demo/2014-undercount-children.pdf. See also Child Trends Data Bank, *Children in Poverty: Indicators on Children and Youth*, December 2015, http://www.childtrends.org/wp-content/uploads/2014/01/04_Poverty.pdf. An additional 23 percent of children under age six live in low-income families, defined as between 100 and 199 percent of the federal poverty level (FPL). Almost half of all young children thus live in poor or low-income families—that is, below 200 percent of the FPL, which is $48,500 for a family of four with two children in 2016. National Center for Children in Poverty, February 2016, http://www.nccp.org/publications/pub_1149.html.

15. Medicaid.gov, "Women's Health," https://www.medicaid.gov/medicaid-50th-anniversary/women/women.html.

16. Jiang, Ekono, and Skinner, *Basic Facts About Low-Income Children*; and Isaacs, *Starting School at a Disadvantage*. Certain factors place children especially at risk of being poor or low income: children under age six living below 200 percent FPL include 69 percent of African American children, 73 percent of children living with a single parent, 72 percent of children

whose parents have only a high school degree, and 87 percent of children whose parents have less than a high school degree.

17. For a discussion of these key factors in reducing poverty, see Lawrence Aber et al., *Opportunity, Responsibility, and Security: A Consensus Plan for Reducing Poverty and Restoring the American Dream*, AEI/Brookings Working Group on Poverty and Opportunity, December 3, 2015, http://www.aei.org/publication/opportunity-responsibility-and-security/.

18. According to the GAO, the federal government spent more than $20 billion on a total of 45 preschool and child care initiatives in 2012. Kay E. Brown, "Early Learning and Child Care: Federal Funds Support Multiple Programs with Similar Goals," testimony before the Committee on Education and the Workforce, US House of Representatives, February 5, 2014, http://www.gao.gov/assets/670/660685.pdf.

19. Katharine B. Stevens, *Renewing Childhood's Promise: The History and Future of Federal Early Care and Education Policy*, American Enterprise Institute, November 2, 2015, http://www.aei.org/publication/renewing-childhoods-promise-the-history-and-future-of-federal-early-care-and-education-policy/.

20. See Aber et al., *Opportunity, Responsibility, and Security*.

21. Head Start, FY2015 Program Information Report (PIR) data, http://eclkc.ohs.acf.hhs.gov/hslc/data/factsheets/2015-hs-program-factsheet.html.

22. Ibid.

23. See Steve Barnett, Megan Carolan, and David Johns, *Equity and Excellence: African American Children's Access to Quality Preschool*, Center on Enhancing Early Learning Outcomes, National Institute for Early Education Research, and Rutgers University, November 2013, http://nieer.org/sites/nieer/files/Equity%20and%20Excellence%20African-American%20Children%E2%80%99s%20Access%20to%20Quality%20Preschool_0.pdf; Department of Health and Human Services, Administration for Children and Families, *Justification of Estimates for Appropriations Committee*, Fiscal Year 2017, 105–106, https://www.acf.hhs.gov/sites/default/files/olab/final_cj_2017_print.pdf; and Christopher Walters, "Inputs in the Production of Early Childhood Human Capital: Evidence from Head Start" (working paper, Natural Bureau of Economic Research, October 2014), http://www.nber.org/papers/w20639.pdf.

24. Revisions to the federal Head Start regulations (called Program Performance Standards) were released in September 2016, reducing them to roughly 1,000 regulations, now consolidated into four broad areas comprising 21 subparts and, within those, 115 sections. See Head Start Performance Standards, 81 Fed. Reg. 172 (Sept. 6, 2016), https://www.gpo.gov/fdsys/pkg/FR-2016-09-06/pdf/2016-19748.pdf. The original, much briefer Head Start Performance Standards (with five subparts and 25 sections) were issued in 1975. See Office of Child Development, "Head Start Program Performance Standards," July 1975, http://files.eric.ed.gov/fulltext/ED122936.pdf.

25. US Department of Health and Human Services, Administration for Children and Families, *Head Start Program Facts Fiscal Year 2015*, August 24, 2016, https://eclkc.ohs.acf.hhs.gov/hslc/data/factsheets/2015-hs-program-factsheet.html. One study, for example, found that poor single mothers who faced an increased need for child care due to increased employment through welfare and employment programs sought other child care arrangements rather than using Head Start. See Young Eun Chang et al., "The Effects of Welfare and Employment Programs on Children's Participation in Head Start," *Economics of Education Review* 26, no. 1 (February 2007): 17–32.

26. Both programs were established through federal welfare reform—the Personal Responsibility and Work Opportunity Reconciliation Act (PRWORA)—passed in 1996. Aid to Families with Dependent Children (AFDC) was replaced by TANF and administered as a block grant that gives states great flexibility in determining how funds are spent. At the same time, four preexisting child care funding streams—the AFDC Child Care Guarantee, Transitional Child Care, At-Risk Child Care, and the Child Care and Development Block Grant (CCDBG)—were consolidated into the Child Care and Development Fund (CCDF), also referred to as CCDBG, aimed primarily to support working parents.

27. Hannah Matthews and Christina Walker, *Child Care Assistance Spending and Participation in 2014*, CLASP, March 2016, http://www.clasp.org/resources-and-publications/publication-1/CC-Spending-and-Participation-2014-1.pdf; and US Department of Health and Human Services, Administration for Children and Families, Office of Child Care, "FY 2014 CCDF Data Tables (Preliminary)," May 26, 2015, http://www.acf.hhs.gov/occ/

resource/fy-2014-ccdf-data-tables-preliminary. In 2014, 89 percent of funds were distributed directly to 853,000 families as child care vouchers, and 9 percent were spent in grants or contracts to providers. A total of 369,606 providers received CCDF funds in 2014.

28. Kay E. Brown, "Temporary Assistance for Needy Families: Update on Families Served and Work Participation," testimony before the Subcommittee on Human Resources, Committee on Ways and Means, US House of Representatives, September 8, 2011, http://www.gao.gov/assets/130/126892. pdf. States can choose to transfer up to 30 percent of their TANF funds to CCDBG to fund child care; those funds are then subject to CCDBG requirements. States can also spend TANF funding directly on child care subject to federal TANF rules, which have no health, safety, quality, or reporting requirements.

29. Herbert Hoover, "Address to the White House Conference on Child Health and Protection" (speech, Constitution Hall, Washington, DC, November 19, 1930), http://www.presidency.ucsb.edu/ws/?pid=22442.

30. For a history of CCDF, TANF, and Head Start, see Katharine B. Stevens, *Renewing Childhood's Promise.*

31. In 2014, for example, CCDBG was reauthorized with strongly bipartisan support (passing in the Senate by 88 to 1), expanding its focus to not only assist parents as a work support but also support the healthy development of children by increasing the percentage of low-income children in high-quality care. The 2014 bill stresses child development and learning (neither "development" nor "learning" were mentioned in the earlier bills), setting out new standards for program design, safety, licensing, oversight, and reporting, and requiring that states define program quality and develop plans for improving it.

32. US Department of Health and Human Services and US Department of Education, *High-Quality Early Learning Settings Depend on a High-Quality Workforce: Low Compensation Undermines Quality,* June 2016, https:// www2ed.gov/about/inits/ed/earlylearning/files/ece-low-compensation-undermines-quality-report-2016.pdf; and Rasheed Malik and Jamal Hagler, *Black Families Work More, Earn Less, and Face Difficult Child Care Choices,* Center for American Progress, August 5, 2015, https://www. americanprogress.org/issues/early-childhood/news/2016/08/05/142296/ black-families-work-more-earn-less-and-face-difficult-child-care-choices/.

33. ChildCare Aware of America, *Parents and the High Cost of Child Care*, 2015, http://www.usa.childcareaware.org/advocacy-public-policy/resources/reports-and-research/costofcare/; and Lynda Laughlin, *Who's Minding the Kids? Child Care Arrangements: Spring 2011*, US Department of Commerce, Economics and Statistics Administration, April 2013, https://www.census.gov/prod/2013pubs/p70-135.pdf.

34. See, for example, Katharine B. Stevens and Elizabeth English, *Does Pre-K Work? The Research on Ten Early Childhood Programs—And What It Tells Us*, American Enterprise Institute, April 2016, https://www.aei.org/wp-content/uploads/2016/04/Does-Pre-K-Work.pdf.

35. Chris M. Herbst and Erdal Tekin, "Child Care Subsidies and Child Development," *Economics of Education Review* 29 (2010): 618–38, http://www.chrisherbst.net/files/Download/C._Herbst_Subsidies_Child_Development.pdf.

36. Jay Belsky, "Effects of Child Care on Child Development in the USA, 2006," in *The Quality of Early Childhood Education*, ed. J. J. van Kuyk (Arnheim, The Netherlands: Cito), 23–32, http://www.imfcanada.org/sites/default/files/effects_childcare_development_belsky.pdf; and Chris M. Herbst and Erdal Tekin, "Child Care Subsidies, Maternal Well-Being, and Child-Parent Interactions: Evidence from Three Nationally Representative Data-sets" (working paper, National Bureau of Economic Research, January 2012), http://www.nber.org/papers/w17774.pdf.

37. See NICHD Early Child Care Research Network, "Child Care and Mother-Child Interaction in the First Three Years of Life," *Developmental Psychology* 35, no. 6 (1999): 1399–413.

38. See, for example, "Framing the Future" published by the Pre-K Coalition, a collaboration of seven national K–12 organizations—the American Association of School Administrators, American Federation of Teachers, Council of Chief State School Officers, National Association of Elementary School Principals, National Association of State Boards of Education, National Education Association, and National School Boards Association—focused on establishing a P–12 public school system. Pre-K Coalition, "Framing the Future: Addressing Pre-K in ESEA," May 2011, http://www.centerforpubliceducation.org/Main-Menu/Pre-kindergarten/Thinking-P-12-The-school-board-role-in-pre-k-education/Framing-the-Future-Addressing-Pre-K-in-ESEA.pdf.

39. Education Commission of the States, "State Pre-K Funding for 2015-16 Fiscal Year: National Trends in State Preschool Funding," January 2016, http://www.ecs.org/ec-content/uploads/01252016_Prek-K_Funding_report-4.pdf.

40. This approach builds on two existing federal programs. The first is the successful Early Learning Challenge, a competitive grants program launched in 2011 and jointly administered by the US Departments of Education and Health and Human Services, which funded the efforts of 20 winning states to design and implement an integrated system to improve the quality of early learning and development services and to close the achievement gap for children with high needs. Several of those states are now national leaders in early childhood policy and practice. See US Department of Health and Human Services, Administration for Children and Families, Office of Early Childhood Development, *Race to the Top—Early Learning Challenge*, www.acf.hhs.gov/programs/ecd/early-learning/race-to-the-top. The second is the Preschool Development Grants program authorized under the ESSA Act of 2015, based in the Department of Health and Human Services and jointly administered with the Department of Education. The purpose of the program is to coordinate early childhood education programs in a mixed delivery system of providers including schools, licensed child care centers, Head Start, and other community-based organizations aimed to prepare disadvantaged children for kindergarten. See Department of Health and Human Services, Administration for Children and Families, *Justification of Estimates for Appropriations Committee*, 118.

41. For more information, see Parent Aware for School Readiness, "MELF Archive," http://www.pasrmn.org/MELF/index; Parent Aware, "Home," http://parentaware.org/; and ParentAwareRatings, "The MELF Story," YouTube video, posted February 15, 2012, https://www.youtube.com/watch?v=19MviDASO9Q.

42. For a similar proposal, see Center for Evidence-Based Policy, *Proposed Social Spending Innovation Research (SSIR) Program: Harnessing American Entrepreneurial Talent to Solve Major U.S. Social Problems*, February 2015, http://coalition4evidence.org/wp-content/uploads/2015/02/Proposed-Social-Spending-Innovation-Research-SSIR-program.pdf.

About the Authors

Douglas J. Besharov is the Norman and Florence Brody Professor at the University of Maryland's School of Public Policy, where he teaches courses on poverty, welfare, children and families, policy analysis and logic models, program evaluation, and performance management (including "pay for success"). He is also a senior fellow at the Atlantic Council, where he leads a program on international policy exchanges. Between 1985 and 2009, he was a resident scholar at the American Enterprise Institute. Between 1975 and 1979, he was the first director of the US National Center on Child Abuse and Neglect. In 2008, he was president of the Association for Public Policy Analysis and Management (APPAM) and, subsequently, APPAM's international conference coordinator. He is now director of the University of Maryland's Welfare Reform Academy and its Center for International Policy Exchanges. Together with Neil Gilbert of the University of California, Berkeley, Mr. Besharov is coeditor in chief of the Oxford University Press Library on International Social Policy. He has written 18 books, including *Recognizing Child Abuse: A Guide for the Concerned* (Free Press, 1990), which is designed to help professionals and laypersons identify and report suspected child abuse. He has written more than 250 articles and has contributed to the *Los Angeles Times*, *New York Times*, *Wall Street Journal,* and *Washington Post.*

Richard V. Burkhauser is the Sarah Gibson Blanding Professor of Policy Analysis in the Department of Policy Analysis and Management at Cornell University and a senior research fellow at the Lyndon B. Johnson School of Public Affairs at the University of Texas at Austin. His professional career has focused on how public policies affect the economic behavior and well-being of vulnerable populations, such as older persons, people with disabilities, and low-skilled workers. He has published widely on these topics in journals of demography, economics, gerontology, and public policy, and he is the coauthor of *The Declining Work and Welfare of People with Disabilities* (AEI Press, 2011). He was the 2010 president of the Association for Public Policy Analysis and Management. He holds a Ph.D. in economics from the University of Chicago.

Douglas M. Call is the deputy director of the University of Maryland School of Public Policy's Program for International Policy Exchanges and its Welfare Reform Academy. He graduated with his master's in public policy from the University of Maryland School of Public Policy in May 2007. He has coauthored articles for the *Policy Studies Journal* and the *Wilson Quarterly*. With Douglas Besharov, he was the coeditor of *Poverty, Welfare, and Public Policy*, the third volume in the *Journal of Policy Analysis and Management*'s Classics series. He is also a lecturer at the University of Maryland School of Public Policy, teaching courses on program evaluation and poverty measurement and alleviation.

James C. Capretta is a resident fellow and holds the Milton Friedman Chair at the American Enterprise Institute, where he studies health care, entitlement, and US budgetary policy, as well as global trends in aging, health, and retirement programs. In 2015 and 2016, he directed two major studies: one on reforming US health care according to market principles and consumer choice, and the second on reforming major federal entitlement programs to promote greater personal responsibility, focus limited resources on those most in need, and lower long-term federal expenditures. Mr. Capretta spent more than 16 years in public service before joining AEI. As an associate director at the White House's Office of Management and Budget from 2001 to 2004, he was responsible for all health care, Social Security, welfare, and labor and education issues. Earlier, he served as a senior health policy analyst at the US Senate Budget Committee and at the US House Committee on Ways and Means. Mr. Capretta was also a fellow, and later a senior fellow, at the Ethics and Public Policy Center. His essays and reports include "Improving Health and

Health Care: An Agenda for Reform" (AEI, 2015); "The Budget Act at Forty: Time for Budget Process Reform" (Mercatus Center, 2015); and "Increasing the Effectiveness and Sustainability of the Nation's Entitlement Programs" (AEI, 2016). His book chapters include "Health-Care Reform to Lower Costs and Improve Access and Quality" in *Room to Grow: Conservative Reforms for a Limited Government and a Thriving Middle Class* (YG Network, 2014) and "Reforming Medicaid" in *The Economics of Medicaid: Assessing the Costs and Consequences* (Mercatus Center, 2014). He has been widely published in newspapers, magazines, and trade journals, including *Health Affairs* (where he is a member of the editorial board), the *JAMA Forum*, *National Review*, the *Wall Street Journal*, and the *Weekly Standard*. His television appearances include *PBS NewsHour*, Fox News, CNBC, and Bloomberg Television. Mr. Capretta has an M.A. in public policy studies from Duke University and a B.A. in government from the University of Notre Dame.

Kevin C. Corinth is a research fellow in economic policy studies at the American Enterprise Institute, where he focuses on homelessness and poverty. He has studied the effectiveness of homelessness policies, the treatment of shared housing arrangements in safety net programs, the role of community in economical rental housing, and ways of improving social services through competition and technology. Before joining AEI, Dr. Corinth was a lecturer in microeconomics at the University of Chicago. He has also worked as a research analyst with the Analysis Group in Boston. He has a bachelor's degree in economics and political science from Boston College and a master's and doctorate in economics from the University of Chicago.

Maura Corrigan is a visiting fellow at the American Enterprise Institute, where she studies and evaluates programs related to child welfare, child support, food assistance, and disability. In addition to her research and writing, she works with human services officials and leaders at the state level to make them aware of the latest federal policy developments and reform ideas relevant to social welfare policy. She also works to educate federal policymakers about promising state-level social services innovations. Ms. Corrigan is a former chief justice of the Michigan Supreme Court and a former first assistant US attorney for Detroit, Michigan. Before joining AEI, after a distinguished legal career, she served as director of the Michigan Department of Human Services, where she oversaw public assistance programs for low-income and vulnerable families and children in Michigan. Programs included food, cash, and medical assistance; foster care and adoption services; child support; and children's protective services. As director of the Department of Human Services, Ms. Corrigan oversaw a 66 percent reduction in the number of individuals dependent on cash welfare, rolled out an innovative program to help the disabled, and left office with nearly 350,000 fewer Michigan residents needing food assistance. She has a J.D. from the University of Detroit Law School and a B.A. from Marygrove College.

Mary C. Daly is senior vice president and associate director of research at the Federal Reserve Bank of San Francisco, where she specializes in employment and wage dynamics, economic inequality and mobility, relative income and subjective well-being, disability and economic well-being, and disability policy in industrialized nations. She is also a research fellow with the Institute for the Study of Labor, a member of the editorial board for *Industrial Relations*, and a fellow with the National Academy of Social Insurance. She has published extensively in a variety of academic journals and is the coauthor of *The Declining Work and Welfare of People with Disabilities* (AEI Press, 2011). She holds a Ph.D. in economics from Syracuse University.

Robert Doar is the Morgridge Fellow in Poverty Studies at the American Enterprise Institute, where he studies and evaluates how improved federal policies and programs can reduce poverty and provide opportunities for vulnerable Americans. Specifically, he focuses on the employment, health, and well-being of low-income Americans and their children. Mr. Doar has served as a co-chair of the National Commission on Hunger and as a lead member of the AEI-Brookings Working Group on Poverty and Opportunity, which published the report titled "Opportunity, Responsibility, and

Security: A Consensus Plan for Reducing Poverty and Restoring the American Dream." Before joining AEI, he was commissioner of New York City's Human Resources Administration, where he administered 12 public assistance programs. Programs included welfare, food assistance, public health insurance, home care for the elderly and disabled, energy assistance, child support enforcement services, adult protective services, domestic violence assistance, and help for people living with HIV/AIDS. Before joining the Bloomberg administration, he was commissioner of social services for the state of New York, where he helped to make the state a model for the implementation of welfare reform. His writing has appeared in the *Wall Street Journal*, *USA Today*, and *National Review*, among other publications. Mr. Doar has a bachelor's degree in history from Princeton University.

Ron Haskins is a senior fellow and holds the Cabot Family Chair in Economic Studies at the Brookings Institution, where he codirects the Center on Children and Families. He is also a senior consultant at the Annie E. Casey Foundation and president of the Association for Public Policy Analysis and Management. He is the author of *Show Me the Evidence: Obama's Fight for Rigor and Evidence in Social Policy* (Brookings, 2014) and *Work Over Welfare: The Inside Story of the 1996 Welfare Reform Law* (Brookings, 2006); coauthor of *Creating an Opportunity Society* (Brookings, 2009); and senior editor of *The Future of Children*. In 2002, he was the senior adviser to the president for welfare policy. Before joining Brookings and Casey, he spent 14 years on the staff of the House Ways and Means Human Resources Subcommittee, serving as the subcommittee's staff director between 1995 and 2000. In 2016, Dr. Haskins and his colleague Isabel Sawhill were awarded the Moynihan Prize for being advocates for public policy based on social science research. In 1997, he was selected by the *National Journal* as one of the 100 most influential people in the federal government. From 1981 to 1985, he was a senior researcher at the Frank Porter Graham Child Development Center at UNC Chapel Hill. He holds an A.B. in history, an M.A.T. in education, and a Ph.D. in developmental psychology from UNC.

Bruce D. Meyer is a visiting scholar at the American Enterprise Institute, where he focuses on poverty, inequality, and social safety net programs. Concurrently, he is the McCormick Foundation Professor at the University of Chicago's Harris School of Public Policy. He is also a research associate at the National Bureau of Economic Research. His past faculty appointments include being a tenured professor of economics at Northwestern University and a visiting professor of economics at Harvard University, Princeton University, and University College London. He has also advised the US Department of Labor and the US Bureau of Labor Statistics. The author of many journal articles and book chapters, Dr. Meyer has also edited two books. He is also a former editor of the *Journal of Public Economics*, the *Journal of Labor Economics*, and the *Journal of Business & Economics Statistics*. He has a Ph.D. in economics from the Massachusetts Institute of Technology and an M.A. and B.A., also in economics, from Northwestern University.

Edgar O. Olsen is a professor of economics and public policy at the University of Virginia, where he served as chairman of the economics department and was heavily involved in the creation of its new public policy school. His research specialty is low-income housing policy. He has published papers on housing markets and policies in professional journals such as the *American Economic Review*, *Journal of Political Economy*, and *Journal of Public Economics*, and he wrote the chapter on low-income housing programs in the 2003 National Bureau of Economic Review volume on means-tested transfers in the United States, the chapter on achieving fundamental housing policy reform in a 2006 Brookings volume on promoting the general welfare, and (with Jeff Zabel) the chapter on US housing policy in the recent North-Holland *Handbook of Regional and Urban Economics*. Dr. Olsen worked on the National Housing Policy Review that led to the US housing voucher program; was a visiting scholar at the Department of Housing and Urban Development (HUD) during its Experimental Housing Allowance Program; has testified on low-income housing policy before congressional committees seven times; has been an expert witness on the topic in two major class-action lawsuits; and was a consultant to the Government Accountability Office and HUD, a member of the 2007 National Academy of Sciences Committee to Evaluate the Research Plan of the US Department of Housing and Urban Development, and a member of the MTO Technical Review Panel.

Angela Rachidi is a research fellow in poverty studies at the American Enterprise Institute, where she studies the effects of public policy and existing support programs on low-income families, continuing the work she did for the New York City Human Resources Administration for almost a decade. A former deputy commissioner for policy research and evaluation for the Department of Social Services in New York, Dr. Rachidi oversaw a team of analysts working on studies used to guide local officials to make informed policy decisions on how work, family, and public policy can reduce poverty and improve the economic situation of poor families. In particular, she studied low-income support programs such as Temporary Assistance for Needy Families, the Supplemental Nutrition Assistance Program, and workforce development programs that provide or fund job training and the development of certain skills. She also evaluated the impact of the earned income tax credit program in New York City, of child-support enforcement programs, and of Medicaid. Dr. Rachidi has a Ph.D. in social welfare policy from the New School's Milano School of International Affairs, Management, and Urban Policy. Her academic work explored the economic disadvantage of unmarried mothers. She also has a master's of public administration from Northern Illinois University and a B.S. in public administration from the University of Wisconsin–Whitewater.

Katharine B. Stevens is a resident scholar at the American Enterprise Institute and leads AEI's early childhood program. Her work focuses on the research, policy, and politics of early childhood care and education; the role of early learning in expanding opportunity for low-income Americans; and the implementation challenges of rapidly growing early childhood education initiatives. Before joining AEI, she founded and led Teachers for Tomorrow, one of the first urban teacher-residency programs in the United States, which recruited and trained teachers for New York City's lowest-performing schools. She began her career in public education as a preschool teacher in New Haven, Connecticut, and St. Louis, Missouri. Her analyses and commentary have been published in *Education Week*, Huffington Post, *Los Angeles Times*, *New York Daily News*, *New York Post*, *US News & World Report*, and the *Wall Street Journal*. Dr. Stevens has a Ph.D. in education policy from Columbia University, a M.Ed. from Teachers College, an M.B.A. from Columbia Business School, and a B.A. in US history from the University of Chicago.

Russell Sykes directs the American Public Human Services Association's Center for Employment and Economic Well-Being. His career in social services spans more than 40 years. Among his many posts, he has worked as an independent consultant on issues related to health, workforce, food assistance, and low-income tax policy; a vice president at the Schuyler Center for Analysis and Advocacy; deputy commissioner of the New York State Office of Temporary and Disability Assistance, where he oversaw SNAP, TANF, LIHEAP, and the SSI State Supplement and Employment Services; and a senior fellow at the Empire Center for Public Policy and the Manhattan Institute for Policy Research. In 2014, he was one of 10 congressional appointees to the National Commission on Hunger, which published its final report in 2016. He has written policy reports and provided testimony over his career on the earned income tax credit, Medicaid, TANF reauthorization, SNAP, subsidized housing, and child support. He has published numerous opinion pieces in major newspapers, among them, the *New York Times*, *Wall Street Journal*, *Albany Times Union*, *New York Post*, and *USA Today*.

Acknowledgments

I thank Andrew Smith, Sarah Crain, and Bradley Wassink for their outstanding research and editorial assistance. Without them, this volume would not have been completed. I thank all the contributing authors for not only their work here but also their years of effort at finding ways to help struggling Americans. Finally, I thank Arthur Brooks and the American Enterprise Institute for allowing me to search for, and offer, ideas that will help America's least powerful be full participants in the life of our country.

Robert Doar